The Weekend that Changed the World

The Weekend that Changed the World

The Mystery of Jerusalem's Empty Tomb

PETER WALKER

Marshall Pickering
An Imprint of HarperCollins*Publishers*

Marshall Pickering is an Imprint of
HarperCollins*Religious*
Part of HarperCollins*Publishers*
77–85 Fulham Palace Road, London W6 8JB

First published in Great Britain in 1999 by Marshall Pickering

3 5 7 9 10 8 6 4 2

Peter Walker asserts the moral right to
be identified as the author of this work

A catalogue record for this book is
available from the British Library

ISBN 0 551 03135 2

Text illustrations by Peter Cox Associates

Printed and bound in Great Britain by
Woolnough Bookbinding Ltd, Irthlingborough, Northamptonshire

Contents

PART III: THE SIGNIFICANCE

List of Figures and Plates

LIST OF FIGURES

Chapter 7

Chapter 10

LIST OF PLATES

Section 1

Section 2

Section 3

Foreword

The Weekend that Changed the World is a superb title for the events of Good Friday and Easter. That weekend did indeed change the world, so much so that now, almost two thousand years later, a third of the world's population, in every country and nationality, worship the carpenter-teacher who was executed and then raised from the dead on that weekend long ago which changed the world for ever.

And if the title is apt, the book is outstanding. Some writers about this famous weekend are academics, some archaeologists, some teachers, some simply enthusiasts. Dr Peter Walker is remarkable for being all four. He is an able New Testament scholar, who teaches at Oxford. He is one of the foremost experts on the archaeology and topography of ancient Jerusalem. He is an attractive and clear teacher with great gifts as a communicator. And he is passionate about Jesus Christ, and longs to make him known.

The plan of this lavishly illustrated book is simple. In the first part the author draws us evocatively into the story of the betrayal and death of the most famous person in all history. He follows this story through that awesome weekend, leading us from the crucifixion and burial to the Resurrection on Easter morning. He faces the enormous improbability that anyone could possibly be raised from death to a new and endless life, and he demonstrates convincingly that no alternative explanation has ever been found to bear critical examination.

The second part of the book looks at the setting of this amazing event. Modern visitors to Jerusalem are shown two alternative sites for the tomb of Jesus, both of which have had their advocates. I have never seen as cool and wise an evaluation of these two possible sites as is presented to us here. Peter is an absolute expert on the subject, and yet he guides even the complete amateur through the intricacies of scholarship and controversy, ancient and modern, with enviable sureness of touch and the fascination of a good detective mystery. In the end he gives us the evidence and leaves us to make up our own minds. He is clear that in the last analysis it is not important. Jesus is not here: he is risen! And therefore neither the Garden Tomb nor the Holy Sepulchre are of critical importance to Christianity, fascinating though the debate undoubtedly is.

The gifts of the teacher, the theologian, and the convinced communicator of the gospel are all combined in the third part of the book, where he draws out the significance of the Resurrection. It means the divine identity of Jesus is revealed, his teaching affirmed and his death given meaning. It shows there is a solid ground for hope – in the God who can raise the dead. And it is like a trailer to the main film; it points to the final victory of God. But Peter will not leave the matter there. He offers us a powerful and moving conclusion. His treatment of the Resurrection in the New Testament is matched by an exploration of the impact of the Resurrection today, and he mingles story, argument and challenge to draw his readers into a personal and deepening experience of the Risen Christ.

I do not think there is any other book like this around. One that tells and evaluates the story, offers a scholarly examination of the site, and elucidates the significance of the greatest event in all history, the death and Resurrection of Jesus of Nazareth in the weekend that changed the world. This is a book to buy, to lend and to treasure.

REVD DR MICHAEL GREEN

ADVISOR IN EVANGELISM TO THE ARCHBISHOPS OF CANTERBURY AND YORK

Preface

The life of Jesus has always fascinated people. It is a story of power and beauty, irony and tragedy, suffering and yet victory, simplicity and yet depth. It has also been retold throughout the world in many different cultures. Yet it will forever remain a story rooted in history – of one 'solitary' man, in one place, at one particular point in time.

This book aims to take that history very seriously, at the same time allowing those ancient events to fire our imagination. It was written with a variety of people in mind:

Those beginning to be interested in the story of Jesus for the first time

Those familiar with the Gospel story, who want to picture it more accurately

Those willing to look in more detail at the issue of Jesus' Resurrection and to think more deeply about its implications for today

Those thinking about travelling to the Holy Land and interested in doing some reading beforehand

Those who have now visited Jerusalem and want something to remind them of their visit, as well as to deal with some of the unanswered questions which any such visit invariably raises.

I have always been fascinated by books about Jesus' Resurrection (such as those by Morison, Anderson and Wenham). So it was a privilege to be invited by the Garden Tomb Association to consider writing on this theme. I also well remember the deep impression made on me by my first visits to the Holy Sepulchre and the Garden Tomb (in 1981) and trust that what follows will be of real assistance to the many who make such visits each year. A big thanks to that Association (especially Peter Wells, Peter Davies, Colin Reeves, Roger Gilbert and John Milne) for their continued help and their giving me the freedom to write a book close to my heart.

The book was written in several locations and I would like to thank all those who helped in different ways. In Cyprus: Michael and Stephanie Wood, for their hospitality. In Oxford: Martin Biddle, for his helpful co-operation on our parallel projects; my fellow staff at Wycliffe, for their patience with my absences (to Jerusalem, again!); so too some keen students (especially Rob, Laurie, Alan, Nick and Anthony) who read through some draft chapters. Thanks too to Alan Millard and Rupert Chapman for their timely help. In London: the team at HarperCollins (especially Elspeth, Jeremy, Kathy and Jo) for their expertise in seeing the book through to publication.

In Jerusalem: my friend, Brian Bush, for all his help with the illustrations; Johnny Giacaman and the Garden Tomb volunteers, for their hospitality; scholars such as Justin Taylor, Jerry Murphy O'Connor and Gabi Barkay, for their fruitful advice; and for my recent fellow-travellers (Tom Wright, Graham Tomlin, friends from Tonbridge and Abingdon, and a student party from Wycliffe Hall) for their inspiration and ideas.

So this book is dedicated to all those who have travelled to Jerusalem with me over the years, but in particular to three family members who have travelled with me in many other ways as well: Patricia Taylor, Sylvia Walker and Georgie Walker. Their support has been invaluable. But, this time, they must not only buy the book –they must read it!

PETER WALKER, DECEMBER 1998

Introduction

There had been some strange happenings over the weekend. If anyone had been keeping a close watch on all the movements in and out of the city, they would have noticed quite a few unusual 'comings and goings'. This one was odd too.

Three women, huddled close together, were silently and unobtrusively making their way out through the Garden Gate long before most people were awake. Where exactly were they heading at this early hour? And what were they carrying, wrapped up in their cloaks?

Now that it was the first week in April, the rainy season was past. So it promised to be a warm, bright day, with the skies crystal clear. But right now, with the sun's rays not yet breaking over the crest of the Mount of Olives, it was still bitterly cold and the atmosphere was decidedly damp.

The small expedition, hoping to be unnoticed, made its way furtively into a garden just outside the city walls. The garden was really one side of a quarry area, long disused, and nearby there was an outcrop of rock which, because of recent events, would always have painful associations for the women and their friends. But for now their minds were on other things. They had a solemn and not very pleasant task to perform.

Ever since late Friday afternoon, when their lives had been broken by a tragedy quite beyond their worst fears, they had been discussing what their next move should be. Something more had to be done for him. It was the very least that they could do. But within an hour or so the Sabbath had begun, restricting their movements and preventing any possible visit to the spice bazaar. True, the shops had then opened on the Saturday evening, but the work they had to do, they all agreed, could not properly be done at night. Now, early dawn on Sunday, was their first opportunity. At long last, after an anxious night waiting for the cock-crow, the fearful women set out.

It was a tiny, insignificant expedition, but it was destined to be a failure – they never achieved what they set out to do. Nevertheless, it would become one of the most famous expeditions in history – a mission aborted because it was overtaken by circumstances quite beyond their control.

The story of their quiet, clandestine arrival in the garden, amidst the early mist of a Jerusalem spring dawn, would come in time to be emblazoned throughout the world. They were about to stumble upon an event which would completely change the way in which countless people in subsequent generations would view themselves – and indeed the whole of history and eternity. Others looking back on it would see that particular dawn as the dawn of a new age, the central point in human history, the moment when God fully revealed his master-plan for the universe. This quiet, otherwise normal, Sunday morning would come to be seen as the most important day in the calendar of the human race – the day that changed the world.

The task of this book is to look again at the events of that unique weekend – the first 'Easter'. What had been going on in Jerusalem in the previous few days? What had been going on in the garden before the women arrived? What happened next? In particular, can we establish where precisely these strange events took place? And what are the implications of those events for today? Are they merely a fascinating part of ancient history, or are they indeed history's central point, meaning that every human life should be focused upon them in some way?

Before we can begin to answer those questions, however, we need to retrace our steps. The story, which on that Sunday morning was about to take such a sudden new twist, was a story which had been growing apace throughout the previous months and years. It concerned a Jewish man from the northern region of Galilee, now in his thirties, who had established a reputation as an authoritative religious teacher, drawing around himself a small group of followers. Amongst the populace he was widely recognized as a 'prophet', following in the long-lost tradition of the famous prophets of the Old Testament. Expectations were rife as to what he would do next – not least when he hinted that this year's visit to Jerusalem for Passover would be the time when matters would come to a head.

So we join this group of Galileans some time after their arrival in Jerusalem. Once again an observer would have noticed a small group leaving the city through one of its gates. But this time the group consisted of 12 men and the time was less remarkable – around 10 o'clock on a Thursday evening, when the many thousands of residents and festival visitors were only just beginning to turn in for the night. But for the group and especially for their leader, this Galilean rabbi called Jesus, the night was but young.

PART I

The Story

When they had carried out all that was written about him,
they took him down from the tree and laid him in a tomb.
But God raised him from the dead.

(ACTS 13:29–30)

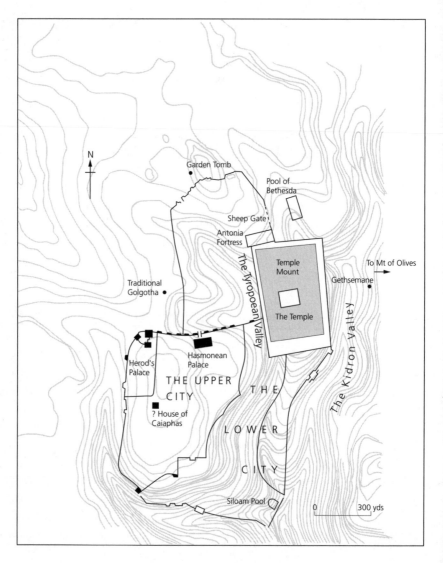

Fig. 1. Jerusalem in the time of Jesus.

Torches in the Garden

Thursday Evening's Rendezvous

The small group who left the city on that chilly Thursday night in April consisted of Jesus and his 11 remaining disciples. Having finished their Passover meal in the upper city of Jerusalem, they were now walking down towards the Kidron valley.

It would be a long night, the details of which still repay close study after all these years, and which none of those connected with this Jesus would ever forget.

THE LONG WALK

As they made their way down through the city streets towards the Siloam gate, several of them may well have been whispering puzzled questions to one another. Above all, what exactly had been going on at that strange Passover meal with Jesus just now? This annual remembrance of the Israelites' escape from Egypt was something which they had celebrated many times before. But this time it had been quite different. What had Jesus been up to?

THE LAST SUPPER

The venue

Modern visitors
are directed
either to the
Syrian Orthodox
Church of St

Mark within the Old City or to the Crusader's Cenacle on Mount Sion.

The Cenacle is quite probably the location for the later events of Pentecost (Acts 1:13; 2:1ff.).[1] At least the Byzantine Christians believed so, building their 'upper church of the apostles' on the site of an earlier second-century building, described as the 'little church of God' by Epiphanius (AD 315–403).[2] If the 'upper room' of the Last Supper (Mark 14:15) could confidently be identified with the upstairs room of Acts 1:13, then the Cenacle would also be the site of the Last Supper.

It is assumed here that this identification is correct and that this is also the home of John Mark (Acts 12:12); Jesus' followers would not have had access to many different homes within the city. Yet it remains possible that there may have been three quite separate sites.

The time

The Synoptic Gospels give the strong impression that it was a Passover meal (Mark 14:12, 16), but John's Gospel (13:1; 18:28; 19:31) indicates that it was on the night before Passover (i.e. 14 Nisan in the Jewish calendar). Perhaps Jesus was following an alternative calendar (used by the Essenes?) so that it was a genuine Passover meal, yet held a few days in advance of the main Jewish Passover. Pixner has therefore suggested that the Last Supper took place on the Tuesday and that Jesus was kept under guard till his crucifixion on the Friday.[3]

More probably John is correct. Jesus' meal was a day ahead of schedule: it was Jesus' own distinctive Passover meal, consciously modelled on the official Passover, but also given a quite new meaning. The next evening would have been too late.

Jesus was almost certainly crucified on a Friday afternoon, the day of Preparation before the Sabbath began at sunset (see Mark 15:42; Luke

23:54; John 19:42). So, to fix the date, we need a year in which the day before Passover (14 Nisan) coincided with the day before the Sabbath. This occurred in AD 30 and AD 33, and both dates are possible. The Last Supper would then have taken place (in the Julian calendar) on either Thursday, 6 April AD 30 or Thursday, 2 April AD 33.

The evidence of Luke 3:12 and John 2:20 strongly favours the later date. Moreover, if Acts 2:20 ('the sun will be turned to darkness and the moon to blood') refers quite literally to the darkness at the crucifixion followed by a lunar eclipse, then this tallies with the astronomical evidence for the year AD 33.[4] Jerusalem residents, waiting to start their Passover meals on the evening of Friday, 3 April AD 33, would not have seen the expected full Paschal moon, but a moon with a red 'bite' removed. A dramatic effect to end a dramatic day.

Fig. 2. The Last Supper: location and timing.

A strange Passover

Jesus had told them that he had been eagerly desiring to share this Passover with them (Luke 22:15), and he had made some quite elaborate arrangements to ensure that it went ahead according to plan. By tradition the Passover meal had to be eaten within the city walls of Jerusalem, but Jesus also needed a place where he and his disciples could be sure of getting some privacy. As it turned out, Jesus had made arrangements with the father of John Mark, a well-to-do man in the upper city (cf. Acts 1:13ff.; 2:41; 12:12). In a cryptic manner, reflecting the caution which the whole operation demanded, he had then given his disciples their instructions: 'look out for a man carrying a pitcher on his head and follow him to his master's house' (Mark 14:13). It had been the strange beginning to an evening which had only got stranger still.

Another strange thing was its timing. Jesus' Passover meal was a day ahead of schedule (see John 19:14). Was this something to do with Jesus wanting to keep his movements undetected? Or was it because he sensed that things were getting dangerous for him in Jerusalem and he might not get the peace he needed the following night? So there had been no lamb on the table. But Jesus clearly thought of it as a Passover and wanted his disciples to remember it as such (Mark 14:14). Indeed, he seemed to be instituting a new Passover of his own. Who did he think he was? Another Moses?

The evening had got off to an awkward start – with Jesus himself washing their feet (John 13:3–11). It was so embarrassing. It had made them all feel a bit uneasy, and a little on edge for the whole evening. This was a slave's task – certainly not the expected role for the meal's host! Stranger things were to follow. A little later, those reclining near him heard Jesus say that he would be betrayed. Moments later one of their number, the man in charge of the group's finances, suddenly got up and left them (John 13:29). Where was Judas off to at this time of night? Next Jesus had taken some bread and wine. Instead of giving thanks in the normal way associated with the Passover liturgy, he had uttered those extraordinary words – 'This is my body', 'This is my blood'. What is more, he had then commanded them to drink it – even though for Jews the drinking of blood was a sacrilege. It was bizarre, even sinister. What could it all mean?

Perhaps the most worrying thing was Jesus' present frame of mind. He was now talking frequently of his 'going away'. When they said they were happy to join him *wherever* it was that he was going, he told them they could not do so. It was 'better' for them, he said, that he went away (John 16:7). So what exactly did he have in mind?

Nevertheless, right now he evidently wanted them to stay with him. So, after singing some hymns and psalms (Mark 14:26), they had left the house as a group and were gradually making their way out of the city – in search, they presumed, of a place to sleep for the night.

Or were they? With Jesus as he was right now, nothing was certain any more.

Reflections in the valley

They had quite a long walk ahead of them. If they were headed, as they thought they were, towards Gethsemane at the foot of the Mount of Olives, it would take a good 40 minutes' continuous walking (see Figure 5, p. 21). As they walked along they sang the occasional Passover hymn. On a couple of occasions they stopped for a while: Jesus made them consider the image of a vine and its implications for his followers (John 15:1ff.); he also stopped to pray for them and their future (John 17).

Much of the time, however, was probably kept in silence, each with his own thoughts, unable to shift the sense of puzzlement or the clouds of gathering gloom. Overhead there was a bright, full moon, lighting up their path, but it did not make what was about to befall them any the clearer.

Some, trying to fathom what was going on and what was passing through Jesus' mind, may have been thinking back to those brighter days in Galilee. There had been opposition to Jesus from the outset. He had never had a honeymoon period in his ministry, but at least there had been a large measure of support from amongst the people. Now Jesus seemed strangely alone. There had been high hopes too when Jesus had first set out for Jerusalem. In Jericho things had reached a fever pitch, with people being convinced that Jesus was going to do a mighty work in Jerusalem: he would usher in the long-awaited 'Kingdom of God', about which he had spoken so much (Luke 19:11). But, looking back on it, there had always been this strange undercurrent, with Jesus predicting that things would turn out rather differently once they got to Jerusalem (Mark 8:31 etc.). Jesus had left Jericho in a determined mood, marching out in front of them, and none of them had dared ask what was really passing through his mind. It was the same feeling now.

Others perhaps, as they looked up to the right and saw the places where the crowds of their fellow Galileans were camping out on the Mount of Olives, thought back to that great moment of their first arrival in Jerusalem – that moment when after all their journeying from Galilee they had at last reached the top of the Mount and caught that special first panorama of the holy city and the Temple. Not surprisingly, the pilgrims had burst forth into singing. On this occasion

Jesus had decided that no harm could come from joining in the celebration and had been pleased to receive the enthusiastic welcome which many wanted to give him. From his contacts in Bethany he had gained the use of a young donkey and entered the city, not on foot as was customary for all pilgrims, but rather on this colt. This certainly gave the lie to any idea that Jesus would be using military force to achieve his ends. So the political and religious authorities were not particularly bothered. Yet in the light of a prophecy in the book of Zechariah ('see, your King comes, riding on a donkey' [Zechariah 9:9]), this was probably a clue that Jesus was claiming to be Jerusalem's true king – a staggering thought. This had all taken place only a few days before, but now it seemed an age away. What kind of throne did this 'king' have in his mind? Why had he not capitalized more on that swelling tide of popular acclaim?

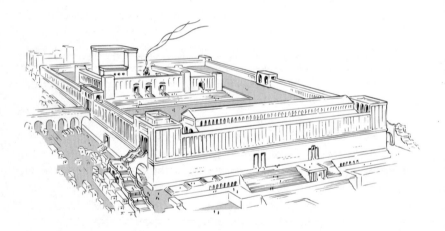

Fig. 3. The Jerusalem Temple in the time of Jesus, looking from the south-west. Herod the Great had recently rebuilt it, extending the platform quite considerably to the south. The archways over the Tyropoean valley enabled access from the upper city; alternatively worshippers could enter through the southern gates and proceed up some covered stairs until coming out in the Court of the Gentiles. Beyond the tall Holy of Holies lay the Antonia Fortress, the Roman garrison overlooking the Temple.

Between the Temple and the tombs

Others, looking up to the left, saw the massive outline of the platform extended by Herod to support the Temple enclosure (see Plates 1 and 7, and Figure 3, p. 8). The disciples' attitude to the Temple could never be quite the same again after that dramatic incident a few days earlier. Jesus had entered its precincts and turned over the tables of the moneychangers (Mark 11:15–17; see Plate 10). From one point of view it had only been a small episode – normal business was resumed within a few hours. But from another point of view, it was charged with significance. At the very least, it showed Jesus' opposition to the High Priest's recent ploy of moving the market from the Mount of Olives and placing it in the outer court of the Temple. The financial extortion associated with the purchase of the Temple's own peculiar currency was bad enough, without the whole enterprise being brought within the Temple precincts – together with all the sacrificial animals! The High Priest's action seemed to reflect a pretty low view of this outer court, the Court of the Gentiles – the only place where non-Jewish visitors to the Temple could stop to pray. So Jesus' action revealed his desire that the Temple's worship should be purified and reformed – after all, it was the place which he had once daringly described as his 'Father's house' (Luke 2:49).

But at the same time did it not also reflect a more radical view towards the Temple in Jesus' thinking? After all, for that brief moment he had brought to a halt the whole system upon which the sacrificial offerings of the Temple were purchased. Was there not some connection with that strange episode when he had cursed the fig tree on the Mount of Olives (Mark 11:13–14, 20–21)? It was as though Jesus had gone to the Temple looking for fruit and his action there was a demonstration that he found it lacking – effectively putting a curse on the place. Who did he think he was to do such a thing? It was like Jeremiah of old, who had pronounced judgement on the Temple; sure enough, not many years later it was destroyed. In fact Jesus had quoted Jeremiah's phrase about the 'den of thieves' and had then taken some of the disciples aside and warned them explicitly that not one of the stones from the Temple buildings would be left in place (Mark 13:2). From down in the Kidron valley, most of what they could now see was simply the Temple platform, not the Temple buildings themselves. Even so, it was an awesome prediction that Jesus had made. Who did he think he was? Would the Temple really come tumbling down, as in the time of Jeremiah?

Others, perhaps, could not help noting the massive tombs which were immediately to their right as they walked up the valley (see Plates 1 and 16). Cut out from the living rock within the previous 100 years (and later to be called the tombs of Absalom and Zechariah), they were an awesome reminder of the reality of death. Jesus' words in the upper room about his 'body and blood' had been macabre, seemingly expressing the morbid state of mind into which he had now entered. As he passed these tombs, was he thinking about death once again? Was he wondering what kind of tomb he would one day be given? For, although they did not know it, this was in fact the last walk he would ever make as a free man.

It was not a short walk, so there was ample time for thought. Yet it was physically quite demanding (with steep steps down into the valley and then a steady climb up towards Gethsemane), and some of them may simply have been too tired to think. But precisely *because* of all that had happened and in the light of Jesus' strange actions and words in the upper room, it is not unfair to imagine that others of them would have used this time to try and work things through in their own minds. What did it all mean? How was it all going to end?

THE LONG WAIT

So they came to Gethsemane. The name 'Gethsemane' means 'oil-press', and John describes it as a 'garden' (John 18:1). So, although it may have been an open stretch of land, it was more probably an enclosed area, incorporating an olive grove, an oil-press, and possibly a few buildings for storage. Unlike the other Gospel writers, Luke does not mention Gethsemane by name, but instead states simply that Jesus 'went, as he usually did, to the Mount of Olives' (Luke 22:39). Was this then the spot where Jesus and his disciples had been sleeping on previous nights? Or had they up till now been returning en masse to Bethany each night?

Either way, it seems likely that this was a favourite haunt of Jesus and, during the coming days of the Passover, they may have been

THE GARDEN OF GETHSEMANE

This was probably an enclosed olive grove. John describes it as being on the 'other side of the Kidron valley' (18:1); Luke simply talks of the 'Mount of Olives' (22:39). So the present church of All Nations (built in 1924; see Plates 3 and 15) is almost certainly in the right vicinity, also being close to the natural route leading from the city to Bethany. Ever since the third century, Christian visitors have used this general area as a place of prayer.[5]

In Jesus' day the Mount of Olives would have been covered with olive trees, but many of these would have been destroyed by the Roman legions under Titus in the siege of AD 70. So the present olive trees, though extremely ancient, probably date from a slightly later period.

Inside the church there is an exposed area of rock that by tradition is the place of the 'agony', when Jesus prayed on his own. No mention is made in the Gospels of such a rock. Nevertheless, it was pointed out to Christian visitors such as the Bordeaux Pilgrim (AD 333) and was incorporated into a 'graceful church' by the time of Egeria (AD 384), and again, much later, into a Crusader church. If this were the correct spot, the scene of Jesus' betrayal by Judas would be a 'stone's throw away' (Luke 22:41), presumably in the direction of the city walls. Byzantine Christians appear to have remembered it further down at the foot of the valley.

Fig. 4.

expecting to sleep here – to ensure that they fulfilled the requirement of sleeping within the greater Jerusalem area for the feast itself. Moreover, if it was enclosed, it would certainly be a useful place to gain some much-needed privacy, away from the many pilgrims camping round about. Not implausibly, some have even suggested that this too was a piece of property made available to Jesus by that well-meaning man in Jerusalem – the father of John Mark.

Praying and waiting

Leaving most of the disciples in one place, Jesus took Peter, James and John so that they could be with him in his time of need. He prayed in their hearing, and once again they were aware of the special way in which Jesus addressed God so personally as his 'Father' (*Abba* in Aramaic). Yet his prayers now, though personal, were full of pain. He asked that this 'cup' of suffering might pass from him. 'Yet not my will, but yours be done.' He prayed so earnestly, we are told, that his 'sweat became like great drops of blood falling down on the ground' (Luke 22:44).

The eight other disciples were soon asleep, puzzled by the evening's events, but seemingly unaware of the drama which was unfolding around them. Peter, James and John, however, had the opportunity to witness Jesus' darkest hour. But they too were probably in the dark as to what was just around the corner. What was Jesus expecting to happen? He had not been like this before; what was so different now? But if they had any such questions, they soon came to an end. For they too were soon fast asleep.

One of the most significant factors, however, in this well-known story is often missed: namely the great length of time that the disciples were in the garden before their sleep was rudely interrupted by the arrival of Judas with some soldiers. Peter, James and John fell asleep no less than *three* times. Given that it was clearly important to Jesus that they keep awake, it is hard to imagine that they fell asleep in a matter of minutes. These were fishermen – quite used to being awake all night. On this occasion, however, they were simply not able to keep their eyes open. Clearly we are dealing here with an extended period of time.

An opportunity – but too late?

In order to answer we now know what the disciples throughout that evening did not know – namely that Judas had left their Passover meal with the express intention of going to Caiaphas the High Priest with the news that Jesus would soon be in Gethsemane. He had in fact left the meal quite early in the proceedings. Since Caiaphas' house was in the same quarter of the city, he would have been able to speak to Caiaphas or his officials while Jesus and his disciples were still in the upper room.

If Caiaphas had then responded to this information straightaway, sending out a party to arrest Jesus, they would have had little difficulty in reaching Gethsemane at a similar time to Jesus – perhaps around 11 o'clock. This was already late enough for most people – though no doubt there might be some advantage in doing this deed a fraction later, at the very dead of night. But Judas and the soldiers probably did not come till one or two o'clock in the morning. What took them so long?

In order to answer this we need for a moment to leave the disciples, sleeping contentedly in Gethsemane, and to consider in a bit more detail what precisely was taking place half a mile away in Jerusalem's upper city.

In all probability there were some important decisions which needed to be taken in the High Priest's house, which simply could not be rushed. A lot of quick thinking and planning had to go on behind the scenes.

Sometimes it is supposed that the religious authorities had all along intended only to arrest Jesus at this last possible moment before the feast; all that they wanted to know from Judas was where Jesus was going to be. Yet this is most unlikely. First, this strange delay in reaching Gethsemane makes it quite clear that the plan was not up and ready, simply waiting for the moment when it could be implemented. If they were simply waiting for the signal, why the delay? And why wait until the last possible moment, when it made the whole operation tantalizingly risky? After all, if there were any hitch in the proceedings and they did not succeed in getting the death penalty implemented speedily, Jesus would end up being in prison for the whole length of the Passover festival – an eventuality which, from their perspective, would be the worst of all possible scenarios.

Almost certainly, therefore, they had been hoping that Judas would bring them word some time well before this. Judas had been on the lookout for several days. This would then explain the rather furtive ways in which Jesus had prepared for his private Passover meal. Jesus was ensuring that Judas could not second-guess his next move. He had to keep his plans close to his chest, because he was being watched. Only now, on the final evening before Passover, did Jesus at last give Judas the advance information that he was waiting for. Yes, after dinner he would be going to Gethsemane. If Judas wanted to find him, that was where he would be.

Yet it may well be that Judas was not simply waiting for a fixed, quiet location. Was he perhaps also looking for some indication that Jesus' arrest would go smoothly? No popular uproar, no resistance from the disciples but, above all, no display of power by Jesus himself. There was no guaranteeing that this task of arresting Jesus would go straightforwardly. After all, this man was reputed to have brought dead people back to life, cursed fig trees and overturned the tables of the moneychangers in the Temple! What would happen if people tried to lay hands on him and arrest him?

So Judas could only be convinced that the time was ripe when Jesus began giving clear signals that he was actually ready *to give himself up*. He began alluding in strange ways to his death, and he effectively invited Judas to go and do what he needed to do. Now at last (at the moment when Jesus said so – not before!) Judas could go to Caiaphas and the chief priests. It was not just that Jesus' night-time location was clear (perhaps he *had* been in Gethsemane on previous nights). It was also that he was in a frame of mind that would not offer them any resistance. *This* was the good news for which they had been waiting.

But it almost came too late. Indeed, on hearing it, some might have concluded that it *was* too late. Perhaps there was more than we have realized to Jesus' parting remark to Judas, 'do *quickly* what you are going to do' (John 13:27).

The urgent question for Caiaphas, then, was: granted that this political prisoner seemed intent on giving himself up, could they be sure that by sundown the next day he would be dead? Many things had to fall into place within the space of the next 21 hours. It would be a close call.

First, the prisoner had to be tried and sufficient evidence brought forward which would justify the death penalty. Secondly, this needed to be ratified by the leading Jewish council, known as the Sanhedrin. Thirdly (and this was the trickiest of them all), the Roman governor had to give his approval. Some 20 years earlier (in AD 6) the Jewish authorities had lost the right to inflict capital punishment themselves; so Pontius Pilate would have to consent to their proposal. He would probably not have many qualms about the deed. But neither was he any lover of the Jewish authorities, and he might choose on this occasion to deny their request. If he did refuse, then potentially the position of the priests would be worse than if they had never arrested Jesus in the first place. Better that Jesus should go back to Galilee than end up in a Jerusalem prison as a natural focus of popular commotion.

It was a lot to accomplish in such a short space of time. Could it be done? Caiaphas might have some degree of confidence about those parts of the plan which were effectively under his control (though it would mean a night-time trial and a hasty summoning of the full Sanhedrin the next morning); but the ultimate outcome rested largely with Pontius Pilate. In these circumstances, something more needed to be done. Before he could give Judas and the Temple guards the go-ahead, he had to be sure that Pontius Pilate would agree to hear the case the next day and ratify the death sentence. There was only one way to know for sure.

Although it was getting late, a visit to the governor's residence was now an urgent necessity.

The secret visit

We know from the account of Peter's denials of Jesus that it was a cold night (Mark 14:67). We may imagine the governor and his wife sitting in their apartment by the fire, when suddenly at some point around 10 o'clock their peace was disturbed. Would the governor receive a most important caller? Who could this be who was troubling him at *this* time of night? Perhaps only one member of the Jewish population could presume upon a welcome at so late an hour – the High Priest himself. And no doubt he gave full assurances to the door attendant that it was a matter of the utmost importance – which simply could not wait until the following morning. Pilate agreed to see him, and after a detailed explanation of the situation, he seems also to have agreed to Caiaphas' request. He would confirm the death penalty for this important prisoner-to-be, and, yes, as it was a holy day within the Jewish calendar, he would agree to conduct the hearing outside the Praetorium headquarters. Caiaphas hurriedly left with the assurances he needed and Judas was despatched on his mission.

There are several further factors which support this reconstruction of these high-level negotiations late on that April evening. First, John records that the arresting party included a detachment of Roman soldiers (John 18:3); *someone*, at least, within the Roman hierarchy had been informed.

Secondly, there was evident consternation on the part of the Jewish authorities when Pilate the following morning, instead of simply confirming the verdict, effectively opened a retrial with the familiar question (*accusatio*): 'What crime do you charge this man with?' 'If he were not a criminal,' they reply, 'we would not have handed him over to you' (John 18:29–30). They had hoped for a simple 'yes' verdict, but were now seemingly caught off their guard by Pilate's determination to conduct a proper hearing. But what had ever caused them in the first place to believe it would be a straightforward 'rubber-stamping'?

Thirdly, there is the otherwise strange episode of Pilate's wife, Claudia Procula, having a bad dream and sending word to him the next morning not to have anything to do with 'that innocent man, for today I have suffered a great deal because of a dream about him' (Matthew 27:19). At first sight this might seem a fanciful story, concocted much later. Yet, if Pilate and his wife had indeed been disturbed by a surprise caller the night before, it looks rather different. Even if Claudia did not herself see Caiaphas, it would be highly unlikely that Pilate would be able to go to bed without being persuaded to let his wife in on the secret. What was all that fuss about at the front door? The next morning she woke up to learn that her husband had already left to do what he had agreed. So she hurriedly sent word to him: 'Have nothing to do with him!' Hence, it seems, his decision to hold a retrial after all.

Fourthly, there is the curious point that when they brought Jesus to Pontius Pilate the next morning the religious authorities were not prepared to enter the Praetorium. They made it plain that this would ritually defile them; they would then not have enough time to perform the necessary cleansing procedures in time for their Passover duties (John 18:28). One can only conclude that in the normal run of events Pilate would not have been expecting to hear *any* trials that day, for it would be absurd to hold judicial proceedings on a day when the principal officers and witnesses could not be present. So he clearly needed to be warned of this special impending case. More importantly, he needed to give his particular consent to their proposal of trying the case *outside* the Praetorium. All of this suggests again that some important deals had been struck the previous night.

Back in the Garden

All of this frantic activity behind the scenes was quite lost on the disciples. They were too busy falling asleep in the garden. But Jesus would have known only too well what was going on. In fact it was he who had set Judas and the authorities the tough deadline. He knew what important decisions and consultations they would need to make before daring to come and arrest him.

Meanwhile, Jesus prayed and waited; he prayed and waited for his 'hour' to come – knowing it would, because in effect he himself had set it in motion. If he had wished to flee what was coming, he could so easily have kept walking over the crest of the Mount of Olives and found a bed for the night in Bethany. Instead he remained as an obvious target – praying.

The long wait in Gethsemane proves, more than anything else does, that Jesus' death was no accident. Despite the agony which it would involve, it was a path which he consciously chose. If he had been thinking only about himself and his own safety, he could so easily have escaped. Instead he stayed. 'The Son of Man,' he had said, 'came not to be served but to serve, and to give his life a ransom for many' (Mark 10:45).

Eventually, just as he expected, Jesus saw the flare of some torchlights in the distance. They gradually came closer, flickering their way out from the city to the rendezvous point which he himself had set. Judas and the various soldiers (both Jewish and Roman) were just across the valley and would soon be upon him. Jesus' 'hour' had come at last.

Crosses on the Skull

Friday's Grief

The disciples woke up suddenly to the noise of the arriving soldiers. What was going on? A few hours earlier Jesus had warned them, using imagery from the book of Zechariah, that he as the Shepherd would soon be 'struck' and his 'sheep scattered' (Mark 14:27). It was time for his prediction to be proved all too true.

To avoid any confusion amidst the darkness of the olive grove, Judas made directly for Jesus and kissed him – an agreed signal for his comrades. But Jesus offered no resistance. He simply asked that his friends be allowed to go free. Peter, only just waking from his sleep, tried impulsively to take control of the situation. Jesus could not give in so easily! – it was time to wield his sword. But within a matter of moments most of the disciples were soon disappearing into the darkness of the neighbouring olive groves – fearful that they too would be arrested, despite Jesus' plea that they be spared. It was all over – almost before it had begun.

As far as we can tell, nine of Jesus' close disciples ran for their lives. We also learn from Mark's Gospel (14:51–2) that one young man fled away naked – possibly a reference to John Mark himself, the subsequent author of the Gospel. If Gethsemane was his father's property, he may have volunteered to sleep there rather than in the busy house. Almost certainly they all raced up the hill on their way to Bethany.

A few minutes later, when they stopped to catch their breath, they would have been able to see the scene below and the procession of flickering torchlights beginning their return to the city. What had happened, they would have wondered, to Peter and John? Well might they fear that they had also been arrested and were being dragged back to the city, surrounded by those soldiers and torches. In this state of confusion, not knowing what would happen next but fearing the worst, they fled to Bethany, where they broke the terrible news to Mary, Martha and Lazarus. Here they could stay – out of harm's way. But it also meant that they were effectively cut off from any further news from the city. In all probability they remained there till some time on the Sunday. These men, who would become key players in the subsequent story, were completely out of the action at the vital moment. They were about to miss what would become Jerusalem's most famous weekend (see Figure 5).

In fact, however, Peter and John had not been arrested. They too may initially have thought of fleeing up the hill, but eventually they took courage and followed along behind the soldiers to see what would happen to their master. We follow them as they go back the same way they had just come – back towards the wealthy upper city, where Caiaphas the High Priest, the leading figure in Jerusalem's religious hierarchy, was waiting to see this much-wanted prisoner.

THE LONG NIGHT

Jesus was first of all taken briefly to meet Caiaphas' father-in-law, Annas (John 18:13). Annas had been the High Priest until a few years previously (though he still retained the title in certain circumstances) and may have asked if he could give the prisoner an initial interrogation. Then Jesus was taken through to another room, to meet Caiaphas himself.

Peter's denial

John and Peter followed a little behind. John actually followed right in to the courtyard of the High Priest's house, and eventually he persuaded Peter to do the same. But the pressure was now too much for Peter and, when asked by different people if he was anything to do

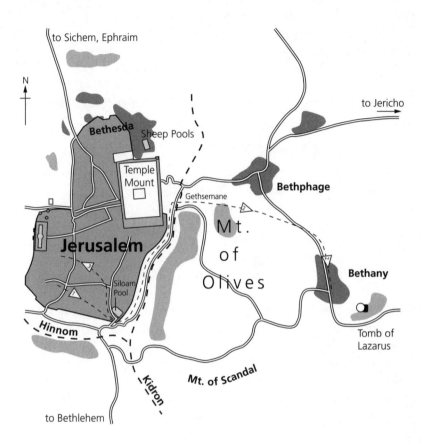

Fig. 5. Thursday evening's movements (cf. Pls. 2 and 6). Jesus and the disciples left the 'upper room' in the Upper City, probably going out of the city by the Siloam gate (1). A few hours later Jesus returned under arrest, followed by Peter and John, to the house of Caiaphas (3). Meanwhile the rest of the disciples fled over the crest of the Mount of Olives to Bethany (2).

with Jesus, he told a barefaced lie – three times. 'You are not one of his disciples, are you?' they quizzed him. 'I am not' (John 18:17).

Peter had sworn such unflinching support of his master, but Jesus had known what he was made of, predicting that this leading disciple would in fact deny him three times before the cock crowed. Suddenly in those dark, eerie hours before dawn, Peter heard the sound of the cock crowing. 'And he broke down and wept' (Mark 14:29–30, 72).

John's home and family

One of the reasons why John seems to have been more at ease in this tense situation was that he was known personally to the High Priest (John 18:15). This may have played a part in strengthening his resolve to risk following the soldiers into the city, and it also meant he had fewer qualms about entering Caiaphas' house.

Quite why Caiaphas knew John is not clear. Some have suggested that John's fishing business was responsible for deliveries to the High Priest's house! More probable, perhaps, is the suggestion that John was himself a priest. It was quite regular for priests to have other secular employment. If he was related to John the Baptist (as suggested just below), then this would be confirming evidence; for the father of John the Baptist, Zechariah, was evidently a priest in the Temple (Luke 1:5).

Another possible reason, which could be combined with either of these, is that John also had a family home in the vicinity. The next day, Jesus would instruct John to look after his mother, Mary; 'from that hour', we read, 'the disciple took her into his own home' (John 19:27). This is often given a less specific sense, but it could mean that there and then John escorted Mary away to his home *in Jerusalem*.

If so, John may similarly have taken Peter there now. Peter was distraught, recriminating himself for feebly denying Jesus at the critical moment. He was also still afraid: what *would* happen to Jesus' followers? As far as we can tell, he now left the scene and remained in hiding throughout the following day – only to re-emerge on the Sunday morning. So yet another disciple – this time the one whom Jesus had appointed as their leader – was kept indoors through fear. He too missed the weekend's dramatic proceedings.

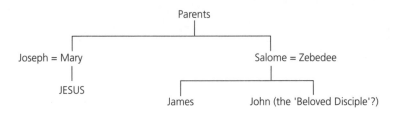

Fig. 6. Jesus' family relationship with Salome, James and John.

If John's family did indeed have a home in Jerusalem, then several pieces in the jigsaw of reconstructing that fateful night fall into place more easily. For there were other close followers of Jesus, quite apart from the 11 disciples, who were in the Jerusalem area at that time and needed a place to stay. The next day we will hear not only of Jesus' mother, Mary, but also of another Mary and of Salome.

From the various ways in which the Evangelists describe these women, it is possible to construct the following family trees, which may be helpful. Salome (Mark 15:40) is also described as 'the sister of Jesus' mother' (John 19:25) and the 'mother of the sons of Zebedee' (Matthew 27:56). This means that Jesus was a 'first cousin' to James and John (see Figure 6).

This in turn might explain the special friendship which seems to have existed between Jesus and John, the 'disciple whom Jesus loved' (John 13:23), as well as why Salome thought that her sons might have a special place in the glory of Jesus' Kingdom (Matthew 20:20). They were, after all, Jesus' cousins.

Meanwhile 'the other Mary' is variously described as the 'mother of James and Joses' (Mark 15:40; Matthew 27:56) and as the 'wife of Clopas' (John 19:25). Clopas (or Cleopas) may be a Greek transliteration of 'Chalphai', which could also be transliterated as 'Alphaeus' (dropping the rough breathing at the start of the name). It would then be possible to identify the son of Cleopas and Mary (called James the 'younger' in Mark 15:40) with the other James within the band of disciples – 'James, the son of Alphaeus' (Mark 3:18) (see Figure 7, p. 24).

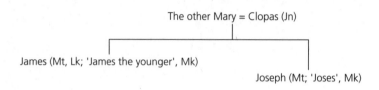

Fig. 7. The family of 'the other Mary'.

Furthermore, there is also an early Christian tradition that Cleopas was in fact the brother of Jesus' 'father' Joseph. If so, a complete family tree of Jesus' relatives might be reconstructed as in Figure 8.

Even if the last point is speculative, this discussion highlights the fact that there were also in Jerusalem that weekend a group of people who belonged to the generation of Jesus' mother, who were part of Jesus' wider circle of followers, and who may all have been related to one another. Given how crowded Jerusalem was at Passover time, it is almost certain that, if they were members of the same family, they would have stayed together. It is also highly probable that, because they were more advanced in age, they would be given preference over Jesus' disciples when a choice had to be made between sleeping in a house, or sleeping rough on the Mount of Olives (or in Bethany). And if James and John did have a family home in Jerusalem, then it is only natural that their parents (Zebedee and Salome) should have hosted the others.

Earlier in the evening Jesus had deliberately celebrated his Passover meal in a different Jerusalem home, the house of John Mark. He wanted to keep this special event just for the twelve. And he may have been concerned, too, with the issue of security: Zebedee's house, the home of James and John, would have been the obvious place for any search parties to begin.

Now, however, as the night wore on, we may imagine the alarm of these older relatives of Jesus when John and Peter returned to Zebedee's house with the news of Jesus' arrest.

In geographical terms, they were actually quite near to where Jesus was being held. Nevertheless, probably only John was able to stay within earshot of the trial. Jesus was effectively deserted in his

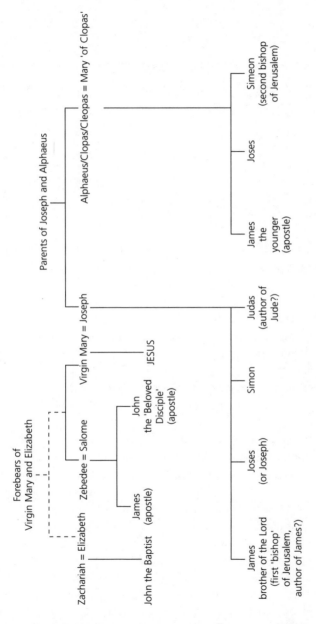

Fig. 8. Jesus' extended family. A possible reconstruction, as in Wenham (1984), p. 40.

hour of need. Although his relatives would be near him the next day, throughout the remainder of this long night he was on his own.

WHERE WAS THE HIGH PRIEST'S HOUSE?

Various suggestions have been made for the location of Caiaphas' house, including some ruins in the Armenian property just outside the Zion Gate, or the church further down the hill called St Peter in Gallicantu.

This latter church (named after Peter's denying Jesus 'at the crowing of the cock') was built in 1931 after excavations had revealed the remains of a sixth-century church, below which there are some chambers that may have been used as a prison. Right by the church are the remains of some first-century steps (see Plate 14), almost certainly marking a route which Jesus would have used with his disciples en route from the Upper to the Lower City, possibly even after the Last Supper.

St Peter in Gallicantu is unlikely, however, to be the 'church of St Peter' known in the Byzantine era. The home of the High Priest was more probably on the top of the western hill where the most luxurious houses were located (not least because of the refreshing breezes from the west). This would favour the Armenian area of modern Jerusalem.

An excellent idea of what a wealthy home would have looked like in the time of Jesus can be gained from visiting the 'Herodian Mansions' (in the Wohl Archaeological Museum nearer to the Western Wall). It was in these luxurious surroundings that a poor preacher from Galilee dared to claim that he was Israel's Messiah.

Fig. 9.

The unusual trial

So the interrogation of Jesus before Caiaphas and his colleagues continued. This so-called 'trial' has been examined in meticulous detail. It is often noted that there were many things about it that were technically illegal. According to a document in the Jewish Mishnah called *Sanhedrin* (late second century AD), the defendant strictly should have been brought to court by the witnesses, not by an armed guard. Technically it was illegal to try a capital charge by night. And, when the evidence of the witnesses had broken down, the judges should have acquitted the prisoner; instead Caiaphas chose at that moment to cross-examine Jesus himself. Part of the difficulty here is knowing how much this later Pharisaic document would truly reflect the practice of the first-century Sanhedrin, which was influenced more by Sadducees. Nevertheless, it is likely that many aspects of the trial were indeed strictly illegal. Far from calling into question whether the Gospel accounts are reliable, this suggests that Jesus was submitted to a trial which was known at the time to be out of order.

Nevertheless, there was at the same time an intention, if possible, to follow some of the basic rules. Attempts were made to get an accusation which, as required by law, was agreed by two witnesses. This of itself suggests that Caiaphas was not all-powerful to work his will in that assembly. It also suggests that they were conscious that their night-time verdict would need to be endorsed by the full Sanhedrin in the morning. It was important, even if other aspects of the trial were out of the ordinary, to get the accusation right.

The first attempts failed. So too did those which focused on Jesus' cryptic statement (probably recorded correctly in John 2:19), 'destroy this Temple, and in three days I will raise it up' (cf. Mark 14:58). These failures at this critical juncture indicate that the whole process had not been carefully orchestrated in advance. Jesus' arrest, though contemplated in advance, had in fact come about quite suddenly, scarcely allowing time to prepare watertight charges. The failure of the witnesses to agree also strongly suggests that they were attempting in their testimonies to offer bona fide statements; they were not trying to concoct something 'out of thin air'. Evidently Jesus had said some such thing concerning himself, the Temple and 'three days'. The trouble was, none of his accusers could get the wording exactly right.

The fact that the concept of the 'three days' is so clearly part of the saying under examination is particularly striking. The other references to 'three days' in Mark's Gospel all concern Jesus' prediction that he would be raised to life 'after three days' (Mark 8:31; 9:31; 10:33). Now, at his trial, an enigmatic saying with this same phrase is acknowledged by his accusers to have come from his lips – a saying which the disciples afterwards clearly understood as referring to his Resurrection. This evidence strongly suggests that Jesus *did* make the seemingly absurd claim that 'after three days' he would rise again, and that his accusers had gained some inkling of the fact.

So at this stage there was still no charge against the defendant which would carry any weight the next day with either the Jewish Sanhedrin or the Roman governor. As a last desperate measure – again technically illegal – Caiaphas placed Jesus under the Oath of the Testimony: 'I put you under oath before the living God, tell us if you are the Messiah' (Matthew 26:64; Mark 14:61). Jesus replied, 'you have said so' – a Hebraic way of saying 'yes'. 'You will see the Son of Man seated at the right hand of the Power and coming with the clouds of heaven' (Mark 14:62). Standing before the High Priest of his own nation, Jesus claimed a status by comparison with which that High Priest was as nothing. Clearly there was here a fundamental and irreconcilable clash. The city was not 'big enough for the both of them'. One of them had to go.

At a personal level, therefore, Caiaphas' violent reaction makes eminent sense; so too at a political level. This was precisely what he needed: on the one hand, a messianic claim (which could be dressed up before Pilate as a form of political insurrection) and, on the other, a claim to enjoy a position at God's right hand (which the Sanhedrin would acknowledge as blasphemous). *Both* subsequent hearings should be well satisfied.

It had indeed been a long night. The cocks were crowing. The dawn was approaching. Few of those present, we can assume, had slept during the night and it was too late for sleep now. Jesus was presumably held prisoner there in the house of the High Priest, awaiting the prospect of the new day. With sunrise, it would be time for the members of the full Sanhedrin to gather (possibly in the great portico on the south side of the Temple: see Plate 11). Their task would simply be to ratify the sentence and then to prepare some charges to take before Pilate. Then, as soon as possible after that, it would be time for the final ratification by Pilate. By sunset it would all have been decided one way or another.

THE PLACE OF JESUS' TRIAL BEFORE PILATE

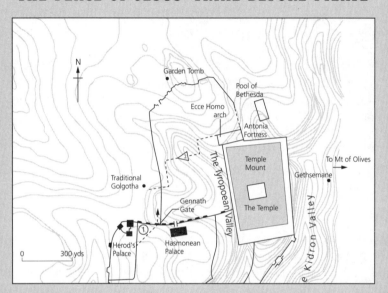

John's Gospel (18:28; 19:13) tells us that Jesus was taken to the 'palace of the Roman Governor' and that Pilate sentenced Jesus when sitting on 'the judge's seat at a place known as the Stone Pavement (which in Aramaic is Gabbatha)'.

For many years this was identified with a stone pavement found to the north of the Temple Mount beneath the convent of the Sisters of Sion. The convent is also popularly known as the 'Ecce Homo' (the Latin for 'Behold the Man!', Pilate's description of Jesus according to John 19:5). On the pavement are various markings including what appears to be the Kings Game, a dice game played by soldiers where the one who landed on the crown was the winner. It was assumed that this was a pavement within the Antonia Fortress and that this was where Pilate tried Jesus – the game perhaps tying in with the way the soldiers mocked Jesus with a 'crown of thorns' (John 19:2).

> Now, however, the pavement has been dated to AD 135 when Hadrian created a forum here. The nearby archway also dates to after Jesus' time, being built by Herod Agrippa in AD 41–4, and the Antonia Fortress is now known to have been somewhat smaller. Instead Pilate probably resided for that Passover weekend in the greater comfort of the palace built by Herod the Great on the west of the city (just inside and to the south of the modern Jaffa Gate; see Figure 1, p. 2).
>
> If so, Jesus' route towards Golgotha would have been more northerly, so that the westward route of the medieval Via Dolorosa is misplaced. Pixner[1] suggests that Pilate was staying in the Hasmonean Palace (and indeed identifies this with the 'Herodian Mansions'), but this was more probably the festival residence of Herod Antipas.

Fig. 10.

THE LONG DAY

Where Pilate was located on that fateful day is still a matter for debate (see Figure 10). Wherever it was, it is likely that Jesus was brought to him at a fairly early hour. It would be good if this episode of the Galilean preacher could all be settled before the streets of Jerusalem were too full of stories about what had happened during the night. Almost certainly, John and some of the others in his household were up early enough to see what happened to their Master next, but those in the general populace who were sympathetic to Jesus were probably quite unaware of what was going on.

Pilate's vacillations

Things did not go quite according to plan. Caiaphas and Pilate had struck an agreement the night before. But now in the cool, early hours of the morning the agreement seemed to have fallen apart. Instead of the expected, quick go-ahead from Pilate, the religious leaders were presented by him with the request for a formal accusation. Their reply betrays their exasperation and can probably be paraphrased as 'Can you not be satisfied with the ruling of our court, that this man is an evildoer?' Why was Pilate reopening the case?

Pilate was already known for his intransigent policies amongst the Jews. He had offended them by sending into Jerusalem the Roman legions, complete with their pagan ensigns. He did this at night, presumably because he knew it would cause trouble. When he needed some extra finance in order to build a much-needed aqueduct for Jerusalem from the Pools of Solomon, he chose to requisition some of the money from the Temple treasury. He similarly caused offence by bringing some votive shields into the Herodian palace. In all of these instances he refused to give way easily, being prepared to use force to maintain his position. So the record in the Gospels (Luke 13:1) that Pilate on some other occasion had executed some Galileans and mingled their blood with their intended sacrifices tallies exactly with what we know of the man. On the one hand, then, he would *not* be especially interested in the finer points of justice in an essentially Jewish trial. On the other hand, he would also not be too worried about causing offence to the religious hierarchy, if need be.

There was probably only one person whom he really feared: the Emperor, Tiberius Caesar. Already the Emperor had been approached twice by people complaining about Pilate's practices, and a few years later (AD 36) he would lose his job when the Emperor was informed of the way Pilate's troops had attacked some Samaritans during a religious ceremony. At the trial of Jesus too it would be his fear of Tiberius which would eventually prove decisive.

However, up until the point when the issue of the Emperor's reaction was raised, Pilate seems to have done as much as possible to renege on the agreement which he had made the night before. Why?

Some of the responsibility for this may well rest with Pilate's wife, Claudia Procula. That dream of hers certainly had an unsettling effect. But even before he received her urgent message Pilate was evidently refusing to go along with Caiaphas' wishes. So perhaps there was something unsettling about this strange prisoner, who talked so little in his own defence and who spoke of another Kingdom (John 18:37). It was uncanny. At one level this prisoner seemed entirely passive and quite resigned to anything that transpired. Yet at another level he seemed to be ominously in control of the whole proceedings. Who was he? What had he done to provoke this damning response from the leaders of his people?

Pilate tried various means of escape. First, he sent Jesus to Herod Antipas, the tetrarch of Galilee who was in Jerusalem for the feast. Antipas was probably staying nearby at the Hasmonean Palace (see Figure 10, p. 29). In due course, however, Jesus was sent back (Luke 23:6–12). Then he offered a Passover amnesty, but Barabbas, not Jesus, was the one who eventually went free. In the end, however, he was taunted with the words, 'If you release this man, you are no friend of the emperor' (John 19:12). It was the ultimate card. It worked. Seated on the stone pavement known as Gabbatha, Pilate washed his hands and condemned Jesus to be crucified. The sentence had been ratified.

Who knows in what mood Pilate returned to his other business that day? Certainly, when he was later challenged about the written charge over Jesus' cross, one senses that he was not prepared to be pushed around for a second time in the space of a few hours. The title 'the king of the Jews' was necessarily ambiguous: was this merely Jesus' claim or did it reflect some paradoxical reality? Pilate trenchantly answered, 'What I have written, I have written' (John 19:22). In other words, let the ambiguity remain. Something about Jesus had made an impression. His detractors might complain as much as they wanted, but Pilate did not care. What he had written, he had written.

The path to the Skull

So Jesus was dismissed from Pilate's presence. He was led out through the Gennath (or 'Garden') Gate to a place which appropriately was known as 'Golgotha', or 'the place of the skull' (Mark 15:22). And there they crucified him.

Despite its enormous significance for their subsequent faith, the Gospel writers are notably restrained in their description of the Crucifixion. The main body of disciples probably remained in Bethany, fearful for their lives and ignorant of the real situation in the city until news filtered through in the late afternoon. Those staying in John's house were surely there, but the absence of any mention of Peter suggests that he too stayed away, filled with both fear and remorse.

THE FAMILY OF THE CROSS-BEARER

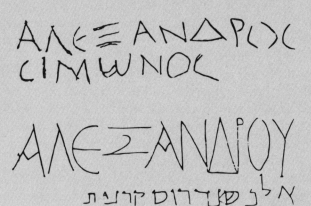

Jesus' cross was carried by Simon of Cyrene. Mark's Gospel adds the detail that he was the 'father of Alexander and Rufus' – perhaps an indication that Mark's readers knew his sons. If Mark was writing in Rome, then one of Paul's greetings at the end of his letter to the church in Rome may be significant: 'Greet Rufus, chosen in the Lord, and his mother, who has been a mother to me too' (Romans 16:13).

Even more intriguing is the possibility that the ossuary of his brother, Alexander, has survived.[2] Ossuaries were stone boxes used to contain a person's bones after the body had decomposed. In 1941 some ossuaries were found in a tomb in the Kidron valley. One of them had several inscriptions (reproduced above): 'Alexander of Cyrene' (in Aramaic) and 'Alexander, son of Simon' (in Greek). Did this contain the bones of the man whose father carried Jesus' cross? If so, we know something about four members of a family, who were influenced by what happened that Friday morning outside Jerusalem's city wall.

Fig. 11.

Those condemned to be crucified normally carried their own
'cross-beam' (or *patibulum*). When Jesus was too weak to do this, the
soldiers conscripted into service a Jewish man visiting Jerusalem from
North Africa, known to us as Simon of Cyrene (Mark 15:21). Victims
were paraded through the city for some distance to endure humiliation by those in the streets. Then, once they had arrived at the place of
execution, they were normally stripped of any clothing. Certainly this
was what happened in other provinces of the empire, but because of
Jewish sensitivities there may have been occasions when this was not
implemented in Judea. Nevertheless, the fact that all four Evangelists
comment on the way the soldiers cast lots for Jesus' clothing may be
their discreet way of hinting that Jesus was indeed naked on the Cross
– for any Jew the ultimate in humiliation.

Although crucifixion had become the regular Roman means of
execution, it is unlikely that there were many crucifixions outside the
walls of Jerusalem at this time. It was quite a rare event. However, it
was only 30 years since some 2,000 people had been crucified in
Galilee when the Romans put down the revolt led by Judas the Galilean
(4 BC), and within a generation the Romans would use the same method
in response to the First Jewish Revolt (AD 70). According to Cicero, it
was a punishment especially reserved for people of the lower classes,
and the word for 'cross' was avoided in polite Roman society.[3] According
to later Church tradition Peter was also crucified, but Paul, because he
was a Roman citizen, was beheaded. So in more ways than one did
Jesus take 'the form of a slave' when he humbled himself 'to the point
of death – even death on a cross' (Philippians 2:7–8). The death that he
would die would be that reserved for the lowest of the low.

Gathered round the Cross

By now the news may have been filtering through some of the nearby
streets of Jerusalem. Many would be busy that day on the other side of
the city, taking their Passover lambs to be sacrificed in the Temple, and
generally getting things ready for the Passover festival. They would
only find out later. But there were some on hand to see what was now
happening to Jesus. Some of those who identified with Jesus' teaching
and claims lined the streets, including 'many women who mourned
and lamented him' (Luke 23:27).

And at some point there arrived hotfoot from Bethany one of Jesus' closest followers – Mary Magdalene. The suspense in that Bethany household may have become unbearable, with Mary eventually insisting that she be allowed to go on a discreet mission, to find out for them all what exactly was happening.

There is some evidence within the Gospels and in later Church tradition that this Mary is to be identified not only with the unnamed woman who, when in Galilee, had tried somewhat unsuccessfully to anoint Jesus (Luke 7:37ff.), but also with the Mary who repeated this action with a deeper meaning when in Bethany (John 12:3ff.; Mark 14:3–9). She was Martha's sister and her true home was in Bethany, but for a while she had lived an independent and notorious life up north in Magdala.

If this identification is correct, then several things in the Gospel narrative make extra sense. It would certainly be fitting if the woman whom Jesus praised so highly for anointing his body in advance for burial was also present at the time of his real burial. It would also not be surprising if the same woman was one of those who three days later was eager to bring spices to complete this solemn task of anointing. It also makes eminent sense that this Mary, having heard the disciples' tale when they returned to Bethany during the night, resolved to make her way into the city the next morning to find out for them just what was going on.

She would have arrived to find her worst fears being fulfilled. She joined Jesus' friends and relatives as they watched the Roman duty soldiers do their job – stripping Jesus of his clothes, nailing him to the cross-beam of wood, and then hoisting him up onto the vertical shaft. They did the same to two common criminals, one on either side. Yet even at this moment of unbearable pain and ultimate humiliation Jesus' followers heard him pray: 'Father, forgive them; for they do not know what they are doing' (Luke 23:34).

CRUCIFIXION

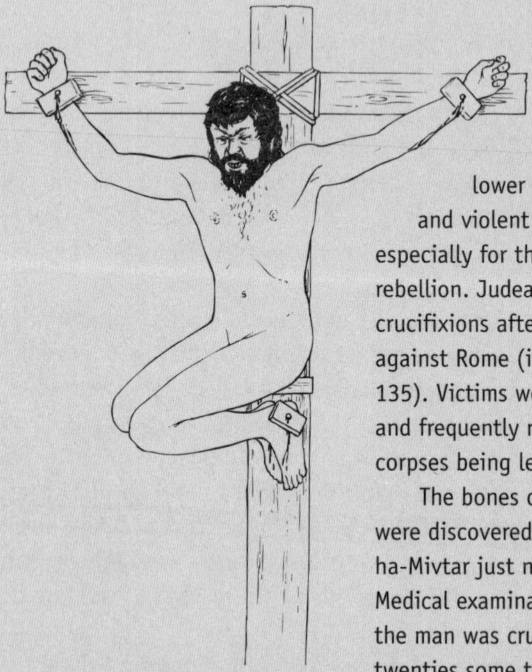

Crucifixion was a form of punishment used by the Romans for the lower classes – for slaves and violent criminals, and especially for those involved in rebellion. Judea was littered with crucifixions after each of the revolts against Rome (in 4 BC, AD 70 and AD 135). Victims were normally naked and frequently never buried – their corpses being left for birds of prey.

The bones of a crucified man were discovered in 1968 at Giv'at ha-Mivtar just north of Jerusalem. Medical examination revealed that the man was crucified in his mid-twenties some time during the middle of the first century AD. His forearms had been nailed above the wrist and his legs had been broken. Even to this day his heel-bones were still nailed together.

From this it has been deduced that victims were made to stand against the cross for the nails to be hammered through their forearms. Their legs were then pushed up (almost certainly to one side, as above) so that their arms were now carrying the body's full weight. This then caused the nails to tear through the flesh of the forearm until they reached the wrist. If there was a slight 'seat' on which the victims could rest, this only prolonged the agony. Eventually they would die of suffocation, unable to pull themselves up sufficiently to breathe.[4]

Fig. 12.

Amongst their number there was also the other Mary (the wife of Cleopas) as well as Joanna. Joanna is named by Luke, along with Susanna (who probably was also present at the Crucifixion), as one of the women who had supported Jesus during his Galilean ministry (Luke 8:3). Since Joanna's husband worked for Herod Antipas, she might well have been staying amongst Herod's retinue during his visit to Jerusalem. Quite possibly she was one of Luke's special sources (e.g. for Luke 23:6–12). She may have been working for Herod during that morning, but was free later in the day to join the crowds at the scene of the Crucifixion.

Luke therefore speaks several times of the 'women who had accompanied him from Galilee' (23:49, 55). He also speaks of Jesus' 'friends' (v. 49), probably referring to his male acquaintances and friends, such as Zebedee, Cleopas, Joseph of Arimathea and Nicodemus. But the fact that he does not use the word 'disciple' strongly confirms our conclusion that throughout this period the majority of the 'disciples' were nowhere to be seen – hiding anxiously in Bethany.

In the midst of all this, Jesus was still able to think of another woman, a third Mary, who was anxiously watching this horrendous spectacle – his own mother (John 19:26–7). She was no longer young and the sight of a crucifixion was no sight for a broken-hearted woman. No doubt despite entreaties from her relatives, she insisted on being there; who could deny her a mother's right to be with her son? But there came the time when Jesus himself spoke to John and bade him to take her home, as if he were now her son. So John for a while left the scene, taking Mary back to his home – helped presumably by his mother, Salome, who was also Mary's sister. Salome then stayed to comfort Mary, but John returned in time to see Jesus' final moments (John 19:28f.).

The death of Jesus

Throughout the preceding couple of hours there had been an eerie darkness over the city – perhaps caused by a dust-storm from the desert. There had also been (so they would learn later) a strange event in the Temple, with the curtain in front of the Holy of Holies being torn 'from top to bottom' (Matthew 27:45, 51ff.). Was this all an outward sign of something more serious, an indication that this was a time of divine judgement? Certainly, it was in keeping with the solemn and grim reality of what was now taking place.

John and the others could do nothing but stand and watch as Jesus, the one whom they had seen bringing healing and life to others, was hung on a cross before their very eyes. His accusers' taunts seemed cruelly to the point: he had saved others, but he evidently could not save himself (Mark 15:31). So the one who had made God's presence so real to them was heard at one point to utter those chilling, unforgettable words: 'My God, my God, why have you forsaken me?' (Matthew 27:46). It was indeed a dark moment – cut off, so it seemed, from so much as a hint of light.

It was not unknown for those being crucified to survive on display for two or three days – in agony, gasping for breath. On this occasion, however, because of the imminent Passover celebrations, the religious authorities were keen that the victims' legs should be broken and their bodies removed before the Sabbath sundown (John 19:31f.). But in Jesus' case this proved unnecessary; the end came comparatively soon. For after some five or six hours of hanging on the Cross Jesus was heard calling out in a loud voice: 'It is finished. Father, into your hands I now commit my spirit.' With that, he 'breathed his last' (Luke 23:46; John 19:30). It was around three o'clock in the afternoon. It was all over.

For those who had believed that Jesus would be their Messiah, this was the final, sickening end to all their hopes. A dead Messiah was no Messiah at all. Many left the scene 'beating their breasts' (Luke 23:48). For some in the crowd this was just another horrid instance of human cruelty and a complete travesty of justice. But others may have been impressed at a deeper level. Jesus' dying moments had been so different from those of others. To the end he had still been trusting God, still calling him 'Father'. Certainly, there was something about Jesus which enormously impressed the Roman centurion who saw him die. Jesus was no ordinary prisoner. 'Truly,' he concluded, 'this man was a son of God' (Matthew 27:54).

Hasty burial arrangements

At some point in the preceding hours an awful realization must have dawned upon Jesus' followers gathered around the Cross. When the end finally came, Jesus' body would simply be thrown into a common grave along with the other criminals who were being crucified that day. Amongst their number was a man who could prevent that from happening – if he was prepared to risk it. His own family tomb happened to be almost immediately nearby – in a garden area not far from the crucifixion-site (John 19:41).

Joseph of Arimathaea is described as a rich member of the Sanhedrin, who had not consented to the council's verdict on Jesus (Luke 23:50–1). Now he had his opportunity of identifying with Jesus' cause – even if too late. He bravely went to Pilate to gain permission to bury Jesus in his own tomb.

No doubt the religious authorities would not have been best pleased with this – not least because it meant that responsibility for Jesus' body was now once again within Jewish, rather than Roman, jurisdiction. But by this stage in the afternoon many of them were involved in the ceremonial 'waving of the first-fruits', and so would only hear about Joseph's manoeuvre some hours later.

Joseph returned with Pilate's permission and consulted with Nicodemus about what to do in the brief time that remained before nightfall and the beginning of the Sabbath. Normally the body would have been washed and anointed with perfumed oils before being redressed in an 'everyday' outer garment. There was no time for all this. Joseph hurriedly purchased a large linen cloth and Nicodemus a huge quantity of dry spices, whilst the women agreed to come back at the first opportunity after the Sabbath to anoint the body properly.

We can then imagine Joseph and Nicodemus, perhaps helped by John or some servants, taking Jesus' body and laying it in the nearby tomb. It was certainly a task for more than one man. The two Marys seem to have watched this from a short distance, not going into the tomb. They probably did not themselves know Joseph and their own social standing may have prevented them from introducing themselves. Joanna and Susanna, however, were part of Herod's court and, according to Luke, they saw 'how his body was laid' (23:55). Perhaps they even accompanied the men into the tomb. And so Jesus was temporarily laid to rest. It was as much as they could do for now. The remainder of the operation would have to wait until after the Sabbath.

The sun was setting in the western sky. There was no time to lose. So they hurriedly crept out of the tomb. They rolled the customary disc-shaped stone across its entrance in order to prevent any thieves (or jackals and wild animals) from disturbing the tomb. They then began to make their way out of the garden area back towards the city gate. It would not be surprising, however, if, as they did so, they looked back over their shoulder to cast a final eye at the scene of that afternoon's harrowing events – painfully aware just how many of their hopes had been buried forever in that cold garden tomb.

The house of mourning

The light of the Passover full moon would soon be in the sky over the Mount of Olives. Joseph and Nicodemus returned to their homes. Joanna and Susanna made their way back to the Hasmonean Palace, the residence of Herod Antipas. It was too late for Mary Magdalene to take word of all this back to the disciples in Bethany. So the other Mary, Cleopas' wife, took her back to the place where she had been staying, the home of Zebedee and Salome. Peter, Cleopas, John and Jesus' mother would all be there too. They would all need each other for comfort and consolation through the interminably long hours of the Sabbath.

No doubt, once all together, they rehearsed in detail the events of the previous 24 hours. So much had happened so quickly; they needed time to take it all in. And behind all the drama of the events, there were the inevitable questions. What did it all mean? Had Jesus seen all this coming, and, if so, how could it all be part of God's purpose? Where indeed *was* the God that Jesus had spoken about with such faith and confidence? What had happened to all their hopes that Jesus was the one who would redeem Israel and usher in the Kingdom of God? Was he really just another failed messiah? Was he really under God's curse, because he had died on a 'tree' (cf. Deuteronomy 27:26)?

For others in Jerusalem it was a high and holy day. All the neighbours were getting started with their evening Passover celebrations. Children were excited. Parents were busy explaining to them how

God had redeemed them from Egypt and would one day act again to redeem his people. It was a time for looking back, but also for looking forward.

For those huddled in the home of Zebedee there was little to look forward to, no sign that God would ever come to their aid – only the sorry confirmation that good did not triumph over evil. It was a day of heart-searching questions. It was a day of almost unbearable personal loss.

It had indeed been a long day – a day which they would have preferred to forget, but which would come to be etched on their memory for ever.

3

Drama in the Tomb

Sunday's Surprise

The next day was a quiet Jerusalem Saturday. Everyone had ample time for reflection. But history suggests that this Sabbath-day was also a day in which some strategic planning was done by most of the people at the centre of this drama. Outwardly all was calm, but amidst the quiet some important plans were afoot.

THE RESTFUL SABBATH?

Jesus' followers

Jesus' followers would have had at least two practical concerns preying on their minds. First, the women at the crucifixion (who throughout this weekend bore the brunt of the crisis) had agreed to meet again at Joseph's tomb as soon as possible after the Sabbath; they wanted to prepare Jesus' body properly for its final rest. That meant that someone had to obtain some more spices and ointment. It is possible that Joanna and Susanna, being more wealthy, already had a supply and so were able to begin to get things ready when they returned to the Hasmonean palace on the Friday afternoon (Luke 23:56). But for the two Marys staying in the home of Zebedee and Salome it was a matter of sending someone out to the market after sundown on the Saturday (Mark 16:1).

Secondly, there was the complete breakdown of communication with the other disciples in Bethany, of whom nothing had now been heard for nearly two days. This too surely required an expedition after the Sabbath had ended on the Saturday evening. We can well imagine Salome offering to buy the spices and to stay in Jerusalem to tend for her sister, Jesus' mother, whilst the two Marys opted to go out to Bethany. After all, Mary Magdalene had a brother and sister there, and the other Mary would be anxious for her son (James the younger). They could set out just before sundown and cover the distance of a 'Sabbath-day's journey' to the crest of the Mount of Olives; they could then complete the rest of the journey under the first light of the stars. Since they would arrive in the dark, it is almost certain that Cleopas would also have accompanied his wife. Once in Bethany, the three from Jerusalem would find that all was well with the disciples. For their part, however, they could only confirm the appalling news that had already been filtering into Bethany: their beloved Master had been dead for more than 24 hours. The only consolation was that Peter and John had not been arrested and that Jesus' mother was in good hands.

The religious leaders

Meanwhile, the city's religious authorities were also coming to terms with the events of the preceding day. They had indeed successfully achieved their principal objective (the Galilean rabbi was dead), but not everything had gone straightforwardly. What were they to make of the strange events surrounding Jesus' death – the dark skies, the earth tremors, and above all the fact that the Temple's inner curtain had been torn in two, laying bare the secret Holy of Holies (Matthew 27:45, 51)?

Moreover, the last-minute intervention of Joseph of Arimathea in placing Jesus' corpse in his own tomb was immensely irritating. If Jesus' body had been cast by the Roman soldiers into a common criminal grave, then it would effectively have become Roman property. As it was, Jesus' body and its tomb were now clearly once again a Jewish responsibility. In more normal circumstances, this would not be much of a problem. But this Jesus had been a popular figure with a sizeable segment of the Passover crowds. When news of his death became known and the Sabbath came to an end, would there be a popular outpouring of grief – or worse, of anger? A few days earlier those same religious authorities had been fearful of how the crowds would react if Jesus were arrested (Mark 14:2; Luke 22:2). We can imagine they might now have been even more fearful, when it became public knowledge that he had been arrested *and* put to death.

In such circumstances the tomb where Jesus' body was resting would inevitably become the clear focus for any voices of protest. Some might want to come and pay their last respects. Some might want simply to confirm with their own eyes that the deed had truly been done. But others might have some more forceful ways of expressing their disapproval.

And so, once again, even though it was a Sabbath, the religious authorities requested an audience with Pilate – this time, in order to obtain his permission for a guard to be set over the tomb (Matthew 27:62–6). Pilate's reply to this further request is unfortunately ambiguous. It could mean 'You (already) have a guard.' This would be a plain refusal (similar to that in John 19:22). More probably, however, he agreed to their request ('Yes, have a guard'). Roman soldiers had been involved alongside the Jewish Temple guard in Jesus' arrest in Gethsemane, and their presence would be a valuable asset now – and for the same reasons. Galilee was a hotbed of messianic expectation and zealot unrest – only the previous year Pilate had taken some drastic action against some Galileans (Luke 13:1). When it came to matters of security and of quashing potential unrest, we may be reasonably certain that Pilate's political instinct would be to take pre-emptive action and make a speedy show of force. Yes, get a guard in place – as soon as possible.

For the religious authorities, if not for Pilate, there was also the not insignificant matter that this Jesus was on record as having said that something strange would happen 'after three days'. Even if the witnesses at his trial had not got the exact wording correct, he had clearly said something like, 'Destroy this Temple and after three days I will raise it again' (Mark 14:58; cf. John 2:19). Some had taunted him with these words when he was hanging on that Roman cross (Mark 15:29). If such rumours were in the air, it would be understandable if those implicated in Jesus' death did not sleep entirely easily until that third day had safely passed. What if, for example, some of his followers latched onto this idea and stole the body? Then this 'last deception would be worse than the first' (Matthew 27:64).

LIGHT IN THE DARKNESS

Pl.1: The full moon over the Kidron Valley (looking south). Jesus walked north-wards up the valley to this point on his way to Gethsemane (100m to the left); he would have been well able to see the Temple platform (right) and the 'Tomb of Absolom' (left) under the full Passover moon.

THE HILL FREQUENTED BY JESUS: TWO VIEWS OF THE MOUNT OF OLIVES (1900 AND 1989), LOOKING EAST ACROSS THE KIDRON VALLEY

Pl.2 (above): The disciples fled from Gethsemane (centre probably to Bethany (over the hill to the right). The summit i the traditional site for the Ascension.

Pl.3 (left): In addition to the two Russian churches (of the Ascension and St Mary Magdalene) note the modern church of All Nations in Gethsemane (1924).

JESUS' LAST NIGHT: TWO AERIAL
VIEWS FROM THE SOUTH-WEST
(1936 AND 1998)

Pl.4 (above): In Jesus' day the walled city came further south, surrounded by
the valleys of the Kidron (right) and Hinnom (bottom). The Mount of Olives
and Judean desert are seen to the right.

Pl.5 (inset): The Holy Land Hotel model of the city in the first century,
showing even more clearly the steep terracing from the Upper City (left) down
to the Lower City (seen in Pl.4; cf. Pl.14).

Pl.6: Jesus'
night-time walk
from the Last
Supper on
Mount Zion (1),
down to the
Siloam gate (2),
and up to
Gethsemane (3).

THE DEPTH OF THE VALLEY

Pl.7: The Kidron valley (c. 1880), looking north, before the extensive building of houses on the right (modern Silwan) and left (the ancient City of David on the Ophel Ridge). When Jesus walked up the valley, the Temple platform (top left) would have appeared even higher, surmounted by colonnaded stoas.

SAFE HAVEN

Pl.8: Bethany (c.1890), looking west. This village, the last before the Judean desert, was the home of Mary, Martha and Lazarus – the place where most of the disciples probably fled after Jesus' arrest. Jesus too could easily have escaped here. Lazarus' tomb (see John 11) is marked by the church up the right-hand pathway.

THE VALLEY OF THE SHADOW

Pl.9: The Kidron Valley (1998), merging with the Hinnom Valley south-east of the city near the pool of Siloam. The late afternoon sun catches the top of the Ophel Ridge (King David's 'Zion'), the golden Dome of the Rock and the Arabic village of Silwan. In the distance lies Gethsemane and, beyond, the modern Hebrew University on Mt Scopus.

JESUS AND THE TEMPLE: CLEANSING, TRIAL AND DESTRUCTION (AS SEEN IN A CONTEMPORARY MODEL AND IN RECENT ARCHAEOLOGY)

Pl.10 (top opposite page): Jesus overturns the traders' tables in the outer court (note the fence or 'wall of partition' preventing Gentiles from entering the Temple 'proper' to the right). This provocative action, together with his prediction of the Temple's destruction (Mark 14:58) precipitated his arrest.

Pl.11 (inset opposite): Jesus on trial before the Sanhedrin at dawn in the royal portico (to the south of the main Temple).

Pl.12 (bottom opposite page): The vast stones which crashed down onto the paved road below in AD 70 (when the Temple was destroyed by the Romans under Titus). Jesus had warned: 'not one stone would be left upon another' (Mark 13:2).

JESUS WEEPS FOR THE CITY

Pl.13 (above): The view of Jerusalem from 'Dominus Flevit', the small church commemorating 'the Lord's weeping' over Jerusalem (Luke 19:41–44). Claiming that his own arrival was the ultimate moment in Jerusalem's history, Jesus announces what will shortly happen 'because you did not recognize the time of your visitation from God'. The window's central cross is focused not on the golden Dome of the Rock, but on the church of the Holy Sepulchre. Despite the crowd's initial welcome he would soon be cast out from the city to be crucified.

Pl.14: The remains of some first-century steps (next to St Peter in Gallicantu), possibly used by Jesus when leaving the Upper City after the Last Supper.

FROM THE TABLE
TO THE TOMB:
REMINDERS OF JESUS'
SOLEMN JOURNEY

Pl.15 (right): The church of All Nations in Gethsemane, commemorating Jesus' agony.

Pl.16 (below): The rock-cut 'Tomb of Absolom', which Jesus passed twice that night – both to and from Gethsemane.

Pl.17 (below right): A rolling-stone by the entrance to a tomb; this one comes from Nazareth (beneath the convent of the Sisters of Nazareth) – a first-century tomb just yards away from where Jesus had spent his childhood. Jesus now knew how things would end.

The scene is set

So as this quiet Saturday draws to a close, the stage is set as follows:

- *In Bethany* (possibly the perspective from which Matthew's Gospel was later composed?): nine disciples, now joined briefly for the night by the two Marys and Cleopas (who sleep uneasily waiting for cock-crow and their planned return to the city in the half-light of dawn).
- *In John's house* (the perspective of Mark and John?): Peter, John, Jesus' mother, Zebedee and Salome (with Salome waiting for the return of the three from Bethany soon after dawn).
- *In the Hasmonean palace* (the perspective of Luke's Gospel?): Joanna and Susanna (intending to rendezvous with the other women at the tomb soon after sunrise).
- *In the garden of Joseph of Arimathea*, and unbeknown to the women: two groups of guards (no doubt tired after the demanding activities of this Passover weekend) beginning their night watch and waiting eagerly for daylight when their shift would be complete...

The question at the centre of human history is: *what happened the next morning?*

The women indeed set out on their expedition. It was still dark when the two Marys set out with Cleopas from Bethany (cf. John 20:1; Matthew 28:1) but somewhat lighter when, having left Cleopas at John's house, they at last found themselves making their way out of the city gate towards Joseph's garden.

But when they arrived, they were – to say the least – in for a big surprise!

THE RISING SUN

The first event that next morning, so Matthew claims, was an earth-quake followed by the appearance of angels who rolled back the stone which had been covering the tomb (Matthew 28:2–4). The frightened guards went running to the chief priests (v. 11), who then had to decide how best to limit the damaging effects of this report.

The event never described

Matthew's text gives the initial impression that this earthquake took place at the moment when the women arrived. More probably, however, it had occurred shortly beforehand. (Matthew's account may simply reflect the difficulty of describing 'relative time' in a language which lacked such literary devices as brackets and footnotes.) Yet even this – the most dramatic account given by the four Gospel writers – falls short of actually describing the precise moment when, so they believed, Jesus' body had been raised by God from the dead. The earthquake breaks open the tomb, but there is no mention of what happened at that moment (or at some previous point) to Jesus' body. As far as we can tell, the tomb was opened not so much to let Jesus *out* (cf. John 20:19) as to let others *in* – to see that it was empty. But again this is, strictly speaking, a conjecture: we do not know what happened at the decisive moment.

This is one of the most remarkable things about the Gospel accounts of those strange early morning events. Not one of them actually describes the Resurrection itself! This is the great event which the women (and eventually others) conclude must have taken place before their arrival on the scene. This is the great event on which the rest of the New Testament entirely depends. It can be deduced by reflecting on the subsequent appearances of Jesus to his disciples (how could he be seen, if he had not first been raised?), but in itself it is never described. It is the great unseen factor, in itself forever mysterious, which yet explains so much else and casts everything in a new light.

This reticence on the part of the Evangelists, however, even if not in keeping with some of our own preferences, serves only in a strange way to confirm their general reliability. A hundred years later an apocryphal work (the *Gospel of Peter*) would try and fill in this obvious gap for the sake of the inquisitive reader. The four canonical Evangelists, however, were content to leave their account as open-ended and rough-hewn as were those original events. They told it like it was. They did not use fine artistry, papering over all the cracks. Instead their accounts to this day bear all the marks of surprise, as they relate with fresh and vivid colours the initially bewildering, almost eerie sequence of events which they believed had taken place in the garden in that early dawn.

Who had moved the stone?

The realism of their accounts is also seen in the way they portray the characters in the story so honestly. For example, there is no attempt to hide the fact that it is only as the women make their final steps towards the garden that they ask the rather obvious question: 'Who will remove for us the stone?' (Mark 16:3). One might have expected them to ask this long before, but all their anxious preparations that weekend had seemingly caused them to overlook the obvious. Despite the women's desire for secrecy, they would clearly need to get some assistance to dislodge this heavy stone from its sunken position over the tomb's entrance.

As it was, it proved unnecessary. For, as they approached, the women were shocked to notice that the stone had been rolled to one side.

Perhaps they had had a sneaking suspicion that something would go awry, and that even now, after his death, their master would not be allowed to rest in peace. Could he not have been given the dignity of being left undisturbed – in death, if not in life? Now, all their worst fears had been fulfilled. Coming as it did at dawn to people whose minds were already filled with grief, this shocking discovery was quite enough by itself to produce a condition bordering on hysteria. Their spirits, already burdened with grief, now had yet another burden to bear. What else could they conclude but that someone had stolen the body?

So, without more ado, the youngest and most impulsive of them, Mary Magdalene, ran back as fast as her legs would carry her to Zebedee's house – to alert Peter and John to the next drama in this series of depressing events which were fast spiralling out of their control. Things were going from bad to worse. What would happen next? Breathless, she blurted out the news: 'They have taken the Lord out of the tomb and we do not know where they have laid him' (John 20:2). John's record of the word 'we' confirms that Mary was accompanied by others, even though in the previous verse he had focused only on Mary – possibly because she was the prime mover in all these proceedings.

The shocking encounter

Meanwhile, back in the garden, the other, older women eventually gathered their wits sufficiently to venture nearer the tomb entrance. This may well have been occasioned by the welcome arrival from the Hasmonean Palace of Joanna and Susanna, with whom they had agreed to rendezvous as soon as possible after dawn. Joanna had probably been inside the tomb on the Friday. So, plucking up courage, the four of them tiptoed into the tomb – only to be presented with another shock. Yes, as they feared, the body had disappeared – the tomb was empty. Yet, as they got used to the light, they became chillingly aware that they were not alone: the tomb was *not* so empty after all. There inside the tomb, sitting over to the right, was a young man.

It is hard to express adequately the complete state of shock which all this must have brought about. Anyone in similar circumstances would have been startled out of their minds – and these were ageing women after an emotionally draining weekend, now caught unawares in a dim, damp tomb at dawn.

What was this man doing here and what did he want? Had he stolen the body? And how would he react to being disturbed by these prying women?

Yet this was not the time for stopping to ask too many such questions (nor was it the time to carefully commit every minute detail to memory for the sake of posterity!). This was a time for getting out of the tomb and the garden as fast as possible. So they turned around and began to make their get-away.

But, as they did so, the man tried to calm them: 'Do not be alarmed. It's all right. I know you are looking for Jesus of Nazareth who was crucified. But why do you look for the living among the dead? Come back; see the place where he lay. He is not here, but has risen' (Mark 16:6; cf. Luke 24:5). We can almost imagine him calling these words out after them – as they scurried away, only half listening to what was being said. He also tried to tell them something about Galilee – about what Jesus had taught them there concerning his going up to Jerusalem and about his desire to meet them again in Galilee. But little of it made any sense.

And then, perhaps when they were just a little distance from the tomb, the 'penny began to drop'. What was it that he was saying? He was claiming that Jesus was not dead, but alive – risen from the dead! What could that possibly mean? And if by some miracle that was indeed what had happened, then this man was not a dangerous thief, who had removed Jesus' body, but... They looked back one last time and, as they did so, it finally dawned on them that this was not just a young man who was calling after them, but in fact ... two angels! Even so, they kept running away from the tomb – their hearts pounding with fear, but also with a twinge of hope. Could what they had just heard possibly be true? At that moment they did not say a word to anyone (Mark 16:8), but clearly there were people in the city who needed to be told immediately. They ran out of the garden area towards the city gate in search of Peter, John and the others.

The whole story is charged with emotion and sudden drama – still found in the primitive Gospel accounts. It would all have happened so quickly – the strange encounter in the tomb possibly lasting little more than a minute. And in that short space of time their emotions had been pulled in almost every direction. No wonder some of the details would forever remain a blur. But the general impact of it all – that would be something which they would never, never forget.

The Risen Lord

Peter and John had in fact already left the house – John running fast, Peter lagging a little behind. Perhaps providentially, they had missed the women amidst Jerusalem's narrow streets. By the time they arrived at the tomb, the angels too had temporarily disappeared. It is as though Peter and John needed to be given space for a more leisurely investigation and to check things out for themselves.

Out of breath, Peter took the lead in going into the tomb and noticed what John had already been observing as he peered in through the entrance. Jesus' grave-clothes were still there – in position, as it were, with the head-cloth separate from the rest – but the body, which till recently had been within them, was simply nowhere to be seen. For John at least, this was evidence enough. No robber would have carefully wrapped up the head-cloth in this way, and no one would have dragged a naked corpse out into the open. The only way to explain what he was now seeing was that Jesus' body had been brought back to life and in some miraculous way had passed through

the grave-clothes (John 20:1–10; Luke 24:12, 24). After a few linger-
ing moments, they made their way with haste back to the city – half-
believing, half-doubting.

Meanwhile Mary had arrived back at the tomb (John 20:11ff.).
After running to Zebedee's house she would have been out of breath.
So she probably lingered to offer Jesus' mother some comfort at the
prospect of this further disaster – the stealing of her son's decomposing
corpse. But soon she made her solitary way back, full of tears at this
final injustice. Unlike Peter, John and the other women, she did not
dare go in to the tomb. But she too suddenly found herself being
addressed by two angels, whom she could see through the entrance.
They were sitting at either end of the place where Jesus' body had
been laid to rest. Still convinced that someone had stolen Jesus' body,
she sobbed through her tears, 'They have taken away my Lord and I
do not know where they have laid him.'

Suddenly, however, she became aware that someone else was
there, not so far behind her. Turning half-around and not daring to
look up, she immediately presumed that this must be the caretaker of
the garden – one of the few people whom she and the other women
might have expected to be up early enough to help them to move the
stone away. 'Sir, if you have taken him away,' she pleaded, 'tell me
where you have laid him.' She was agitated, desperate, longing for this
nightmare to be over. Then she heard a word. It was a single word,
which would change her whole life. It was her own name, but spoken
with a knowing love as only one person could ever speak it: 'Mary!' he
said. She turned to face the one who was speaking to her, believing
neither her ears nor her eyes. And in that moment she recognized
him: 'Master!'

THE RESURRECTION SUNDAY

So the first person to meet with the Risen Jesus was Mary Magdalene
– almost certainly the same person who a few days earlier had prema-
turely anointed his body for burial (John 12:3–8). It was true. Jesus,
though crucified three days earlier, was now alive again. Death had
not destroyed him. Other appearances would take place throughout
that Sunday.

Somewhat later in the morning Jesus appeared to some of the

other women (Matthew 28:9–10). Quite possibly this took place as one or two of them were making their way out to Bethany – for someone surely needed to tell the main body of disciples what was happening. By the time they reached the disciples, however, they had something amazing to report. It was not just that the tomb was empty. They had now *seen* the Lord! To the disciples, of course, this seemed like an 'idle tale and they did not believe them' (Luke 24:11). Nevertheless, this strange message was enough to force the disciples out of their self-imposed confinement in Bethany. At long last, perhaps slightly sheepishly, they returned to the city, arriving perhaps at around lunch-time. A lot had happened since they were last there – there was a lot to catch up on.

Back in the early morning, however, we may reasonably imagine that *all* the women who had been at the tomb made their way first of all to Zebedee's house. When they arrived, they would have found that Peter and John had already departed for the tomb. But they still had the opportunity to tell the others staying in the house what had happened in those few moments after Mary Magdalene had left the garden. Not much later, Peter and John returned with their own report, confirming what Mary and now the other women had witnessed – the tomb *was* empty. But what did it mean? Could it be that Jesus really *had* been raised from the dead?

The road to Emmaus

Surprisingly, it was at just *this* moment (i.e. before Mary arrived back once more with a yet more startling report) that two of the people gathered in Zebedee's house decided that they really must be on their way – to Emmaus, a village to the north-west of Jerusalem (Luke 24:13ff.; see Figure 13, p. 52). One of them was Cleopas; the name of the other person is unknown (though possibly it was his wife, Mary). What we do know, however, is that it must have been something very important which caused them to leave at just this juncture, when the whole household was awash with rumour and speculation. As they set out, however, their mood was still decidedly depressed (v. 17). These strange Sunday morning events had clearly done nothing as yet to dislodge the atmosphere of gloom and despondency which had prevailed in that household throughout the weekend.

THE LOCATION OF EMMAUS

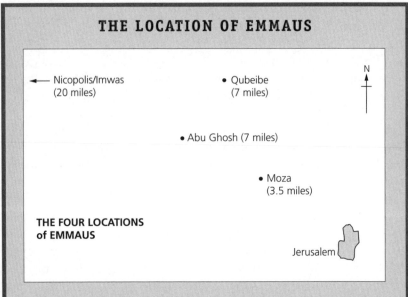

No less than four different places have been suggested for the village of Emmaus. It is described in Luke 24:13 as being 'sixty stadia from Jerusalem'. A stadion is just over 200 yards, so this suggests a distance of 7.5 miles (11.5 km). A few manuscripts, however, read 'one hundred and sixty stadia' (20 miles or 31 km).

There was indeed a place called Emmaus 20 miles from Jerusalem (later called Nicopolis; modern Latrun). This site was favoured by the Byzantines. The manuscripts, however, strongly favour the shorter distance; the copyists may have introduced the longer distance precisely because they knew of this more well-known Emmaus.

Josephus[1] refers to another Emmaus, on the site of ancient Mozah, which is just 3.5 miles north-west of Jerusalem. This is probably the correct site. Luke was thinking of the 'round-trip' distance which the disciples covered in their journey both to and from Jerusalem. When Vespasian's troops founded a colony there after AD 70, the town changed its name and was thus forgotten. Christians in the Middle Ages, however, focused on two sites (Abu Ghosh and Qubeibe) because they were 7 miles from Jerusalem. Neither of these is supported by any preceding tradition.

Fig. 13.

So when a stranger came up to meet them on the road, they expressed their disbelief at how Jesus had been treated by Jerusalem's authorities. But they also acknowledged (vv. 22–4) the two reports they had received that morning – that of the women ('a vision of angels who said that he was alive') and that of Peter and John ('some of those who were with us found it just as the women had said'). Eventually they reached their destination. But soon they were hurrying back along the very road they had just travelled – all the way back to Jerusalem! For the stranger who had walked and talked with them along that road turned out to be none other than Jesus himself! They had recognized him at last when he had broken bread in his characteristic manner in their own home. Whatever it was that had been so urgent in Emmaus was now completely eclipsed by something immeasurably more important: they had seen the Risen Lord!

When they got back to Jerusalem, events had moved on. Possibly in keeping with plans made earlier in the day, the rendezvous-point for the 11 disciples was evidently the upper room in John Mark's house – the place where they had last been together (for the Passover meal). This, they reckoned, was the venue where they were least likely to be disturbed. So when the two travellers from Emmaus returned to the city, it was to John Mark's house that they directed their steps.

Jesus with his friends

In the meantime the Lord had been seen by Peter (Luke 24:34; cf. Mark 16:7 and 1 Corinthians 15:5). Jesus' leading disciple had spent the whole weekend behind doors, chiding himself for his threefold denial of his Master. So his encounter with the Risen Jesus was bound to be a singular and poignant moment. Perhaps, therefore, the Gospels' silence about the details of this meeting is entirely appropriate – it was an event too sacred and personal to be made a matter for public knowledge. Evidently, however, at some point in the day Peter had taken himself off from the others and found a quiet place (such as Gethsemane?) where he could gather his thoughts in the light of all that had happened. And it was there, on his own, that Jesus met him – speaking words, we may presume, of forgiveness and reassurance (cf. John 21:15ff.).

It is hard to imagine the atmosphere in that upper room, as the disciples gathered in the evening: a mixture of excitement, fear, disbelief, joy and plain bewilderment. They were fearful of the religious authorities who, ever since the guards' report that morning, might well be anxious to know the movements and plans of Jesus' friends. So the disciples had made sure that the doors were securely locked (John 20:19).

Now there was a knock at the door.

Who could it be? Friend or foe? Could it even be ...?

No, it was Cleopas and his friend – but with the same story, experienced quite independently. First, there had been Mary Magdalene, then the other women, then Peter, and now these two back from Emmaus – all with the same unbelievable story – that their Master was back from the dead! What on earth would happen next? Was that another knock on the door?

It was just then, 'while they were still talking about all this', that suddenly Jesus himself appeared in their midst.

The doors were locked, but here he was! 'They were startled and terrified, and thought that they were seeing a ghost,' but Jesus calmed their nerves, speaking his characteristic greeting in his familiar tones: 'Peace be with you. It is I myself! Touch me and see.' They 'still could not believe it because of joy and amazement', so Jesus ate some of their fish supper. Then they 'rejoiced when they saw the Lord' (Luke 24:36ff.; John 20:19ff.) – perhaps one of the greatest understatements in ancient literature! What a reunion! The party could now begin.

Jesus stayed with them for a while. He began to teach them how the dramatic and totally unexpected events of the last three days were nevertheless all part of God's plan and purpose – both for Israel and for the world. It would be the first of several such encounters during the next five weeks or so, both in Galilee and back in Jerusalem. These encounters would be experienced by people such as Thomas and James and, on one occasion, by over 500 people (John 20:24; 1 Corinthians 15:5–9). Eventually, however, they would come to an end when Jesus bade then a final, fond farewell on the Mount of Olives, bequeathing to this small group of men and women the task of taking this extraordinary message to the unexpecting world.

But for now we leave the disciples in that upper room, struggling to come to terms with the day's remarkable events. For those who had helped the various women get ready for their undercover dawn visit to the tomb, it had been a long day. But it is hard to imagine any of them taking an early night! For, when eventually they did fall asleep, it would have been with the realization that, because of what had happened in the last 24 hours, their lives could never, ever be the same again. In one sense the day was over, in another it was the dawn of a quite new day. Any previous plans which they had had for their lives were now to be discarded because of this one Passover weekend in Jerusalem. Indeed, it would go down in history as the weekend which changed the world.

✟

4

Solving the Mystery

Was Jesus Really Raised?

It is indeed a remarkable story. And if it *is* true, then this is an event which will come to affect our *own* plans for our lives – just as it did for those first disciples. Not surprisingly, therefore – precisely because the stakes are so high – it is a story which has been subjected to endless questions.

Even for those who accept the Resurrection-claim, there inevitably continue to be many questions. What precisely was the nature of Jesus' risen body? If it was not identical to his body before death, in what way was it different? Where was it when it was invisible? These are important questions.

But for those who wish to dispute this claim, there are yet more pressing questions, and it is these which we need to consider here in more detail. Can this Easter story stand up to scrutiny? Is there not another more down-to-earth explanation? After all, dead men do not rise from the dead – normally!

WAS THE BODY STILL IN THE TOMB?

In modern times one of the first questions which is frequently asked is: *was the tomb really empty?* Perhaps the women went to the wrong tomb? Or perhaps the disciples knew full well that Jesus was dead and buried but decided to pretend otherwise? So Jesus' body, all along, was still in the tomb.

To question the empty tomb is natural enough. Yet, surprisingly, it does not seem (from what evidence we have) to have been a question asked by sceptics in first-century Jerusalem. The only rumour of an alternative explanation is the charge made that the disciples must have 'stolen the body' (Matthew 28:11–15). In other words, the emptiness of the tomb was conceded even by those who would have loved to scotch this rumour. The only point of dispute was how this empty tomb was to be explained.

Many of the alternative explanations which are offered today falter on this key point – namely that there were many in Jerusalem who would have loved to prove the story false by producing the body or, if there was any confusion about the tomb, by showing the correct tomb. But they did not – because they *could* not.

Was it the wrong tomb?

For example, could the women really have gone to the wrong tomb? Was the 'man' whom they met at the tomb actually a helpful gardener trying to point out their mistake to them ('He is not here; behold the [true] place where they laid him')? To be sure, they may have been in a state of emotional turmoil and it may still have been a misty dawn. Yet it was only 36 hours since they had witnessed Jesus' burial in the tomb. It is not a long time for forgetting a most important fact. Moreover, this was no mass graveyard, but a distinctive tomb earmarked for Joseph of Arimathea. So there may not have been much room for confusion. Yet, even if there was, and the women *did* in fact make this ghastly mistake, would not someone soon have been able to correct them? Did John and Peter make the same mistake? Would not the local authorities have gladly shown them the error of their ways, perhaps by producing the gardener as a witness?

Sometimes it is suggested that the women made this mistake, and then failed to report back to the other disciples. The other disciples, it is argued, had already disappeared off to Galilee – only to be greeted with this surprising report of a supposedly 'empty' tomb when they returned to Jerusalem a few weeks later for the feast of Pentecost. Yet even if Jerusalem was not an especially welcoming place for Jesus'

THE NAZARETH INSCRIPTION

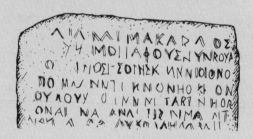

The so-called Nazareth Decree has aroused considerable interest.[1] The stone slab (which was brought to Paris from the Nazareth area in 1878) is dateable to the first century and is inscribed with an order from the Emperor:

> *it is my will that graves and tombs lie undisturbed for ever... Respect for those who are buried is most important; no one should disturb them in any way at all. If anyone does, I require that he be executed for tomb-robbery.*

Could rumours about the disappearance of Jesus' body have reached the Emperor, resulting in this decree? Perhaps it was deliberately set up in Nazareth because it was known to be Jesus' home town? Some have suggested that it came from the Emperor Claudius (AD 41–54), once Galilee was again under direct Roman rule. Is this evidence of the effect which the disciples' preaching of the Resurrection had already had by that time?

The connection with Nazareth, however, is not fully certain, and the Emperor may have been responding instead to tomb-robbing in general. Nevertheless, it does reveal that the authorities viewed the disturbing of tombs as a very serious crime. In such circumstances would the frightened disciples really have dared to perform such a feat? And why were they not punished for this crime which could carry the death penalty?

Fig. 14.

disciples, it is most unlikely that the men deserted the women at this critical juncture. Possibly the men were slightly more at risk of reprisals than were the women, but the women themselves were not entirely safe. Did the disciples really sink so low as to leave some of the key women in their party to cope with the Jerusalem authorities on their own? And when they did return to Jerusalem, they would in any case have had ample opportunity to prove that the women were wrong and that Jesus' body was still resting in peace.

The theory of a simple mistake breaks down. For anyone could have corrected the mistake in an instant. That was not the tomb – but this *is*!

Was it the disciples' trick?

Perhaps, then, Jesus' body was still in the tomb, but the disciples deliberately claimed the contrary? Was it a pure invention?

Few today would make this accusation. There is nothing in the disciples' character up to this point in the story that suggests they were either willing or able to pull off such a charade. Fear and flight are written into the narrative. The men were fearful for their lives, leaving the Sunday morning expedition in the capable hands of the women – perhaps hoping they would attract less opposition. And if, by some extraordinary about-turn, they *had* suddenly decided to court opposition and disbelief with such a monstrous tale, is it likely that they would have persisted with it all the way to their death? For in the coming years many of those first disciples would suffer a great deal – including, for some, martyrdom. Was all this the result of a prank? Was their new-found courage based on a palpable lie? Is it not likely that one of them, when under pressure, would spill the beans and divulge the secret?

No. What turns a coward into a person of courage is not a demonstrable lie but a conviction based on an assured fact. Others might think them wrong, but the disciples who preached the Resurrection of Jesus were themselves convinced that they were right. They were not playing a silly game.

Was it a spiritual experience?

More often, however, the disciples are not charged with outright deceit. Their preaching of Jesus' Resurrection (whilst his body was really mouldering in the grave) is given a more charitable explanation. It all depends on what you mean (so we are told) by this talk of 'resurrection'. Perhaps we have misunderstood them to be referring to a physical resurrection of Jesus' body, when in fact they were never claiming any such thing!

What they were really trying to say was that Jesus' mission went on unhindered even though he was dead. His spirit lived on, and somehow through that spirit those who followed Jesus gained a sense that he was alive. God was perpetuating the presence and power of Jesus among his disciples after his death. Truly 'his soul went marching on'. *This* was what they meant by their talk of 'resurrection'. If there were some resurrection-appearances of Jesus, they were either a form of hallucination, or perhaps something of a mystical nature beyond comprehension, but either way Jesus' body was still in the tomb.

On this reckoning there was no actual event in the experience of Jesus which corresponded to the Resurrection. 'Resurrection' was just a word used by the disciples to describe a *spiritual* conviction that had now dawned on *them*. Perhaps it was only afterwards, when trying to convince others, that they began to propose that an actual, objective, physical Resurrection had taken place in that garden outside Jerusalem. Or perhaps, all along, they never intended these stories to be taken so literally. The tomb was never really empty, but they wanted somehow to express their hope that for Jesus death had not been the ultimate end.

The idea that the disciples were each subject to hallucinations, by the way, is in itself highly unlikely. Even if one were to allow that, statistically, one or two of them might conceivably have been prone to this kind of thing, this would hardly apply to all of them. And they would scarcely all have had a shared common hallucination – a string of isolated, different visions is far more likely. Moreover, it is surprising that these so-called hallucinations took place over an extended period of time which then came to a sudden and abrupt halt – something quite out of keeping with what is observable when people are prone to hallucinations today. But what of the idea that perhaps only Peter and one or two others had such hallucinations? What if as a result of their testimony Jesus' other followers became convinced that Jesus was in some way 'alive' (even though they knew that his body was still in the tomb)?

Was it a 'spiritual body'?

In this connection it is sometimes argued that St Paul appears not to make much of the 'empty tomb' in 1 Corinthians 15 (his famous chapter on the Resurrection). Perhaps Paul would have been shocked to learn of these stories about mysterious disappearances in Jerusalem! Perhaps Paul provides us with evidence that the first Christians were quite content to accept that Jesus' body was still in the tomb. If so, then what Paul was talking about was again just a spiritual resurrection both for Jesus and for believers – hence his use of the term 'spiritual body' (v. 44). If this were true, needless to say, this would be enormously important. It would confirm that the claims for a physical Resurrection were a later development – out of keeping with the claims and beliefs of the first apostles.

Yet a close reading of this chapter reveals that Paul's whole argument depends for its validity on Jesus' being raised from the tomb in a manner which included his physical body: 'If Christ has not been raised,' he argues, 'then your faith is futile!' (v. 17). Paul's conviction 'that Jesus was buried, that he was raised on the third day' (v. 4) implicitly presumes that the place of burial was thereafter physically empty. Given Paul's background in Pharisaism (for Pharisees 'resurrection' necessarily involved the physical body), it is clear that Paul is not talking about a vague, unprovable piece of wishful thinking – that somehow after his death Jesus experienced an invisible spiritual resurrection.

No, he is talking about an event which he and the first apostles believed to have taken place in physical history. And he coins the phrase 'spiritual body' to try to describe the body of Jesus after the Resurrection – a body which was somehow a physical *body* (able to eat food and still bearing the marks of crucifixion) and yet also imbued with a distinctive, *spiritual* dimension (able to move through doors etc.). It proves to be in fact a way of saying that the physical and spiritual realms, which so often are thought to be opposed to one another, are instead seen in Jesus to be in principle both compatible and interconnected.

Was the empty tomb a later addition?

It is also true that the early Christian proclamation of the Resurrection tended to focus more on the Resurrection appearances than on the emptiness of the tomb (see, e.g., Acts 2:32; 3:15; 5:30; 10:39–41). But this is because an empty tomb, in and of itself, did not prove the Resurrection – only that the tomb for some reason was now empty. Nevertheless, had the tomb *not* been empty (with Jesus' body still being wrapped up in its burial cloths), then this *would* have *dis*proved the apostles' claim. (Peter, for example, implicitly lays down this challenge in his Pentecost speech, when alluding to the fact that David was still buried in *his* tomb [Acts 2:29].) In other words, the emptiness of the tomb is a necessary part of Resurrection belief, but in itself it is not a sufficient proof. As a result, it was only natural for the apostles, whilst strongly affirming the tomb's emptiness, to focus on what for them was the otherwise inexplicable fact – that they had seen Jesus.

So the fact that some of these earliest witnesses do not expressly mention the emptiness of the tomb does not mean that this was a later invention. On the contrary, it is a sign once more that this was 'taken as read'. What was at issue was where the body had gone and what this might mean for those who put their faith in this Jesus.

Playing with words

The argument, then, that the idea of an empty tomb took some time to develop is most unlikely. So too is the argument that the apostles did not quite mean by this what almost everyone ever since has presumed they *did* mean. It may be that one or two modern thinkers are able to believe in Jesus' Resurrection whilst affirming that his body long ago decomposed in a Jerusalem grave, but most ordinary folk see these two things as incompatible. In their eyes it has become a mere playing with words – with 'Resurrection' suddenly meaning something very vague, abstract and academic.

The important point to note is that anyone within the world of first-century Judaism would have fully agreed with this objection. 'Resurrection' (*anastasis* in Greek) was a word which had already developed a clear meaning. It referred to the physical raising back to life *within this world* of those whom God chose – the 'resurrection of the just' 'on the last day' (cf. Matthew 22:28; John 11:24). So when the disciples claimed Resurrection for Jesus, they were claiming that God had done for *one* man what they were expecting him to do for *all* his faithful people at the end of time (what Paul refers to as the 'hope' of Israel [Acts 23:6; 26:6]). If they had meant merely that Jesus was a good fellow who did not deserve to die and whose effect on people would surely continue beyond his death, they would have used some other word. They would not have dared to use this word, which meant one thing and one thing only – God's act of raising from physical death. That is what they meant. And that is what they would have been heard to mean.

Underlying this modern argument (that Jesus' body was still in the tomb, but the disciples still believed in his Resurrection) there is a deliberate confusion. People who take this position claim to adhere to a belief in the Resurrection-event but, when pressed, this so-called Resurrection-event proves not to be the physical Resurrection of Jesus but rather the new Resurrection-faith of the disciples – the rediscovery of his impact on their lives and the awareness of his 'livingness'. *This* is the Easter-event, these thinkers claim. Christ is risen – but only in the *faith* of the disciples.

Against such a position, it needs to be urged that in all the New Testament writings the Resurrection is first and foremost a real experience *within the life of Jesus himself*; only then does it secondarily become the basis for the subsequent Resurrection-conviction of the disciples. The Resurrection only became a series of experiences for believers because it was first an event for Jesus.

So there is no way, I suggest, that the disciples could have honestly believed in the Resurrection whilst also accepting that Jesus' body was in the tomb. To hold these two beliefs simultaneously would be nonsense. If they had taken this line with any of their contemporaries, they would soon have been told as much! In talking about 'resurrection', they knew that they would be heard as making a claim for Jesus' physical body – a claim which, on this view, they knew to be false.

This modern view claims to be more polite: the Resurrection is not a palpable lie made up by the disciples, but rather a legend – a story with a 'spiritual' meaning. Yet it effectively charges the disciples again with plain invention – deliberately confusing people at the outset, knowing that the distinction between fact and faith would soon become irretrievably blurred. The story of that first Easter morning becomes again a pious fraud – intended to make a theological point but not describing any series of events which actually happened.

Once again a key question becomes: were they really prepared to suffer and die for a legend that had now become a lie? We may also with good reason ask: if they were intent on creating a convincing legend, why on earth did they invent this story about the Risen Jesus being first seen by women, when for many of their Jewish hearers the testimony of a woman would almost automatically be dismissed? The whole thing bristles with improbabilities.

DID THE BODY SOMEHOW DISAPPEAR?

So the arguments that the tomb was not really empty are far from strong. The only other alternative is to accept that for some reason the tomb *really was empty*. Jesus' body really did disappear. Did someone then steal the body? Or perhaps Jesus was never really dead and simply vacated the premises after a suitable period of restful recovery?

Did Jesus revive?

The latter idea (the 'swooning' theory first advanced by the German Venturini) can be quickly dismissed. Jesus may indeed have died slightly sooner than was expected (cf. Mark 15:44), but there is no way in which the Roman soldiers would have left this matter in any doubt. The thrusting of the spear into his side (John 19:34ff.) was intended for just this purpose. Instead the fact that the water within Jesus' blood had begun to separate is telling evidence (though not scientifically understood at the time) that Jesus was indeed dead.

Yet, even if by some remarkable oversight, Jesus was not in fact fully dead when he was laid in the tomb, is it at all conceivable that he could have recovered from his ordeal sufficiently to set himself free from the grave-clothes wrapped around him? And then to remove the rolling-stone from the front of the tomb – an almost impossible feat even if one were in full health? Lying on a cold slab in April with numerous untended wounds is an unlikely precursor to such a recovery. As was said over a century ago by Strauss (himself no friend of the Christian faith):

> It is impossible that a being who had stolen half-dead out of the sepulchre, who crept about weak and ill, wanting medical treatment, and who still at last yielded to his sufferings, could have given the disciples the impression that he was a conqueror over death, the Prince of Life – an impression which lay at the bottom of their future ministry. Such a resuscitation could ... by no possibility have changed their sorrow into enthusiasm, have elevated their reverence into worship.[2]

Was the body stolen?

So the only alternative is that Jesus' corpse must have been removed. But by whom?

The disciples? But for the reasons already noted, this charge against the disciples will not stick – even though it is the oldest one. Jesus may have hinted at his Resurrection 'on the third day', but there is nothing to suggest that the disciples understood this or were expecting it. On the contrary, it made no sense to them (Mark 9:10). And when the empty tomb was discovered, Mary's immediate presumption was that someone *else* had stolen the body. No, their morale was low. This was clearly not the time for taking the law into their own hands. Through the kindness of Joseph of Arimathea, their Master had received a more decent place of burial than they could possibly have hoped for. Where else could they take him? Above all, if the disciples really did steal the body, what accounts for the transformation of Peter and the other disciples – from being those who denied him to being those who would spread his message throughout the world? Was this all based on an elaborate hoax?

Perhaps, then, it was the Jewish authorities? But a few hours earlier, at least according to Matthew, they had set a guard on the tomb. Is it really likely that they then decided to do the very deed which they were fearful might be done by others? This would indeed be to 'shoot themselves in the foot'! So too, if they suddenly wanted to remove Jesus to a less conspicuous or wealthy tomb in order to prevent the veneration of Jesus' tomb. By doing so they only ended up playing a part in bringing about a far greater veneration of Jesus – as the one who was claimed to have been raised from death. Above all, when a few weeks later the apostles were preaching Jesus' Resurrection in Jerusalem, why did these religious authorities not quickly own up to their removing the body? What the apostles were saying under their noses certainly cast them in a bad light – because of their supposed involvement in Jesus' death. An invitation to the public to view the corpse of this crucified criminal would soon have stifled all this talk of Resurrection!

Much the same can be said of the Roman authorities. Like the Jewish authorities, they too were involved in placing the guard; they too would have benefited enormously from being able to produce the body. If there *had* been a sudden change of mind and Jesus' body was removed under official auspices, why did the Jewish authorities resort to claiming that the *disciples* had stolen the body? Surely it would be much more impressive to state that the Roman authorities had done the deed for their own official reasons? And why did they not produce it?

Perhaps, then, instead it was Joseph of Arimathea? Perhaps he was not such a friend of Jesus after all and had only wanted Jesus to be buried in his own tomb for the sake of ritual purity? But if so, why did he not bother to dispose of the two men crucified with Jesus in the same way? And if he really did want to remove Jesus' body as soon as possible, is he really likely to have done the job during the night – requiring a party of men to begin this difficult work under torchlight? It is far more likely that he would have set to work at first light – at the earliest. But the women arrived on the scene to find the body already gone. And if they had been working through the night, why did they leave the grave-clothes behind, so that they had to carry Jesus' corpse to its new venue naked?

No, it is far more likely that Joseph was indeed an admirer of Jesus, who had bravely seized his last fleeting opportunity of casting in his lot with Jesus. He believed that in future years his own conscience would be able to take comfort from the fact that he had finally done what was right – albeit at the eleventh hour. If so, it is almost unthinkable that, having blotted his copy-book forever in the sight of his colleagues because of his loyalty to this Galilean prophet, he was willing after just 36 hours to part with his glory. Having risked their censure once and for all, there was little point in back-tracking now. Psychology speaks entirely in the opposite direction.

An obstinate truth

So whichever way we look, we come back to this mystery. Within seven weeks of Jesus' death a new movement began in Jerusalem, taking as its foundation charter the daring claim that this recently crucified Galilean had in fact been raised by God from death – in a garden which was just a couple of minutes' walk outside the city wall. Then, as now, this meant, to any who knew the plain meaning of words, that a claim was being made for the disappearance of a body. This claim was a non-starter if the body was actually sitting in the tomb. It was open to empirical falsification, as they say. Produce the corpse and the claim would be null and void – allowing everyone in the city to get back to their day's business without further silly interruptions.

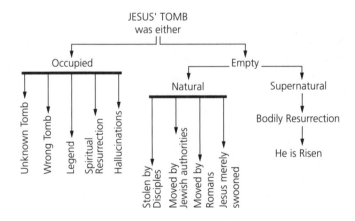

Fig. 15. The only solutions to the Easter enigma (following McDowell [1988], p. 125).

But no one produced the body. This means it was fully agreed at the time that the tomb was empty. But where was it? Either it was elsewhere (and could be produced by someone opposed to the disciples, or a suitable explanation offered for its absence) or some of his followers had stolen it. Or, thirdly ... the body had indeed been raised by God from the dead. Those were the options then and they remain the same to this day. The Easter message is either a pious hoax or the centre-piece of history.

CONCLUSION

Christians are those who have become convinced that only the third option fully fits the facts. Jesus' body was not stolen by his enemies nor removed by his friends, but rather was raised miraculously from death by God himself.

They read the Easter accounts and sense that they have about them the ring of simple, unadorned authenticity. They go back to study the life and teaching of Jesus and conclude that no one has ever lived or taught in the same way as Jesus did. They also read on beyond the Easter story, noting how Jesus' followers departed from their ancestral custom of observing the Sabbath on Saturday and began to honour Sunday instead. In particular, they note how their unlikely message of a crucified Messiah succeeded in making an impact on the far-flung parts of the Roman Empire within a generation. They look at first-century Judaism and ask what explains the emergence of the Christian Church – something which has thoroughly Jewish roots and yet is ultimately intended for all people.

And they conclude that the missing piece of the jigsaw is precisely what the New Testament writers claim – Jesus' bodily Resurrection.

Only this makes sense of what went before – the surpassing beauty, power and spiritual authority seen within Jesus' life. Only this makes sense of what happened next – the incredible vitality of the Christian message, launched like a rocket into places and cultures far removed from that original Jerusalem garden. Only this too makes sense of their experience that this Jesus seems to walk out of the pages of history and into the very journey of their own lives nearly 2,000 years after he was supposed to be dead and gone.

So Christians throughout the centuries have looked back to those strange dawn events and have seen them not just as factual and historical, but even more than that – as the central events within their own life's story and the story of the world.

It is hardly surprising, then, that many of them in due course have not just shown an interest in *what* happened on that first Easter weekend, but have also gone on to ask *where* it all happened.

In the early years after the Resurrection we can well imagine that, if ever they had the opportunity, some of Jesus' new followers would have sought out that garden tomb. In fact, however, we have no *explicit* record that they did so. Instead, as far as the written record of history goes, from the moment that Mary left the garden, the tomb of Jesus strangely passes into complete oblivion – at least for a long while. We may know what happened next in the story of the Easter message spreading out to the world, but what happened next to that garden tomb just outside Jerusalem is something of a mystery. Did it survive? Can it be identified today?

Having considered the *story* of the first Easter, it is time to focus on its *site*.

PART II

The Setting

Come, see the place where he lay.
He is not here; for he has been raised.
(MATTHEW 28:6)

5

An Ancient Find

The Church of the Holy Sepulchre

So the message of the Risen Christ began its historic journey from those few first disciples in Jerusalem 'to the ends of the earth' (Acts 1:8). It was a message that would gradually spread throughout the Roman Empire and beyond. In the course of time it would come to be accepted by the Roman emperors themselves, and ultimately would survive the collapse of their empire, living on in the hearts and minds of Christian people through the centuries until our own day.

But what happened back in Jerusalem? Whatever became of the tomb? Did it survive intact despite the tumultuous events that raged all around it in the next 100 years? And what happened to Jesus' followers and to the developing Christian Church in Jerusalem during this period? These are some of the questions that must concern us in Part II as we ask the question: *where* precisely did the Crucifixion and Resurrection take place?

In the year AD 325 a tomb was uncovered which from then until recent times has generally been accepted as the authentic tomb of Jesus. In this chapter we will describe the discovery of that tomb and the building of what has come to be known in the Western Church as the 'Church of the Holy Sepulchre' (though in the Eastern Church it is always referred to, perhaps more appropriately, as the 'Church of the Resurrection'). In Chapter 6 we will describe the discovery in the late nineteenth century of another tomb, now generally known as the 'Garden Tomb'. The debate as to which (if either) of these two sites is the correct one will be left until Chapter 7.

Before we can understand the story of the Holy Sepulchre, however, it is necessary to find out a little more about the history of Jerusalem and its Christian community during the first three centuries of our era. Much happened in the years between that fateful weekend in or around AD 30, when Jesus' tomb was found to be empty, and the year 325, when a tomb was found and immediately identified as Jesus' tomb.

JERUSALEM AFTER JESUS

Jesus' warnings about the future

As we have seen, Jesus lived at a time of increasing political tension. The issue of how the Jewish nation was going to respond to the continued occupation of their land by the Roman authorities was not going to go away. The group that came to be known as the 'Zealots' was growing during this time and many were looking for the time when Jerusalem would be free from pagan domination. As Luke records in his opening chapters, there were many godly people in Israel at the time of Jesus' birth who were longing for the 'redemption of Jerusalem' and to be 'saved from our enemies and from the hand of all who hate us' (Luke 2:38; 1:71; cf. 2:25). Jesus' own teaching had a distinctive cutting edge because it related directly to this burning contemporary issue. Far from being a 'pale Galilean' who calmly spoke of timeless ethereal truths, Jesus stood in the strong biblical tradition of being a prophet who warned the Israel of his day that the course which many of them were pursuing in opposing Rome would court disaster. Worse still, just like Jeremiah before him, he had the audacity both to predict this disaster and to assert that, when it came, it would need to be seen as demonstrating the hand of Israel's God:

> If you, even you, had only recognized on this day the things that make for peace!... The days will come upon you, when your enemies will set up ramparts around you and hem you in on every side ... because you did not recognize the time of your visitation

from God... When you see Jerusalem surrounded by armies, then know that its desolation has come near.

LUKE 19:42–4; 21:20

These are just two of an estimated 34 passages in the Gospels where Jesus warns his contemporaries of the future that lies in store for Jerusalem and Israel (see also, e.g., Luke 13:33–5; 23:29–31). Set against this backdrop, much of Jesus' teaching can be understood as offering the Israel of his day another way of being Israel, the true people of God – an alternative route through the coming cataclysm. 'The gate is wide and the road is easy that leads to destruction,' he said, 'but the road is hard that leads to life'; 'repent and believe the good news'; 'follow me!' (Matthew 7:13–14; Mark 1:15, 17).

Jesus' predictions came true. In the years that followed, the tensions only increased. In the year AD 39/40, for example, there was a major crisis caused by the insistence of the Emperor Caligula that a statue of himself should be placed within the Jerusalem Temple. For the Jews this only brought back painful memories of the Maccabean crisis in 164 BC when Antiochus Epiphanes had tried a similar thing (often thought to be alluded to by Jesus in his referring to the 'desolating sacrilege' [Mark 13:14]). As then, so now, they were adamant in resisting this imperial whim. As a result, the imperial legate, Petronius, noting their complete resolve, eventually decided that he could not implement the Emperor's wishes. For someone in his position, this was the equivalent of writing his own suicide note. Fortunately for him, he was spared the need to take his own life because news reached Palestine just in the nick of time to tell him that the Emperor himself had died. In another incident ten years later, when Cumanus was procurator, there were such violent clashes in Jerusalem that Josephus records[1] that over 20,000 people were killed at Passover time (this may be what Paul is referring to in 1 Thessalonians 2:14–16). The numbers may be exaggerated, but not the fact that the tensions between the Jews and Rome were fast careering out of control.

Matters came to a head in AD 66 with various provocative acts under the procurator Gessius Florus. The Zealots seized Masada and brought to an end the daily sacrifice that had been offered for the Emperor in the Jerusalem Temple. It was a final act of defiance, inciting a military response from Rome. After some initial successes, the Zealot cause became increasingly hopeless. The Romans laid siege to Jerusalem. Eventually Titus' troops stormed the Temple area in August AD 70, and within a month the final bastion of the upper city had been burnt to the ground. Jerusalem was then systematically destroyed.

The extent of this destruction was almost total. The Jerusalem that grew out of the rubble would be a much smaller city. Thirty years earlier, in the reign of Herod Agrippa (AD 41–4), a new wall had been built on the northern side of the city, bringing the area of the (later) Holy Sepulchre well within the city. In the years after AD 70 this area continued to be part of the city, but the southern half of the city (the ancient city of David and the upper city now known as Mount Sion) was left largely in ruins. By this means, the city's location effectively (but confusingly!) moved some 300 metres to the north (see Figure 16).

The disappearance of the Jerusalem Jesus knew

Yet not all was calm after the year AD 70. Sixty years later history repeated itself. Evidently the opposition to Rome had not disappeared. It was simmering, only to return. Simon Bar Kokhba was heralded by some leading rabbis as the true 'Messiah', and his revolutionary policy against Rome was pursued, leading to the Second Jewish Revolt (AD 132–5). Again the result was disastrous.

This time the Roman Emperor concerned was Hadrian, who, having quashed the rebellion, tried to ensure that it could never happen again. In accordance with a scheme which he may have been entertaining even before the Revolt, Hadrian now refounded Jerusalem as a pagan city. He called it Aelia Capitolina, and laid it out on the regular pattern of a Roman camp, divided by two main roads known as the Cardo Maximus and the Decumanus (see Figure 17, p. 78).

The area of the later Holy Sepulchre, being so close to the central place where these two roads crossed, was a natural site for the building of a Roman forum (or market-place) and a temple to the Capitoline gods (of Jupiter, Minerva and Juno), flanked by a shrine to Venus. Meanwhile all Jews were exiled from the city by   specific ruling.

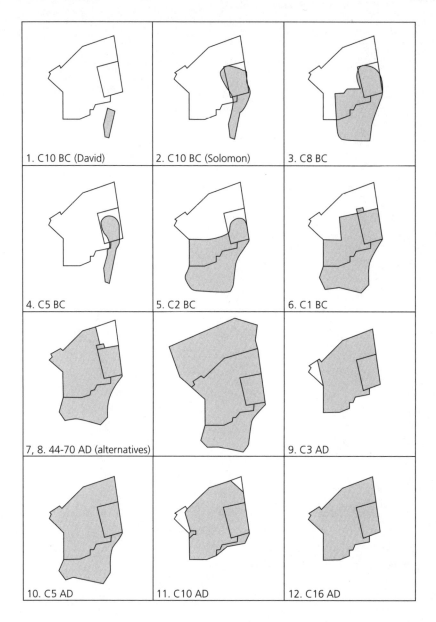

Fig. 16. The 'moving walls' of Jerusalem (after Murphy O'Connor). In the 4th edition of his guide-book (1998) Murphy O'Connor now omits the larger alternative (no. 8).

Fig. 17. Jerusalem after AD 135, when refounded by Hadrian as 'Aelia Capi-tolina'. Apart from the Roman camp, the city in fact may have been unwalled through much or all of this period. Note the street pattern, which survives within the Old City to this day (cf. Pl. 36).

It is forbidden for all circumcised persons to enter or stay within the territory of Aelia Capitolina; any person contravening this prohibition shall be put to death.[2]

The full implementation of this ruling may have grown lax in subsequent generations (there is some evidence of a *small* group of Jews occasionally resident in the new city). But effectively the mass of the Jewish population moved elsewhere – especially to Galilee, which became the new centre of Rabbinic Judaism.

Thus, within almost exactly 100 years of the crucifixion, the Jerusalem that Jesus knew had completely disappeared. Instead there was a new pagan city, Aelia Capitolina, which was much smaller and located only in the northern sections of the former city. To the south of the area previously marked by Herod's Palace was now the camp of the Tenth Legion, who kept a careful eye on the local situation, and the residents were now Gentiles. Some of these might have lived in the city before 135, but many would have been colonists (including army veterans?) resettled there from elsewhere by the Roman authorities. Throughout this period after 135, it is unclear whether Aelia was considered important enough even to have a city wall. Instead, as far as the provincial administration was concerned, the centre of gravity had moved decidedly towards the coastal city of Caesarea Maritima, which became the metropolitan city of the Roman province of Palestine. Caesarea retained this position of pre-eminence well into the fourth century.

THE CHURCH IN JERUSALEM (AD 30–325)

The first generation after Jesus (AD 30–70)

In all of these winds of change, what was happening to the city's Christian community? We know from the book of Acts that, after some initial response to the preaching of Jesus as Israel's Messiah, Jerusalem became an increasingly difficult place for his followers. After the death of Stephen a persecution broke out which caused many Christians to leave the city. For a while the apostles continued to use Jerusalem as their headquarters, but increasingly they too dispersed with their commission to go 'to the ends of the earth'.

The leadership of the local, indigenous Christian community was then delegated to James, the originally sceptical brother of Jesus (Acts 12:17; 15:13; 21:18; cf. Mark 3:31). Within that community there were probably many who observed the Jewish law rigorously (Acts 21:20) and who wanted Gentile believers to be circumcised as a sign of their being true members of the people of God. James himself, however, at the historic apostolic council convened in Jerusalem in AD 49 to resolve this very issue, took a different line. The evidence of the Holy Spirit in the lives of Gentile believers convinced him that God was indeed doing a new thing; this was now the time when the long-awaited 'ingathering of the Gentiles' could take place and Gentiles could be part of the people of God as Gentiles (i.e. without being circumcised). The door into the Kingdom was via faith in Jesus, not via the hallmarks of Judaism (Acts 15:19; cf. Galatians 2:9–10).

James' stance on this issue was brave. It would not be popular with the wider Jewish community who, in those years of increasing political tension, would be extremely cautious about any movements which began to blur the boundary-lines between Jew and Gentile. It would also not be welcomed by some within his own flock. From then on James would have to perform quite a delicate balancing act.

This can be seen in the episode of Paul's 'collection'. Paul had been collecting money from his various congregations as a means of supporting the poorer Christians in Jerusalem and of showing solidarity with them (2 Corinthians 8–9). Even if Paul might have wished that these Jerusalem Christians would take a more relaxed position on certain matters, there was no denying that they had continued the witness to Jesus in the city where it all began. They needed all the support they could get.

Yet not all went straightforwardly when he arrived to deliver this collection during Pentecost AD 57. Almost inevitably he became embroiled in some of the tensions within the city's Christian community. Some of the more conservative believers insisted that Paul meet certain conditions before his gift could be received (Acts 21:20ff.). Also, of course, he met the opposition of non-Christian Jews. They recognized Paul and presumed that, because Paul was known to encourage Gentiles to enter the people of God, he must also have encouraged Gentiles to enter into the inner enclosure of the Temple reserved only for Jews (Acts 21:27ff.). Within a few days of his arrival,

Paul was whisked out of the city in the dead of night, never to return again (Acts 23:31ff.).

Meanwhile the tensions for James and the Christian community will only have increased in the rising tide of nationalism which was sweeping the city and leading inexorably towards the clash with Rome in AD 66. James himself was sentenced to death in the year 62 by the Sanhedrin, who were taking advantage of an interregnum between the appointment of two procurators.[3] Tradition has it that he was thrown down from one of the corners of the Temple platform.[4]

Once the revolt finally started, the Christian community soon realized that there was no future for them in the city. This was the time which Jesus had warned them about: it was time to 'flee to the mountains' (Mark 13:14). Although some have questioned it, the account of Eusebius in his *Ecclesiastical History*[5] is normally accepted. He says that the Jerusalem Christian community fled to the area of Pella (just south-east of Lake Galilee in modern Jordan) for the duration of the siege (see Figure 18, p. 82).

After the siege was over many may have returned to their homes in Jerusalem. Some, however, will have resolved to make a new life in this new location – far from the hassle of Jerusalem life. It is possible, for example, that Matthew's Gospel might be a document associated with this dispersed refugee community in the regions of southern Syria (cf. Matthew 4:24) – the Gospel of Jesus as it was remembered by the Jerusalem church 'in exile'.

Between the Revolts (AD 70–135)

After the death of James the leadership of the Jerusalem Christian community seems to have been kept within the 'family of the Lord' for as long as possible. In Eusebius' list of the first 30 bishops of Jerusalem he records that James' immediate successor was Simeon, a cousin of the Lord.[6] Little is known about the church in this period, except for one incident (c. AD 95) when the Emperor Domitian became convinced that two surviving relatives of Jesus (the grandsons of his brother, Jude) might pose some political threat. When they were brought before him, he soon concluded that these two rural farmers from Galilee were nothing to worry about, and sent them on their way.[7]

Fig. 18. Palestine (AD 70–300).

What we do know is that when in the 130s Simon Bar Kokhba claimed that he was the Messiah, the Christians refused to follow him.[8] As a result they experienced some measure of persecution from their fellow-Jews. Once again the Christians resolved that, even if Jerusalem was important to them for many reasons, they had a higher loyalty which prevented them from taking up arms in defence of the city against their Roman overlords.

Gentile Christians in Aelia Capitolina (AD 135–325)

In the aftermath of Hadrian's edict of 135 (see above), the Christian community in the renamed city of Aelia Capitolina would have been entirely Gentile. This is reflected in the non-Jewish names of the bishops in the second section of Eusebius' list.[9] One of the important questions is then: did this changeover of population mean that the location of Jesus' tomb was now totally forgotten? Were all such memories lost at this time? Or was the tradition passed on – perhaps by Gentile Christians who had been living in the city before 135? We return to this later (see below, pp. 96 and 161).

Throughout the second century the Christian community in Aelia remained fairly small. It was eclipsed in size by the church in the cosmopolitan capital, Caesarea, where the Christian faith began to put down strong roots. In the following century Caesarea would become the home of one the greatest Christian scholars of antiquity, Origen (c. 185 to c. 254), becoming famous for its library and theological school. So if ever the bishops of Caesarea and Aelia were engaged in Church Council meetings during this period, their names were always listed in that order – Caesarea first, Aelia second.

Around the year 200, however, two of Aelia's bishops, Narcissus and Alexander, began to develop the prestige of the Christian community in Aelia – a process of development which continued throughout the third century. As a result, by the beginning of the fourth century the scene is set for some tension between the two sees of Aelia and Caesarea. The bishops of Aelia suggested that their position in the former city of Jerusalem should give them a natural pre-eminence over Caesarea.

During this period there was a steady trickle of interested Christian visitors to Aelia. We know the names of just four of them. Around

AD 170 Melito, bishop of Sardis, came to Palestine in order to establish the true extent of the Old Testament canon[10] and made an intriguing comment about the site of the crucifixion (see below, p. 161). Alexander, who during a visit to Palestine found himself consecrated as bishop of Aelia, had originally come from Asia Minor, so Eusebius says, with the express purpose of seeking out 'the places' and 'to pray'.[11] In the 230s Origen, whilst based in Caesarea, probably visited Aelia at some point – at least, he refers to the nearby 'cave' at Bethlehem.[12] There was also his contemporary, Pionius, who used his eye-witness experience of visiting the land of the Bible in his defence of the faith prior to his martyrdom in Smyrna.[13]

Nevertheless, as one scholar has put it, 'the volume of devout tourism must have been much greater than these isolated examples suggest'.[14] Indeed, Origen speaks of Jesus' birth-place in Bethlehem as being 'pointed out' to visitors from 'all over the world', and Eusebius speaks of Christians visiting both the Mount of Olives[15] and Bethlehem.[16]

In the city of Aelia itself Christian visitors might be shown a small Christian library, an episcopal throne reputed to date back to James himself,[17] and probably a small church in the uninhabited and ruined area of Mount Zion; this was where Christians had assembled at least since 135 and possibly from the days of the apostles (see Figure 1, p. 2 and Figure 17, p. 78). But what of Golgotha and the site of Jesus' tomb? What had happened to these during these long years of changing history?

What about Golgotha and the tomb?

In his gazetteer of biblical places Eusebius simply says concerning 'Golgotha': this is 'the place of the skull where Christ was crucified; this is *pointed out* in Aelia to the north of Mount Zion'.[18] Neither here nor anywhere else in his writings does he ever record that anyone *visited* it. Why?

The simplest answer is this: the site was currently inaccessible. Its general location could be 'pointed out', but Golgotha and the tomb itself were 'out of bounds'. The local Christians had become convinced that Golgotha and the tomb were buried underneath the forum and temple which Hadrian had built at the centre of Aelia in 135. For

Hadrian it may only have been a suitable site. But for Christians it had been none other than the place of redemption. Ever since then, however, it had been buried from view.

However, in the year 324 Constantine (the Roman Emperor in the West since 312) won a decisive battle at Adrianople over the Eastern Emperor, Licinius. From then on, until his death in 337, he would be sole Emperor of both East and West. Regardless of our own estimates as to the motivation and sincerity of his publicly embracing the Christian faith, the result for Palestine was highly significant. The land of the Bible now came under Christian rule for the first time. Aelia Capitolina would gradually revert to its historic name of 'Jerusalem'. Moreover, with the collapse of pagan rule the way was now open for an increased flood of Christian visitors and for the open demarcation of various biblical sites.

Not surprisingly, the first on the list was the tomb of Jesus. Where was it? Was this tradition about its being buried under Hadrian's temple reliable or would they be looking in entirely the wrong place? And even if they were not far off the mark, would there be anything left to find after all these years? Could Christians successfully bring back to light this place which meant so much to them?

THE TOMB AND GOLGOTHA

So began one of the most extraordinary episodes in history – one of the few archaeological excavations in the ancient world! Work is likely to have begun in the second half of 325 or early in 326. The task assigned to them was nothing less than the complete demolition of the pagan temple and forum, and then the search for a first-century tomb which fitted the description in the Gospels. Was it a 'mission impossible'?

The Council of Nicaea: Macarius' golden opportunity

First, however, there was the not unimportant point that they needed the Emperor's permission! There is some evidence that during the reign of Licinius the local Christian community had already been bold enough to request the removal of Hadrian's temple. In the early years of Licinius' reign there had been signs that he was pursuing a more favourable policy towards the Church, but this soon changed. Nothing came of this request. With the coming of Constantine, however, the time looked right. Moreover, the bishop of Jerusalem, Macarius, was conveniently invited to meet Constantine – as were around 300 other bishops, called to discuss the important issues of the Arian controversy at a Church Council meeting at Nicaea. During one of the breaks in the theological proceedings, Macarius plucked up courage to ask the Emperor his question: would he help them uncover the tomb of Jesus? Would he mind if this involved the small matter of destroying a pagan temple built by his illustrious predecessor, Hadrian?

That Macarius did indeed take this opportunity to gain the Emperor's permission is confirmed in two ways. First, it was to Macarius that Constantine subsequently wrote about the project (see below, p. 89). Secondly, one of the resolutions passed by the Council seems also to have been the result of Macarius' personal intervention. It concerned the relative status between himself as the bishop of Aelia/Jerusalem and the bishop of Caesarea:

> Since a custom and ancient tradition has held good that the bishop of Aelia should be honoured, let him have his proper honour, saving to the metropolitan [i.e. Caesarea] the honour peculiar to it.[19]

We noted above that there had been an increasing tension between the sees of Caesarea and Aelia. Macarius thus probably went to Nicaea with the express intention of achieving two important goals, and he returned having been successful on both accounts: the Emperor's permission to destroy Hadrian's pagan temple in the quest for Jesus' tomb, and the Council's backing for his bishopric to be given the recognition which he thought it deserved.

We may well ask, however, what the metropolitan bishop of Caesarea made of all this! – especially when we remember that this was none other than Eusebius. Eusebius was not only the man whose *Ecclesiastical History* has become our indispensable guide to the first 300 years of the Church's history; his *Life of Constantine* is also our chief source for what took place around the Holy Sepulchre! When it is further remembered that Eusebius went to the Council of Nicaea under threat of excommunication for his Arian sympathies, Macarius comes across as something of an opportunist. Eusebius, as the metropolitan of the province and as the Church's leading historian, might well have been geared up to speak *himself* to the Emperor on this score. It appears that Macarius got there first and 'stole his thunder'!

So it was a good day for Macarius. Constantine gave his permission. In future years the Emperor would order the destruction of a few other pagan temples. In this first year of office in the East, however, he might well have needed quite a bit of persuading. Were they sure they were on the right site? Was the destruction of the temple really necessary or might the tomb be under Hadrian's forum rather than under the temple itself? No, Macarius would have replied, the temple would have to go.

On the other hand, Constantine had already publicly espoused the Christian cause, and we know that one of the first things he intended to do after his success at Adrianople was to journey to the East.[20] Was that already a sign of his interest in the Holy Land as a place of Christian origins? Later, on his death-bed, he would regret not having been able to be baptized in the River Jordan.[21] If this reflects his general attitude towards the places of the Gospels, then he may well have already been well disposed to agree to Macarius' request. Nevertheless, we may well imagine that Macarius had various persuasive arguments up his sleeve, should they become necessary: 'Your Imperial Majesty, what behaviour could be more fitting for the first Christian emperor than to be responsible for the uncovering of Christ's tomb? What better opportunity could an emperor have of sending an important signal to his subjects throughout the Empire as to the intentions and nature of this new regime?'

So Macarius returned to Jerusalem with good news for his parishioners, perhaps even with an imperial edict in his hands. Not long after, the workmen set to work.

Eusebius describes the discovery

For what happened next we are indebted to the account of Eusebius. He too returned from the Council with some good news for his parishioners. He had won an order for the production of 50 Bibles. And although he had been out-manoeuvred by Macarius in some ways, at least he had not been excommunicated – which so easily might have happened. We have a letter that he wrote to his home church, explaining how he had been able, without compromise, to sign his agreement to the Creed of Nicaea. We also have his account of what happened next in Jerusalem. The following extract intersperses direct quotations with my own summary (in italics) of Eusebius' fascinating longer account.[22]

The pious emperor addressed himself to another work truly worthy of record, in the province of Palestine. He judged it incumbent on him to render the blessed locality of our Saviour's Resurrection an object of attraction and veneration to all. He issued immediate instructions therefore for the erection in that spot of a house of prayer...

Certain 'impious men' had attempted to 'consign to oblivion that divine monument of immortality ... from which the angel had rolled away the stone for those who still had stony hearts' and 'stony-hearted unbelief'. They had covered the entire spot with a great quantity of earth 'brought from a distance' and with paved stone, erecting a 'gloomy shrine of lifeless idols to the impure spirit whom they call Venus' over the 'sacred cave'. Yet they could not conquer him who conquered death. Constantine, opposing this malice, ordered a thorough purification of the whole site and the destruction of the temple, zealously ensuring the complete transference of its 'stone and timber' and even of the polluted soil to a 'far place'.

Then once down to bed-rock, there appeared immediately and contrary to all expectation the venerable and hallowed monument of our Saviour's Resurrection. Then indeed did this most holy cave present a faithful likeness of his return to life, in that, after lying buried in darkness, it again emerged to light, and afforded to all who came to witness the sight, a clear and visible proof of the wonders of which that spot had once been the scene, a testimony to the Resurrection of the Saviour clearer than any voice could give.

Constantine then ordered the building of a house of prayer near the Saviour's tomb, sending instruction to the governors of the East and the following letter to the 'bishop who at that time presided over the church in Jerusalem':

VICTOR CONSTANTINUS, MAXIMUS AUGUSTUS, TO MACARIUS:

No power of language seems adequate to describe the wondrous circumstance ... that the monument of his most holy passion, so long buried beneath the ground ... should now reappear... For this cause it is ever my first, and indeed my only object, that, as the authority of the truth is evincing itself daily by fresh wonders, so our souls may become more zealous ... for the honour of the divine law. I desire, therefore, especially, that you should be persuaded of that which I suppose is evident to all beside, namely, that I have no greater care than how I may best adorn with a splendid structure that sacred spot, a spot which has been accounted holy from the beginning in God's judgement, but which now appears holier still, since it has brought to light a clear assurance of our Saviour's Passion. It will be well therefore for your sagacity to make such arrangement and provision of all things needful for the work...

Accordingly, on the very spot which witnessed the Saviour's sufferings, a new Jerusalem was constructed, over against the one so celebrated of old, which had experienced the last extremity of desolation. It was opposite this that the emperor now began to rear a monument to the Saviour's victory over death. And it may be that this was that second and new Jerusalem spoken of in the predictions of the prophets...

First of all then he adorned the sacred cave itself, as the chief part of the whole work, and the hallowed monument at which the angel radiant with light had once declared to all that regeneration which was manifested in the Saviour's person. The monument therefore, first of all, as the chief part of the whole, the emperor's magnificence beautified with rare columns...

The next object of his attention was a space of ground of great extent, and open to the pure air of heaven... Then, at the side opposite the cave, which was the eastern side, the church itself was erected... Besides this there were two porticoes on each side... Their gates, placed exactly east, were intended to receive the multitudes who entered the church. Opposite these gates the crowning part of the whole was the *hemisphairion*, which rose to the very summit of the church... In the next place he enclosed the atrium...

This temple, then, the emperor erected as a conspicuous monument of the Saviour's Resurrection and embellished it throughout on an imperial scale of magnificence.

'Contrary to all expectation' – a tomb!

So a tomb was discovered and a great church was built in honour of
him who had been raised from the dead. The site has been marked
ever since by the 'sepulchre' (or 'edicule') at the west end of the
church of the Holy Sepulchre. Eusebius probably wrote these words in
his *Life of Constantine* around the time of the church's dedication (at
which he himself spoke) in September 335, but certainly no later than
339 (the year in which the *Life* was published and the year of Eusebius' own death). The time-gap is little more than 10 years, at the
most. There is therefore no good reason not to accept the general reliability of his account. Nevertheless, there are a few peculiarities which
suggest that Eusebius had particular agendas of his own.

Of course, the most remarkable part of the story is the thing which
Eusebius himself almost found hard to believe: namely that after all
those years there was anything left to find! – let alone a tomb that
could be identified with the tomb of Jesus. The whole account
breathes an air of awesome excitement and wonder. This ambitious
excavation project had paid off! They had something to show for it –
nothing less than a tomb that could be the tomb of Jesus himself!

It is hardly surprising if Eusebius finds it hard to put into words the
wonder of the occasion, and it is only natural that he wants to detect
in this whole event the hand of God himself – vindicating his truth
once again, just as three centuries earlier he had vindicated his Son in
raising him to life. Hence the parallels which Eusebius draws between
the uncovering of the tomb (buried in darkness, now brought to light)
and the Resurrection (the Saviour himself buried, but then brought
gloriously to life).

The question as to whether this was indeed the authentic tomb of
Jesus will be discussed in more detail below in Chapter 7, but several
points must be made briefly at this stage.

First, the phrase 'contrary to all expectation' does not mean, as
some would have us believe, that Eusebius and his contemporaries

knew all along that this project had been an elaborate hoax. It was not a quickly invented tale to persuade a gullible emperor to destroy a pagan temple in the heart of the city. Far more likely, it reflects the great relief and excitement of the local Christians that after all these years there was anything left to find. Till that point they had passed on to their children the tradition about the site, but it lacked any kind of proof. It could so easily have been wrong. Now before their very eyes, the tradition appeared to have been wonderfully vindicated. Contrary to their wildest dreams, there was a tomb!

Secondly, the same excavations revealed some other tombs. Some of these are still visible in the chapel used by the Syrians to the west of the sepulchre (see Figure 19, p. 92 and Plate 22).

So it seems reasonable to suppose that there was some good evidence to support their conclusion that *this* tomb was probably the right one. This particular tomb must have fitted the Gospel evidence sufficiently to convince people that this, not one of the others, was the authentic tomb of Jesus. The Gospels contained the only record of what they were looking for and a tomb which blatantly failed to fit the description would hardly have been convincing.

This means, for example, that we should probably not be too disturbed by Eusebius' referring to the tomb as a 'cave'. The Gospels give the impression that the tomb was cut into the rock by human hand, and Eusebius' terminology is not intended to deny this. For, as is clear from the context within the *Life of Constantine*,[23] Eusebius' motive in using this term was simply his desire to draw together a neat triad of such 'caves' to mark the central places of the Christian Creed – namely here, at Bethlehem, and on the Mount of Olives. The birth, death/Resurrection and Ascension of Jesus had all, so Eusebius would have us note, been strangely associated with caves – though in this particular case it was strictly a man-made tomb. This intriguing way of linking the three main sites of the Creed is unique to Eusebius and gradually lapses in subsequent generations.[24]

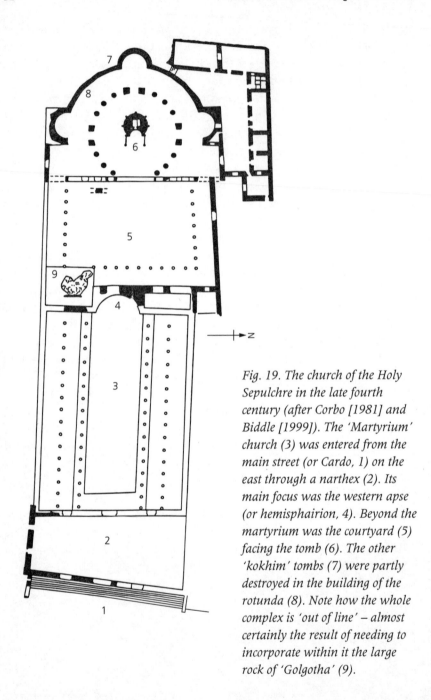

Fig. 19. The church of the Holy Sepulchre in the late fourth century (after Corbo [1981] and Biddle [1999]). The 'Martyrium' church (3) was entered from the main street (or Cardo, 1) on the east through a narthex (2). Its main focus was the western apse (or hemisphairion, 4). Beyond the martyrium was the courtyard (5) facing the tomb (6). The other 'kokhim' tombs (7) were partly destroyed in the building of the rotunda (8). Note how the whole complex is 'out of line' – almost certainly the result of needing to incorporate within it the large rock of 'Golgotha' (9).

Golgotha and the 'wood of the Cross'

So they found a tomb – indeed several tombs, though only this one is ever mentioned. What else did the excavators find? Here Eusebius' account begins to be intriguing. For the strong impression he gives is that this was *all* that they found – a single tomb, which then became the focus for the entire edifice built up around it. Yet any visitor to Jerusalem at the time when he was writing would know that this was only half the story.

For a start, there was a mammoth rock, standing up some five metres above the ground. The Constantinian builders had carefully incorporated this within the overall building – though not without considerable difficulty! Indeed, the whole alignment of the building complex was slightly askew as a result of this rock being preserved intact (see Figure 19). This is, of course, the rock which Bishop Cyril of Jerusalem, speaking just a few years later in his *Catechetical Lectures* (AD 348 or 350), would straightforwardly refer to as 'Golgotha'. Yet for some reason Eusebius' account studiously avoids any reference to it! For Eusebius, if there was a subsidiary focus to the Constantinian buildings after the tomb itself, it was not this rock of Golgotha but rather what he calls the *hemisphairion* – namely the apse at the west end of the adjoining basilica. Why this failure to focus on, or even mention, what to us would seem to be the obvious other point of supreme interest – the possible place of Jesus' crucifixion?

Partly this may reflect the greater emphasis that Eusebius gave to the Resurrection compared to the Cross – something that can be seen from his writings elsewhere. Hence he may have wanted the building to be understood in this more positive context as the place which witnessed primarily to the victory of the Resurrection, rather than to the suffering of the crucifixion. Yet other reasons have been suggested. Did it reflect his doubts as to the authenticity of this Golgotha? Was this precisely the point, that it was only a *possible* place for Jesus' crucifixion? Or, even if not denying its possible authenticity, did he want to hold his peace because, in contrast to the tomb, it simply was not possible to be that confident? After all, who was to say that Jesus had been crucified on *top* of this rock, rather than in the general vicinity to which this rock had given its name? A straightforward and assured identification could not be made beyond any reasonable doubt.

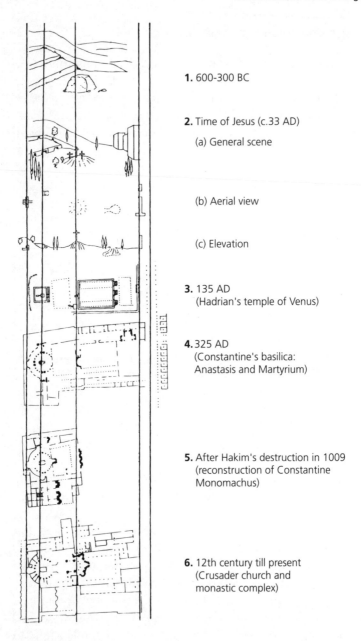

1. 600-300 BC

2. Time of Jesus (c.33 AD)

   (a) General scene

   (b) Aerial view

   (c) Elevation

3. 135 AD
   (Hadrian's temple of Venus)

4. 325 AD
   (Constantine's basilica:
   Anastasis and Martyrium)

5. After Hakim's destruction in 1009
   (reconstruction of Constantine
   Monomachus)

6. 12th century till present
   (Crusader church and
   monastic complex)

Fig. 20. The site of the Holy Sepulchre (AD 30–400) from the south (after Conant [1956]).

However, some have suggested another possible reason. This is connected with yet another intriguing omission within Eusebius' account. In those same *Catechetical Lectures* (delivered actually within the new building), Bishop Cyril makes it quite plain to his baptismal candidates that something else had also been discovered during those excavations: namely the famous 'wood of the cross'.[25] Please note immediately that he never associates this famous relic with Constantine's mother, Queen Helena, nor indeed does anyone else until the very end of the fourth century. So the many legends that have subsequently grown up concerning Helena and the cross can probably be dismissed without further ado. But that there was some wood identified at an early date as belonging to Christ's cross, Cyril is quite clear. Indeed, by the time he talks of it here, he can claim that this relic has already been spread by returning pilgrims 'all over the world'! Eusebius makes a passing reference to the removal of 'stone and timber' from the site, but he makes no reference to the discovery of any such 'wood of the cross'. Why not?

Was he worried about a potential cult of relics? Or was he perhaps a little concerned about how the Jerusalem church would promote this artefact to boost its own ratings and popular appeal (with negative consequences for his own reputation as the chief bishop in the province)? Or, more likely still, was his chief concern the whole issue of authenticity? After all, he knew there had been lots of 'timber' found, but was it not going a little too far to think that the wood of Jesus' cross had been left so conveniently on the site? After all these years, could it really be correctly distinguished from other stray pieces of old wood which happened to be lying around?

Whatever the reason, Eusebius was almost certainly disturbed by the over-enthusiastic identification of this relic. Contrary to what has often been thought subsequently, Eusebius' silence cannot be explained away as simple ignorance. On the contrary, Eusebius' own text (as quoted above) unwittingly betrays the fact that he knew about it only too well. For, despite what Eusebius would have us believe, Constantine's letter to Macarius (a letter which Eusebius was compelled to include in his imperial biography, because of its testimony to the Emperor's religious devotion) appears not to be talking about the discovery of the Resurrection tomb at all.

Instead it is all about a discovery associated with Jesus' 'most holy *passion*'. Constantine also expresses his amazement at the 'fresh

)nders' which were occurring 'daily'. This pardonable exaggeration ongly suggests that, at the very least, he had been informed of more than just *one* archaeological find. He was responding to a second discovery. In all probability, then, he had already been notified about the tomb. Now he was responding to a further report concerning the discovery of the wood of the cross – a 'fresh wonder'. So Eusebius' account probably alludes to this discovery after all!

These puzzling features in Eusebius' account are thoroughly intriguing. They also reveal that from the very outset this most famous church in Christendom inevitably attracted rival opinions. Yet they also have an important consequence for our own purposes, revealing some of Eusebius' qualities as a historian. For if he was so sceptical about other people's claims for these pieces of wood, then by contrast his acceptance of the tomb's authenticity may be taken as reasonably reliable. At the least, even if he were ultimately mistaken, we can be reasonably certain that his enthusiasm was not the result of simple incredulity. Eusebius was not a man to be swept along on a tide of popular emotion.

Hadrian's motives?

A few other features in Eusebius' account deserve comment. First, it was only natural for him and the local Christians to assume that Hadrian's choice of this site for his pagan temple was an act of conscious malevolence towards the Christians of his day. But this may not be fair.

If this was indeed the authentic site of Jesus' burial, then we may reasonably suppose that Christians before AD 135 identified the spot in some way, perhaps simply using it as a place for prayer (though in fact there is no sure evidence of any kind to confirm this [see below, p. 161]). If they did so, however, there is little likelihood that the Roman Emperor would have been aware of this local custom. And if he had, it is still unlikely that he would have drawn any distinction between non-Christian Jews and Jewish Christians (even if he had cause to be grateful that the latter had actually refused to rebel against him). No, if he was informed that this was a special site for some of Jerusalem's inhabitants, then his choosing to build over it must be interpreted as all part of his blanket opposition to Judaism. The Jewish Christians would simply be 'tarred with the same brush'. Were they not all Jews in any case? So his choosing this particular spot was not an act of conscious anti-Christian malice.

In fact the site was almost certainly chosen for quite other reasons. It was simply the most obvious spot, located on some quite high ground immediately adjacent to the centre of his new city. If so, the fact that it covered the tomb of Christ may have been just one of those accidents of history – though Christians no doubt immediately gave it a more sinister interpretation!

The Christians' victory?

Secondly, there is an interesting parallel between what Eusebius presumed Hadrian's motives were in the second century and Constantine's motives in the fourth. Hadrian's building of Aelia Capitolina had sought to express in stone the victory of paganism over Judaism. In a similar way, Constantine's new church now expressed for Eusebius the victory of the Church over the 'Jerusalem of old'. He noted how the church was built on the 'opposite' hill overlooking the Temple mount and (perhaps somewhat with tongue in cheek?) wondered if this new church building might be described as the 'New Jerusalem' mentioned in the prophets (see Isaiah 65:17ff.).

Whatever we make of this extraordinary piece of exegesis, it certainly serves to show the triumphalistic attitude of the Christians at that time. Perhaps this was not unnatural, given that the one in whom they believed, though rejected by Jerusalem three centuries before, had now effectively been vindicated through the conversion of none other than the Emperor himself. Jesus' true kingship had at last been recognized. This was an amazing turnaround from the situation in the first century. Not surprisingly, they sensed in this the hand of their God.

This would, however, be the beginning of an attitude which would continue in the following centuries – not always with happy results. Perhaps the most vivid expression of this attitude is the fact that Hadrian's exclusion of Jews from the city was continued by the new Christian regime – except that they were allowed back on the anniversary of the Temple's destruction.[26]

It would also, of course, leave a painful legacy for the subsequent history of the city from then till now, with religious controversy so often being expressed in the very stones of the city's buildings. And it rebounded on the Christians. Just over three centuries later, that same Temple Mount (deliberately left deserted by Christians in order to make their point) was built on by adherents of another faith in their desire to make a very similar point: namely that their religion was the true one, and their God more powerful than the God worshipped either by the Jews or the Christians. And so the sorry saga of the city would continue down the centuries until the present.

Holy places?

Thirdly, we note the beginnings of an understanding that Gospel sites might be considered as 'holy places'. Eusebius speaks of the 'blessed locality', the 'venerable and hallowed monument' and the 'sacred cave'. Constantine in his letter speaks of the 'sacred spot ... accounted holy from the beginning'. In the wake of such an amazing discovery, fraught with religious significance, such language is hardly surprising. We would probably have used it ourselves! Yet it does mark a watershed in Christian thinking.

In the following decades the concept of Gospel 'holy places' would develop dramatically, till by the end of the century Palestine was littered with such 'holy' sites. Previous to Eusebius, however, this concept of sacred space was comparatively rare within the Christian Church, whether as applied to normal church buildings or as applied to the Holy Land. Christian visitors to the Land were no doubt prayerful; but they seem to have been motivated more by a spirit of historical enquiry than by what we might now refer to as religious 'pilgrimage'.

To be sure, this was partly because the Christian faith was still a persecuted, minority affair; Christians were not able to earmark many buildings in a public way. However, an even more influential factor may have been the way in which the New Testament could be seen as having broken down the concept of 'holy places'. The New Testament writers emphasized the person of Jesus and the universal availability of the Spirit. The passage in John 4 had had a powerful effect: true worshippers did not need to focus on Mount Gerizim or even Jerusalem but rather were required to 'worship in spirit and in truth' (v. 24).

Now, however, as Christians came back to the Land in their droves, all this would change in a dramatic way. Eusebius' account marks an important point in that process. As argued elsewhere, he himself seems by and large to have belonged to the 'old school', emphasizing Christians' general disinterest in the religious significance of physical places, and perhaps being a little critical of Constantine's quite strong obsession with holy objects and places.[27] But now, aged 75, he could not help but use some such language himself in order to do justice to these recent amazing discoveries.

Within a matter of years, however, his much younger contemporary, Bishop Cyril, would be articulating a clear and emphatic theology of 'holy places'. Cyril was possibly just five years old when Constantine came to power in AD 324 and therefore very much a child of the new era. During his episcopate, pilgrimage would take off as never before. This can be attested best by reading the journal of the nun Egeria[28] who, when describing her visit to Jerusalem in AD 384, speaks continuously of the 'holy places' and the religious services held at them.[29] From the fourth century onwards, to an extent which contrasted with earlier practices, 'holy places' would become a regular ingredient in the way Christians viewed the Holy Land.

In all these ways the discovery of the Holy Sepulchre had many important repercussions – not only for the city of Jerusalem but also for the Christian Church throughout the world.

CONSTANTINE'S BUILDINGS

But what exactly was built on the site of Christ's tomb? What did the whole complex look like after Constantine's workers had completed their unique assignment? Here the contemporary church of the Holy Sepulchre can be quite misleading (see Figures 19–21, pp. 92, 94, 100).

The present church is a small, truncated version of the original – the best that the Byzantine Emperor and then the Crusaders could manage after so much of the Constantinian buildings had been destroyed at the order of the Fatimid Caliph Hakim in 1009. Moreover, the structure (or 'edicule') built over the tomb itself is almost entirely a construction of the early nineteenth century after the great fire of 1808.

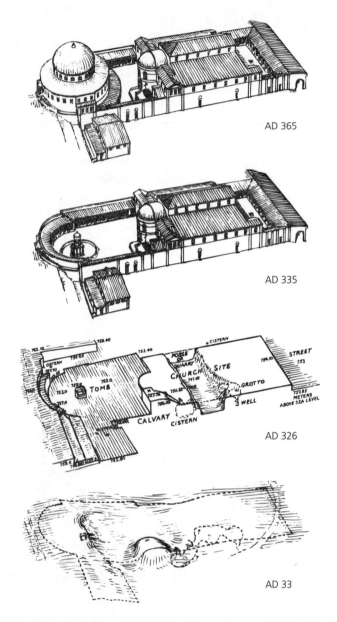

Fig. 21. The changing appearance of the area now covered by the church of the Holy Sepulchre (after Mackowski [1980], p. 156).

The tomb itself

For Eusebius it was clear that the tomb was the 'chief part of the whole work'. In order to emphasize this, the Constantinian architects did something that to us may seem quite strange. Instead of leaving the tomb in its natural surroundings, set into a rock-face or escarpment, they proceeded to cut it free from the living rock, leaving it as a free-standing edifice – not unlike the so-called Tomb of Absalom and Tomb of Zechariah (which can still be seen in the Kidron valley) and the Tomb of the Virgin at Gethsemane.

No doubt this was chiefly done for practical and liturgical reasons, allowing for a steady procession of pilgrims around the tomb (though the newly quarried stone would also come in useful for their vast building programme!). This concern for pilgrim processions can also be seen in the original design of the Church of the Nativity, built just a few years later but subsequently altered by Justinian in the sixth century. Yet there may also have been a sense that this was entirely appropriate, giving the tomb an unrivalled centrality and perhaps too an air of royalty for him who, though crucified in weakness, was now worshipped as the King of Kings.

One of the consequences of this decision (apart from the obvious fact that this destroyed some of the natural aspect of the area) was that they also removed an 'outer hollowed-out rock' or shelter which had been a kind of antechamber in front of the tomb. This was done, says Cyril, in order to 'make room for the present adornment' of the tomb.[30] The result, so Eusebius recounts in another place, was that the tomb was left 'standing erect and alone in a level land, and having only one cavern in it'.[31] The stone identified as the rolling-stone was also placed to one side (now placed in the centre of the Chapel of the Angel just in front of the tomb).

The drawing on p. 102 (Figure 22) gives us some idea of what it may have looked like. This reconstruction is based on some of the later pilgrims' reports and also on the depiction of the tomb as found on a series of pilgrim-flasks now kept in the cathedral treasuries of Monza and Bobbio. These have been dated to the sixth century and show what the edicule would have looked like before the building was set on fire by the Persians in 614 (though the subsequent restoration by Patriarch Modestus made no significant changes).

Fig. 22. The traditional tomb of Christ in the Holy Sepulchre, as it may have appeared in the fourth century (reconstructed in Wilkinson [1972]). For a more recent depiction see Biddle (1999).

In 1009, however, Ibn Abu Zahir 'worked hard to destroy the tomb ... and did in fact hew and root up the greater part of it'.[32] Recent analysis of the texts (especially of what was seen in 1809–10) suggests that more of the original rock may have survived than has often been feared – perhaps simply protected by the mound of fallen stones and rubble which covered the area on that sad day in the eleventh century. It is also suggested that the subsequent restoration of the tomb's *interior* by the Byzantines during the eleventh century has survived to the present day, though the reconstructions of the *outer* edicule by Boniface of Ragusa in 1555 and by Kommenos of Mytilene in 1810 have changed the exterior considerably.

Few today are complimentary about the present appearance of the monument. Regardless of aesthetic tastes, the edicule's structure has been severely damaged over the years – not least by the rainwater pouring down on to it in the decades before the dome of the rotunda was successfully rebuilt in 1868. The earthquake of 1927 has also taken its toll, leading to the installation of the supporting metal frame in 1947 under the British Mandate. In fact it is now structurally so weak that a further reconstruction is an urgent necessity in the coming years. If this were to come to pass, it would presumably become possible to discover exactly how much of the original rock remains. Moreover, if the new design were based on what we know of the Constantinian pattern, visitors might then be able to gain some idea of how the tomb looked in those important years immediately after the tomb's first discovery in 325.

In those early years the tomb was left open to the elements. Within a generation, however, the rotunda had been constructed over the tomb (see Figure 20, p. 94). This was almost certainly part of the original plan – simply delayed by financial concerns and some of the inevitable difficulties involved in its construction. This rotunda would have appeared more spacious than the present arrangement (in which the area between the columns and the outer wall, which was previously open space, is filled with side-rooms). Its outer walls have largely survived, but the columns and dome had to be reconstructed in the eleventh century.

The courtyard

The diagrams of the whole building complex indicate that the area around and in front of the tomb was an open courtyard. This is something which is very hard to imagine today. Most of the present church occupies the space which till the twelfth century was open to the sky! Yet some idea of its appearance may be gained from noting the slender Byzantine columns which stand immediately adjacent to the Crusader ones on the north side of the present church. Although some have seen this as a Constantinian 'garden', it was almost certainly paved over. Cyril himself claims that the excavators had found traces of a 'garden' (perhaps patches of soil which showed signs of having been cultivated),[33] but there is no indication that this aspect of the original scene was recreated.

Golgotha

Located in the south-eastern corner of the courtyard/garden was the rocky knoll which was immediately identified as 'Golgotha', the place of the Crucifixion. The flaw in the rock that resulted in its being left unquarried can still be seen. Not unnaturally, it posed quite a problem for the architects. They decided to cut away the superfluous rocks that formed its slopes and to incorporate it within the courtyard, thus enabling visitors to see from a distance both Golgotha and the tomb at the same time.

Despite Eusebius' personal preferences, it was clearly the second most important feature of the entire site and in Cyril's day it was probably surmounted by a large cross. It was especially a focus for prayer on Good Friday, when it was also customary for the clergy to display the 'wood of the Cross' for the faithful to file past. By Egeria's day this was an activity requiring some important security measures – a few years previously one devotee had succeeded in biting off a portion to take back home![34]

The main church ('Martyrium')

We have yet to describe the main basilica. This was known as the 'Martyrium' (or 'witness') because of its role as the place where Christ's death and Resurrection could be commemorated. As can be seen in Figure 19 (p. 92), this was a massive building which, together with its atrium, stretched all the way to the Cardo, the main north–south street of Hadrian's Roman city, which followed the line of the present *souk* (Khan ez-Zeit, see Plate 20).

At the time of its completion this basilica ranked with St Peter's in Rome for its sheer enormousness. It had five aisles, the outer ones covered by galleries. In contrast to normal Christian practice, it faced westwards, with its main apse being adjacent to Golgotha. This unusual arrangement again is paralleled in St Peter's, where the need to preserve Peter's tomb led to a similar reorientation. The three great entrance gates to the atrium therefore faced the rising sun and five steps led down to join the main street (the Cardo). Archaeological confirmation of this can be found in the property of the Russian Mission (and especially behind Mr Zelatimo's cake shop!). These steps can also

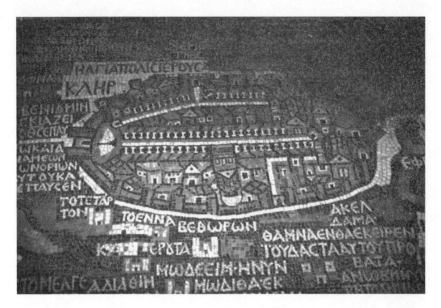

Fig. 23. The Madaba map. This sixth-century floor-mosaic depicts 'the holy city of Jerusalem' from a bird's-eye view, looking from west to east. Note the two main collonaded streets converging at the Hadrianic column just inside the Damascus Gate. The area of the ruined Temple is noticeably absent. The church of the Holy Sepulchre lies in the middle at the bottom and can best be recognized by turning the figure upside down! Note the steps leading up to its three entrance doors and the rotunda at the western end of the building.

be clearly seen (as can the rotunda) in the 'bird's-eye' depiction of the church in the famous mosaic sixth-century map discovered in Madaba (see Figure 23).

Buried underneath the church were rock-cut spaces or 'cisterns' which since the twelfth century have been accessible to visitors (the Armenian 'crypt of St Helena'). As this modern name suggests, this was the place which subsequently became associated with the tradition of Helena and the discovery of the cross, but there is no mention of this in the original sources. In this area one can see some of the basilica's foundation as well as the natural rock. The Armenian excavations, which are behind and below their chapel, also reveal foundation-work from the time of Hadrian and Constantine, as well as the famous graffito of the ship (see further below, p. 162). The fact that this whole area was buried by Constantine's architects underneath their basilica suggests that at the time little significance was given to what was found there.

HISTORY AND SIGNIFICANCE

The overall complex was hugely impressive, attracting pilgrims from all over the world. One of the first such international visitors was the so-called Bordeaux Pilgrim whose brief travelogue of his journey to Palestine in AD 333 makes fascinating reading. Visiting only eight years after the initial excavations (when the site would have resembled a builder's yard), he writes:

> On your left is the hillock Golgotha where the Lord was crucified, and about a stone's throw from it the vault where they laid his body, and he rose again on the third day. By order of the Emperor Constantine there has now been built there a basilica, which has beside it some cisterns of remarkable beauty.[35]

Two years later a host of bishops interrupted their important Church Council meeting at Tyre in order to attend the basilica's dedication. Constantine, who never in fact visited the Holy Land to see the results of his imperial benevolence, would no doubt have loved to be present. Instead Eusebius, the master of ceremonies, travelled almost immediately afterwards to the new imperial capital, Constantinople, where on the thirtieth anniversary of the Emperor's accession he gave an extended oration on the Holy Sepulchre; this incorporated material from the speech which he had earlier delivered in the church.[36]

One of the ironies of history is that this dedication service for the Holy Sepulchre was also the occasion when the bishops formally reinstated Arius, who had been excommunicated for his heretical views about the divine origin of Christ at the Council of Nicaea in 325. This action led to quite a protest, not least from Athanasius, the great champion of orthodoxy, and was subsequently overturned. Yet once again it shows how this church from the outset became embroiled in ecclesiastical disputes.

Some other magnificent churches would soon be built both in Jerusalem (the 'Pentecost' church on Mount Zion around 340) and throughout Palestine (especially the churches in Bethlehem and on the Mount of Olives, started just a year or two later after the visit of Queen Helena). None, however, would ever eclipse the church of the Holy Sepulchre for both its splendour and its abiding significance. Bishop Cyril used it as the natural place for his baptismal classes in 350, and by the end of his episcopate an elaborate pattern of liturgical celebrations had been developed. As can be seen in Egeria's detailed description (AD 384), to celebrate Holy Week in Jerusalem was a colourful experience – and also pretty exhausting! Other places in the vicinity (such as Gethsemane, or the summit of the Mount of Olives) were also used in these celebrations. But at the centre of them all was the Martyrium and especially the Anastasis (as the rotunda over the tomb came to be called).

Anastasis simply means 'resurrection', and in this place the Resurrection of Jesus has been remembered ever since. There is no denying that, precisely because of its importance to so many, it has also been the scene of Christian squabbles. Representatives of the different historic churches have sought to establish a foothold in this central Christian site – Greeks, Armenians, Syrians, Copts and Latin Catholics. Nevertheless, the fact that they are all together under one roof (though admittedly the Ethiopians are on *top* of the roof!) is in its own way a testimony to a far greater unity than might be found in other contexts or religious disputes. The casual visitor may be confused by this, or even appalled. But the alternative – a church used only by one denomination – might be even worse.

There is also no denying that the ravages of history have left the building in a state which can hardly be described as aesthetically pleasing. The refusal in AD 638 of Caliph Omar to pray within it ensured that it was not turned subsequently into a mosque; so it survived the arrival of the Muslims unscathed. The devastating work of Caliph Hakim, however, the ravages of fire, and the endless 'wear and tear' of pilgrims have all taken their toll. Not surprisingly, many visitors in the nineteenth century, especially Protestants, gave fairly depressing accounts of the building. Very little had been done to restore the building after the fire of 1808, and we can imagine something of its appearance by noting the present state of the unrestored chapel, used by the

Syrians, to the west of the edicule. At least in recent years the various parties have come to an agreement about the church's refurbishing. The most recent example of this is the magnificent redecoration of the rotunda, officially 'unveiled' only in 1997.

Regardless of one's aesthetic or liturgical tastes, it has to be admitted that this church, for all its faults, for all its history, is quite unique. Leaving aside the issues of its historical authenticity, we have to acknowledge that for more than a millennium and a half this is the place where Christ's Resurrection has been remembered. As a complex building structure it may seem far-removed in appearance from the events of that first Easter morning. Yet its history, its solidity, and the fact that it has survived at all, serve at the very least to witness to something else – namely the ongoing significance of the Resurrection and its central importance for Christians throughout the centuries.

Although Jesus was rejected by Jerusalem's authorities and led outside its city walls, it is also perhaps appropriate that this church has been able for so long to proclaim by its presence *in the very heart of Jerusalem* the divine vindication which, so Christians believe, was given to Jesus 'on the third day'. This message of the Risen Christ was something which the first followers of Jesus realized had to be preached 'in all Judea and Samaria, and to the ends of the earth', but it was also inevitably a message for 'Jerusalem' (Acts 1:8). It was a message of 'peace', not only for those who were 'far off' but also for those who were 'near' (cf. Ephesians 2:17). So the church of the Holy Sepulchre, or more truly the Church of the Resurrection, simply through being in the heart of the city, proclaims that the Resurrection of Jesus is not just of central significance for the world, but also for Jerusalem.

THE TWO ALTERNATIVE SITES

Pl.18 (top): aerial view (from north-west, 1998), showing both the Garden Tomb enclosure (bottom left) and the grey domes of the Holy Sepulchre (middle right).

Pl.19 (bottom): Jerusalem AD 44–70 (from south-west, in the Holy Land Hotel model), showing how both sites may have been brought within the expanded 'third wall'. Traditional Golgotha is depicted as a crop of unquarried rock (middle right) outside the 'Garden' Gate. The rock-face of Skull Hill (top left) lies outside the Damascus Gate.

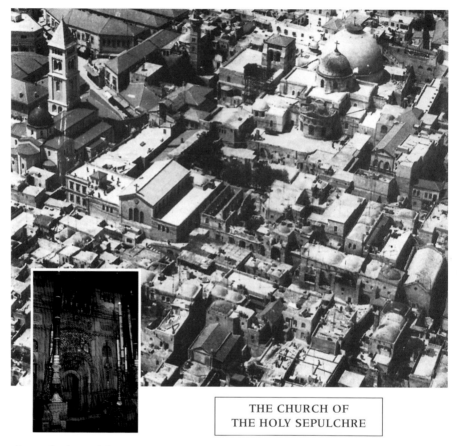

THE CHURCH OF
THE HOLY SEPULCHRE

Pl.20: The line of the main street (the Cardo Maximus, now the modern *souk*) can be seen (from middle left to bottom right). Constantine's basilica extended westwards from this to the large rotunda. The Crusaders' reconstruction (with its smaller dome) occupied only the western third of the area. Note, in front of this, the Ethiopian monastery on the roof of the church's crypt, the tower (left) of the Lutheran church of the Redeemer (1898) and, between them, the excavation area owned by the Russian Church.

Pl.21 (inset): The 'edicule', constructed in 1810 by Kommenos of Mytilene over the traditional tomb of Jesus.

Pl.22 (top opposite page): The 'kohkim' shaft-tombs on the south side of the Syrian chapel. These would have been unearthed in the fourth century when the rounded wall of the rotunda (just visible on the left) was constructed.

Pl.23 (bottom opposite page): The spacious rotunda at the end of the 17th century (de Bruyn). The edicule (as reconstructed by Boniface in 1555) looked quite different before the fire of 1808.

THE AREA OF THE GARDEN TOMB IN THE LATE 19TH CENTURY

Pl.24 (left): The northern walls of the Old City as seen from Skull Hill (c. 1887). Note the Damascus Gate (to the right) and the Spaffords' house just inside the city wall (to the left), frequented by Gordon in 1883. The building (foreground, right) still stands south of the Garden Tomb platform.

Pl.25 (below left): The Garden Tomb enclosure as seen from Skull Hill (c. 1900); this was possibly taken by Peder Beckholdt, showing the walls which he had built round the enclosure.

Pl.26 (inset below): The enclosure as seen from the grounds of the Ecole Biblique, looking south; taken after a fall of snow in 1898 (note the building work on the Lutheran church tower).

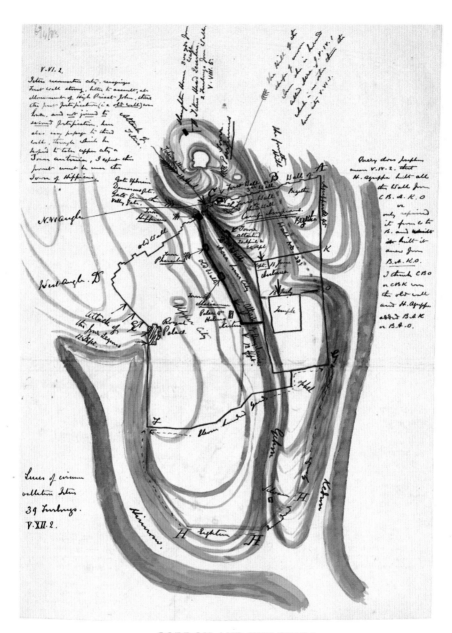

GORDON AND THE SKULL

Pl.27: An original sketch by General Gordon (1883), showing how Jerusalem's contours give the impression of a human skeleton on its side (cf. Fig.25). His markings relate to Josephus' account of the sack of Jerusalem by Titus in AD 70.

FRIENDS OF THE GARDEN TOMB

Pl.28 (above): A sketch made in 1849 by J. H. Wallace of one of his daughters, probably nine-year old Louisa Hope.

Pl.29 (above right): General Charles Gordon, the Governor-General of Khartoum, taken shortly before his death in 1885.

Pl.30 (right): Solomon Mattar (warden of the Garden Tomb, 1948–67) in February 1953.

Pl.31 (below): Conrad Schick, a few years before his death (in 1901).

Pl.32 (below right): General Booth (centre) in 1898 after preaching on top of Skull Hill in front of the Salvation Army flag.

**IN AND AROUND
THE GARDEN TOMB**

Pl.33 (above): Two women inside the tomb (c.1890). The vertical slab was soon removed (see Pl.50), but the groove can still be clearly seen (see Pl.54).

Pl.34 (left): The small 'Venus-stone', uncovered from in front of the tomb by Charlotte Hussey in 1923.

Pl.35 (below): Hanauer's photo (1924) of some artefacts, believed to have been found by Beckholdt in 1904 in front of the tomb, but which disappeared, according to Hanauer, during the First World War.

A Modern Discovery

The Garden Tomb

The church of the Holy Sepulchre appeals to many for the reasons stated at the end of the previous chapter. For others, however, the very same factors tell in the opposite direction. Rather than speaking of Christian unity, the presence of the various denominations within its walls speaks of disunity. Instead of witnessing to the solidity of the Resurrection message as believed by Christians throughout the last 2,000 years, its ancient masonry and its accumulated decorations speak of human religiosity and a form or worship alien to their taste. And the fact that it lies so squarely in the middle of the city, far from being a virtue, only reveals its greatest weakness – the possibility that this is not, after all, the true site of Jesus' crucifixion *outside* the city wall.

It was for reasons such as these, combining both genuine archaeological doubt and a certain spiritual unease, that Protestant travellers to the Holy Land began to ask the question in the middle of the nineteenth century which for the previous 1,500 years had seldom been raised. Was there somewhere else nearby, waiting to be discovered at last after 1,800 years, which marked the true site of these momentous events? Such a discovery, to say the least, would be quite sensational. Not surprisingly, the pursuit for this alternative site and the debate concerning the traditional site began to occupy the attention of a vast number of scholars and travellers. The nineteenth century saw the rise simultaneously both of biblical archaeology and of a greater concentration amongst Christians upon the human, historical Jesus, shorn of subsequent accretions. The combination of these two factors would lead almost inevitably to the traditional site coming under a spate of heavy questioning. Would not archaeology be able to uncover a site less encumbered by religious trappings and more readily connected to the Jesus known from the Gospels?

A century and a half later the question of the true location of the Crucifixion and Resurrection continues naturally to be one of the first questions asked by the modern Christian visitor. It would be so good to know for sure! In this chapter we trace the developments by which a substantial number of people came to focus their attention on just such an alternative site: the Garden Tomb with its neighbouring 'Skull Hill', both set a little to the north-east of the Damascus Gate.

THE SEARCH FOR GOLGOTHA

Ancient doubts?

There are a couple of instances which have survived of writers in antiquity who commented on the strangeness of the church of the Holy Sepulchre lying in the heart of the Old City. Given the clarity of the Gospel records on this point, this was a natural enough question. It is perhaps surprising that there were not more such comments. In AD 724 Willibald wrote:

> Calvary was formerly outside Jerusalem, but Helena, when she found the cross, arranged that place so as to be within the city.

Some interpret this as a sign that Willibald was questioning the authenticity of the site (Helena 'moved' the *place*). Though not impossible, it is equally probable that he thought Helena caused the line of the *walls* to be moved, so as to bring the authentic Calvary within them. He may therefore simply be trying to explain an important point that would no doubt have been noticed by scores of pilgrims.

The same goes for the various maps of Jerusalem in the Middle Ages that depict the site of the crucifixion outside the city walls. In many instances this does not betray some alternative tradition, but simply the desire somehow to reconcile the information of the Gospels with the topography of Jerusalem. Some of the maps in the period after the Reformation are intriguing, however, because they depict Calvary as being on the north side of the city, or at least to the north-west. Does this reflect, after all, some local knowledge or even doubt about the traditional site?

Modern questions

Nevertheless, the authenticity of the Holy Sepulchre went substantially unchallenged until the dawn of the modern period. Then, in 1738 Jonas Korte visited Jerusalem and in a subsequent book concluded that Jesus' tomb must lie somewhere outside the Turkish city walls. This was followed in 1801 by Edward Daniel Clarke, later Professor of Mineralogy in Cambridge, who concluded from his few days in Jerusalem that the crucifixion had instead taken place on Mount Zion; Jesus' tomb was somewhere on the slopes of the opposite hill, across the Valley of Hinnom. These lone voices soon became a flood.[1]

With travel to Palestine becoming much easier for Western visitors in the 1830s (under the Egyptian pasha, Muhammed Ali), the volume of traffic increased substantially and so too the number of people who were prepared to question the traditional site. This was not perhaps very surprising, given the forlorn state of the Holy Sepulchre after the fire in 1808. One of the most famous of these was Edward Robinson who in 1838, soon after his appointment as Professor of Biblical Literature at the Union Theological Seminary in New York, set out to visit the Middle East with Eli Smith, a missionary amongst the Arab peoples.

In writing subsequently about the Holy Sepulchre,[2] he expressed some surprise that the sites of the Crucifixion and Resurrection had been located quite so close together. Even if this were possible, however, he objected to the host of other traditions which were also supposed to be located within this one building:

> the stone on which the body of our Lord was anointed for burial, the fissure in the rock, the holes in which the crosses stood, the spot where the true cross was found by Helena...

This story concerning the discovery of three crosses particularly attracted his scorn. He saw this as the result of 'an age of credulous faith, as well as of legendary tradition and invention, if not of pious fraud' – this latter phrase being one which he repeated frequently. Drawing into the debate the testimony of Josephus[3] that the 'second wall' of the city at the time of the Crucifixion had 'encircled' the northern part of the city and thus had included the area now covered by the Holy Sepulchre, he advocated that the modern scientific reasoning of archaeology should be used instead to determine the true site. Could this young science enter the arena and succeed where the ancients had failed?

Robinson's arguments caused quite a stir and inevitably paved the way for a continuous debate between the modern scientific approach (often identified with Protestantism) and the traditional approach espoused by the Catholic and Orthodox churches. Even within supposedly Protestant ranks, however, the traditional site found its defendants. George Williams, chaplain to the first Protestant bishop in Jerusalem, read Josephus differently and emphasized the continuity of Jerusalem bishops and tradition in the early period. George Finlay suggested that Constantine would have needed some good evidence for the authenticity of the site before giving the dramatic order to destroy the Temple of Venus which had since been built over the site. And even John Henry Newman (before his 'conversion' to Rome) joined in, claiming that the Jerusalem Christians in the fourth century were not unprincipled hypocrites. Instead they were far more likely to be in touch with genuine tradition on the spot, even after 300 years, than was someone like Robinson from the distance of the 'Antipodes'. Robinson retorted by similarly questioning Newman's credentials, 'seated in his arm-chair' in Oriel College, Oxford! And so the debate began – a debate which has gone on ever since, often in just such colourful terms.

Robinson himself did not offer an alternative site, except that it was probably on one of the main roads leading to either Joppa or Damascus. A few years later, in 1848, an architect named James Fergusson (though he had never visited Jerusalem) made the intriguing suggestion that the Dome of the Rock on the Temple Mount was the true site. He argued that this mosque, with its brilliant dome modelled in some respects (as we now know) on the pattern of Byzantine churches, was Constantine's original church built over Calvary.

The desire to prove this claim prompted Fergusson in 1865 to be involved in setting up the Palestine Exploration Fund. In the following decades the *Quarterly Statement* of this organization would contain numerous articles devoted to this one question of the authentic crucifixion site. Yet it soon became clear that Fergusson's initial suggestion was not sustainable. In fact it was convincingly refuted by the very man sent out by the Fund in 1867 to investigate around the Temple Mount, namely Charles Warren. A short while later (in 1884) there was also the amazing discovery of the Madaba map, which clearly showed Constantine's basilica of the Holy Sepulchre in its present location (see Figure 23, p. 105). No longer could anyone seriously suggest that the Holy Sepulchre was merely a Crusader invention. It might be but a shadow of its former self, but it was clearly on the site of the tomb uncovered in AD 325.

Skull Hill

Back in the 1840s, however, soon after Robinson's critique of the Holy Sepulchre, another site had begun to attract people's attention, which seemed far more convincing than either the Holy Sepulchre or the Temple Mount. To the north-east of the Damascus Gate there was a rocky escarpment facing the city walls which was already associated in local tradition with 'Jeremiah's grotto', the place where the prophet had supposedly composed his Lamentations over the destruction of Jerusalem. Intriguingly, some of its features caused it to look like a skull. Was it not far more likely that Jesus was crucified here, rather than on the rock shown in the Holy Sepulchre? It not only resembled a skull, but there was also no doubt that it lay outside the city wall of Jesus' day.

Credit for being the first to make this suggestion is normally given to a German, Otto Thenius, who visited Jerusalem in 1842. There were also several American visitors around this time who were coming to a similar conclusion: Rufus Anderson (1845), Fisher Howe (1853), Charles Robinson (1867) and Selah Merrill (1875–7), together with the Englishman Henry Tristram (1858) and the famous Frenchman Ernest Renan, author of the *Vie de Jésus* (1863). Charles Robinson (no relation of Edward!) spoke out strongly against the liturgical 'postures' practised in the Holy Sepulchre.[4] He had been influenced by Howe's ideas, and a few years after his first coming to this conclusion he had taken some friends to the Mount of Olives, hoping that they too would be struck independently by the rock's skull-shape. They were. His conviction was confirmed. Meanwhile Merrill argued that the traditional line of the second wall would have made Jerusalem too small for its crowded population. He also thought that there was something providential in the summit of this alternative Golgotha having been preserved from the subsequent building of churches by the presence of a Muslim graveyard.

One of the first British scholars to endorse this identification was a young man sent out in 1872 by the Palestine Exploration Fund to conduct a topographical survey of Palestine. Claude Conder was particularly impressed by the fact that, according to the researches of Thomas Chaplin, Sephardic Jews apparently still identified this site with the 'place of stoning' known from the Mishnah (*Sanhedrin* 6:1–4). This suggested that this had indeed been Jerusalem's execution-ground in the time of Jesus. Conder's *Tentwork in Palestine* (1878) was recognized as one of the best statements of the case in favour of Skull Hill (followed, for example, by Besant's *Thirty Years Work in the Holy Land* [1895]). Conder vigorously maintained this view to the end of his life, as can be seen in his final book, *The City of Jerusalem* (published posthumously in 1909).

General Gordon

The next Briton to mention is perhaps the most famous of all: General Charles Gordon (see Plate 29). Gordon was one of the most intriguing persons of his day. A famous soldier with remarkable success in various parts of the world, he was also a Christian. He spent most of 1883 on personal retreat in Palestine – the first six months of it in the village of Ein Karem (some seven miles to the west of Jerusalem). In subsequent years this alternative site for the Crucifixion would come frequently to be known as 'Gordon's Calvary' (he himself referred to it as 'my Golgotha'). There is no doubt that the endorsement of this site by a man who was one of the most famous and intriguing Christians of his day did much to cement its credentials in the popular imagination. Yet it is equally clear that Gordon was, as we have seen, far from being the first one to make this identification.

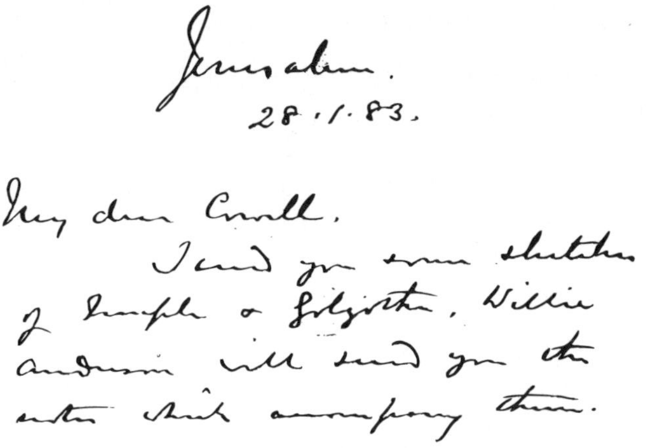

Jerusalem.
28 . 1 . 83 .

My dear Connell,
I send you some sketches
of Temple & Golgotha. Willie
Anderson will send you the
notes which accompany them.

Fig. 24. One of the many letters sent by General Gordon from Palestine to Lord Connell, a member of the Queen's household. This one included 'sketches of the Temple and Golgotha'.

Gordon wrote hundreds of letters during these 12 months, including what he called a 'deluge' to Conrad Schick, one of the leading archaeologists in Jerusalem at the time (see Figure 24).

In reading all these letters we discover not only some of his own distinctive reasons for identifying this site with Golgotha; we also realize that he had already come to this conclusion some time beforehand ('ere I came here').

Gordon arrived in Jerusalem on 17 January 1883. On the very next day he wrote to his sister, Augusta:

I feel, for myself, convinced that the Hill near the Damascus Gate is Golgotha... From it, you can see the Temple, the Mount of Olives and the bulk of Jerusalem. His stretched-out arms would, as it were, embrace it: 'all day long have I stretched out my arms' [cf. Isaiah 65:2]. Close to it is the slaughter-house of Jerusalem, and quite pools of blood are lying there. It is covered with tombs of Muslims. There are many rock-hewn caves and gardens surrounding it. Now, the place of execution in our Lord's time must have been an unclean place ... so, to me, this hill is left bare ever since it was first used as a place of execution.

His distinctive arguments

Gordon was well aware of the traditions associating this place not only with Jeremiah's Lamentations but also with the 'place of stoning'.[5] However, he gave even more weight to an argument drawn from typology and topography. This can be best understood by studying his careful drawings (see Figure 25 and Plate 27).

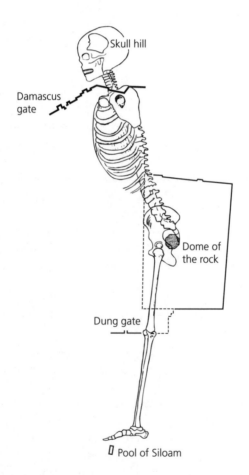

Fig. 25. Gordon's imaginative depiction of Jerusalem (simplified). Viewed from a bird's-eye perspective he saw the contours in terms of a human skeleton with 'Skull Hill' in the place of the skull. For all its fancifulness, it correctly shows how Skull Hill, prior to the quarrying in front of it, was the natural extension of the ridge on which the temple was built.

Evidently he believed that the topography of Jerusalem, when looked at from a bird's-eye view, resembled the shape of a human skeleton. In this configuration the Temple Mount corresponded to the pelvis, his Golgotha to the 'skull'. The fact that it also resembled a skull in actual appearance only confirmed this – as seen in the following note:[6]

> This northern end [of the eastern hill] is marked by an apex of uncovered rock — a rocky knoll resembling in form the human skull — and from this 'skull hill' the crown of the eastern hill follows a line which is aslant, or askew, to the valley of Kedron until it reaches, at about two-thirds of its entire length, another bare rock, now covered by the Mosque of Omar.
>
> I think that the cross stood on top of the skull hill, in the centre of it, and not where the slaughter-house now stands. Leviticus [1:11] says that the victim was to be slain 'on the side of the altar, northward before the Lord', and literally they were to slay the victims 'slantwise to the altar northwards'. The altar was on the second knoll within the Haram enclosure, and if the cross were placed in the centre of skull hill, the whole city, and even the Mount of Olives, would be embraced by those stretched out arms... The whole outline of this sacred eastern hill ... bears a rough resemblance to the human form. From the skull hill, on the north-west, the body lies — as did that of the victim — aslant or askew to the altar of burnt sacrifice.

Gordon's thinking was guided by his mystical and deep devotion to the details of Scripture ('I get imbued with scripture, history, never think of anything else'). He was also influenced by his belief that Christ was the key to the Old Testament, such that many Old Testament details pointed forward to Christ typologically. Hence, for example, he wrote in one of his letters:

Christ is all in all! He is the key to the Scriptures. The victims were slain at north of altar [Leviticus 1:11], therefore he was slain north of Jerusalem and scripture goes out of its way to tell us that the hill was shaped like a skull. His church came from his side; his heart therefore as the Temple was a type of him; the stones would be taken from a place corresponding to his heart ... Christ was and is the true Temple.[7]

Few have followed him in this distinctive line of reasoning, and he received criticism for it even from sympathetic friends during his lifetime. Lawrence Oliphant, a friend whom he visited in Haifa during the year and again in December before returning to England, agreed with Gordon about the site of Golgotha; but he viewed the skeleton theory as a 'singular and mystical conception'. Even so, he described Gordon as 'the most Christ-like man I ever knew'.[8]

At the same time, many of his judgements pursued sound reasoning. He had read Josephus carefully (concluding, with many after him, that the 'third wall' was far to the north of the present Turkish walls). And his insight as to where the Empress Eudocia might have built her church in honour of St Stephen was almost immediately proved correct when the Dominicans discovered its remains just to the north of the present Garden Tomb enclosure in 1885.

A lasting impression

So this famous soldier, soon to die himself at Khartoum, would frequently sit opposite this hill on the roof of a house belonging to the Spaffords, an American missionary family, and contemplate the place where he believed his Saviour had died. It clearly absorbed him deeply. It also left a lasting impression on the Spaffords' five-year-old daughter, Bertha Spafford Vesper, who has left us this endearing account:

> Five is not too young for hero worship, and my hero was a frequent visitor to our house, General Charles George 'Chinese' Gordon, the 'fabulous hero of the Sudan'. He was fulfilling a lifelong dream with a year's furlough in Palestine, studying biblical history and the antiquities of Jerusalem. This was the only peaceful time the general had known in many years, and it was to be his last...
>
> No road led from Ein Karim in those days ... and General Gordon came often from his village home to Jerusalem riding a white donkey... A chair was put out for him on our flat roof and he spent hours there, studying his Bible, meditating, planning...
>
> He gave Father a map and a sketch that he made, showing the hill as a man's figure, with the skull as the cornerstone... Father did not agree with the general's visionary ideas, but ... they were good friends.

Mother wanted General Gordon to have peace when he was meditating on the roof, and cautioned me not to disturb him, but I would creep up the roof stairs and crouch behind a chimney; there I would wait. I watched him reading his Bible and lifting his eyes to study the hill, and my vigil was always rewarded, for at last he would call me and take me on his knee and tell me stories. He was not very tall, and had fair, curly hair, and I remember how blue his eyes were, and the blue double-breasted suit he wore... I did not know General Gordon was famous, only that he was my friend, and I loved him.[9]

Gordon's *Reflections in Palestine 1883* were published early in 1885. His death at Khartoum on 26 January 1885 only served to increase the interest of the British public in this enigmatic figure and his distinctive views. Some may think that Gordon pushed some of his arguments too far. Yet there were now several indications that perhaps the true Golgotha had at last been discovered. Here, outside the city wall, was a skull-shaped hill, clearly visible both from the city walls and from the road that ran in front of that wall to the east; it was also reputed to be a traditional 'place of stoning' and associated with Jeremiah. And Gordon's emphasis on its integral relation with the Temple Mount, the place of sacrifice a little further to the south, remained an intriguing and suggestive idea.

Many were convinced that the true Golgotha had been discovered, including such famous writers as Cunningham Geikie (1887) and Alfred Edersheim (1883), as well as Lew Wallace, the author of *Ben-Hur* (1881). Not surprisingly, when the American evangelist Dwight Moody was in Jerusalem in 1892 and had the opportunity of going to the top of Skull Hill for an Easter Day service, he began his sermon with these words: 'I have preached for thirty years, but have never felt the awe of God as I do at this moment.'[10] In the course of 50 years the initial idea, first sown by Otto Thenius in 1842, had taken a deep root. A convincing Golgotha had been found. But where, then, was the tomb?

THE SEARCH FOR THE TOMB

'Now there was a garden in the place where he was crucified, and in the garden there was a new tomb in which no one had ever been laid' (John 19:41). Given the growing consensus as to the location of Golgotha, it was only natural that there would soon develop a comparable interest in the location of the tomb – which, according to this clear biblical statement, could not be very far away. During 1881 Conder, convinced as he was of the 'new' Golgotha, discovered a *loculus* tomb 200 yards to the west of Skull Hill which had evidently been closed by a rolling stone (see Figure 26). It had since been visited by many travellers (including 'their Royal Highnesses Prince Edward and Prince George of Wales'), and he appealed for funds to purchase it.[11] But he was unsuccessful, and the land was soon bought by the Franciscans (now the White Sisters on the west side of the Nablus Road).

Of far more interest was a tomb some 500 feet to the east which had first been discovered in 1867 and which was actually set in the western escarpment of Skull Hill itself (see Figure 27).

Fig. 26. 'Conder's tomb', based on his own drawing (in Palestine Exploration Quarterly *13 [1881], p. 202).*

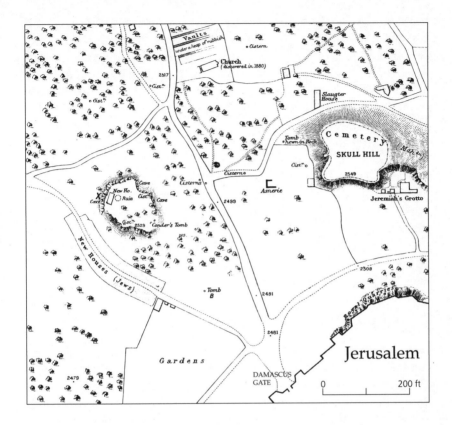

Fig. 27. The area north-west of the Damascus Gate as shown in Palestine Exploration Quarterly *17 [1885], p. 75. The Garden Tomb is the 'tomb hewn in Rock'. A few years later the remains of the basilica of St Stephen were discovered in the Dominican property to the north of the Garden, together with the tombs close to the Garden Tomb itself. Note the city's slaughter-house referred to by General Gordon (above p. 115). Conder's tomb (cf. Figure 26) is further to the west, close to a knoll which also attracted attention as a possible site of the crucifixion.*

One of the intriguing questions is whether Gordon himself ever came to any conclusions about this recently discovered tomb. When a few years later an appeal was made in England for its purchase, it is not surprising that Conder was opposed to it, nor perhaps that he denied that Gordon had shown any interest in it. Yet Conrad Schick, the one who, as Gordon himself admitted, had received a 'deluge' of correspondence from Gordon on Jerusalem matters, claimed the contrary. In one of his letters and several times in the *Quarterly Statement* of the Palestine Exploration Fund (between 1890 and 1892), Schick asserts that Gordon was indeed convinced that this was the tomb of Jesus. Moreover in *The Times* editorial devoted to the subject (8 October 1892), there is an allusion to a Mr Hanbury who had considered purchasing the property surrounding the tomb (for £1,200) precisely because he was inspired by 'Gordon's faith'. Finally, we note that Conder himself at the end of his life conceded that Gordon had thought that a 'tomb in the cliff – now known as the Garden Tomb – must be the true site of the holy sepulchre'.[12] Unless all of this was a false rumour, Crawley-Boevey was probably correct to say some years later that Gordon's 'belief in it as the real place of Christ's burial has done more than anything else to make the Garden Tomb widely famous'.[13]

Conrad Schick and the tomb's first discovery

Conrad Schick himself was integrally involved in the tomb's discovery (see Plate 31). Schick, a native German, had come to Jerusalem in 1846 under the auspices of a Swiss missionary organization from Basel. He was a clockmaker, but over the years he became a local expert on Jerusalem archaeology (especially the Temple Mount). In 1892 he was asked to do a thorough survey of the area around the tomb; and a few years earlier he had also gone down into the two cisterns within the property, one of which was quite vast (measuring 66 by 30 feet at its base, and with a capacity of over one million litres). Although there was one particularly large Christian cross on one wall, he reckoned that the cistern was originally of Canaanite origin (see Plates 42 and 43).[14]

However, 25 years earlier, immediately after the discovery of the tomb itself, he had also been the first person approached for his opinion by the Greek owner of the property. The owner wanted to know whether this 'cave' could be used for a cistern. At the time it was filled to within two feet of the ceiling with rubble, bones and mould. Despite his advice to close it up, a few months later Schick returned to find that it had been substantially cleared out.

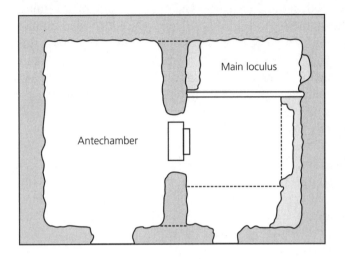

Fig. 28. Interior plan of the Garden Tomb.

Fig. 29. The small Byzantine cross inside the Garden Tomb.

His description[15] matches what can be seen today: a five-foot-high doorway leading into one (the left-hand) of two chambers; around the walls of the right-hand chamber were the positions of three graves (see Figure 28). He also reported that a cross had been painted in red on one wall surrounded by four Greek letters (see Figure 29).

Very soon after its discovery some masonry had been used to repair the broken front of the tomb (between the present door and the small window above to the right). The striking difference (compared to its modern appearance) is that there had also been some slabs about three inches thick which stood vertically around the grave *loculi*, thereby creating grave-troughs; some of these slabs had been removed by the time of Schick's writing (see Plate 33). There was a similar grave-trough located against the far wall of the left-hand chamber.

A solid mound of earth remained in front of the tomb until the 1890s, making access quite difficult, whilst the surrounding area was an unenclosed piece of waste ground. Schick suggested that the bed-rock might be as much as a further five feet below the doorway, and also that the original entrance had been much smaller. Also he was convinced that an arched building had at some point been in front of the tomb.

Schick had been sceptical for many years about the Holy Sepul-chre. By the time he wrote this report in 1892, however, he had changed his mind back in favour of the traditional site as a result of doing some excavations in the area owned by the Russians to the east of that church. Nevertheless, he still gives his opinion that this newly discovered tomb near Skull Hill was originally Jewish – even if it had then been altered by Christians some time after AD 400. Conder too had investigated the tomb in 1873 (see below) without identifying it with that of Jesus' burial. Nevertheless, a growing number of people in the 1880s, perhaps influenced by the opinions of Gordon, became convinced that this was quite probably the authentic tomb of Joseph of Arimathea. These included the Revd J. E. Hanauer, an Anglican Hebrew Christian resident in Jerusalem; Maurice Day, Bishop of Cashel and Waterford, who addressed the Church of Ireland Conference in 1887 on the subject; and some English Christians (such as Henry Campbell, Haskett Smith, Louisa Hope, Evan Hopkins and Charlotte Hussey) who began negotiating for its purchase.

Towards the purchase

After the death of the former owner in 1870, the property had come eventually into the possession of an elderly German banker named Frutiger, described by the later *Times* editorial as a 'shrewd German speculator'. In his failing health, negotiations had to be conducted with his son-in-law Herr Fäber, who was less inclined to sell the prop-erty at a normal market rate. An initial appeal for subscriptions seems to have been made, but when negotiations failed in Jerusalem the sub-scriptions were returned.

Then a deal was struck by Smith and Hussey with Frutiger's wife whereby half the property could be bought at once, the remaining half when funds had been raised (this requirement was soon changed so that they had to buy two-thirds in the first instance). News of this came to Louisa Hope in England who, together with Hopkins and Smith (now back from Jerusalem), formed a committee and asked the original subscribers if they would subscribe again. According to Hussey's later account (1919) the majority of the subscribers did indeed repledge their support. Nevertheless, the amount of money to be raised remained substantial and there was a time limit set for the completion of the transaction.

Helped by the publisher John Murray, Haskett Smith brought the issue clearly into the public gaze. Both in *Murray's Magazine* (1891) and in *Murray's Handbook for Travellers in Syria and Palestine* (1892) he argued strongly that this was indeed Joseph's tomb. It evidently dated from the Herodian period. Although originally intended for Jewish use, it clearly had been of interest subsequently to Christians. Moreover, it appeared never to have been properly finished. The recent discovery (in 1889) of an inscription in the neighbouring Dominican property was also pressed into service. This read: 'The private tomb of the deacon Nonnus Onesimus of the Holy Resur-

rection of Christ and of this monastery' (see Figure 30).

Was this not an indication that this Christian's tomb was near the place of the Resurrection and that he had wanted to be buried 'near his Lord'? Haskett Smith concluded that 'there can be said to be actually not a link missing in the chain of evidence which connects this tomb with the Sepulchre of Christ'.

Fig. 30. The inscription over the tomb of Nonnus Onesimus (as drawn by Lagrange in 1894, reproduced in Vincent [1925], p. 409).

Controversy in *The Times*

So it was that on 22 September 1892 a letter appeared in the London *Times*, written by Henry Campbell and John Murray, which appealed for funds:

> Sir, Many of your readers are doubtless acquainted with the spot lying outside the Damascus Gate at Jerusalem, which is commonly known as 'Gordon's Tomb', from the fact that General Gordon, amongst many others who have made a special study of the question, believed it to be the actual Sepulchre of Our Lord. This question of identity is one of deepest interest, and although all archaeologists are not agreed, and in the existing state of our knowledge a complete solution of it cannot perhaps be looked for, the probability that this tomb may be the Holy Sepulchre renders it very desirable that it should be preserved from destruction or desecration.
>
> The tomb, together with its enclosure in which it stands — an area of about four acres — is now for sale, and the time for which we have obtained the refusal of it has almost expired. The price for the freehold is £4,000. The object and desire of those who have taken the most active part in the negotiations is to purchase this site, to carry out such excavations and restorations as may be considered advisable by the most competent authorities, to lay out the garden, and to vest the property in the hands of trustees, with a view to maintaining it as far as possible in its present simplicity.
>
> In addition to the purchase money, it is estimated that the sum of about £2,000 would be required to meet legal expenses, to place the tomb and its surroundings in order, and to provide for the maintenance of the garden. Nearly £1,000 have already been collected privately, and we would ask to be allowed to seize an opportunity, which may never occur again, of securing and preserving a locality which must be of the highest value and interest to all Christians.
>
> The following gentlemen, in addition to many others, without committing themselves to any confident opinion as to the identity of this tomb with the Holy Sepulchre, have expressed their cordial approval of the purchase of the site, and in many cases have already subscribed to the fund: — The Archbishop of Canterbury, the Bishops of Salisbury, Rochester, Ripon and Cashel, the Archdeacons of London and Westminster, Canon Tristram, the Hon. Rev. E. Carr-Glyn, Professor R. Stuart Poole, the Rev. Sinclair Paterson MD, the Rev. F. B. Meyer, Lawrence Hardy Esq. MP, F.A. Bevan Esq., Hon. H. Dudley Ryder. Subscriptions may be sent to either of the honorary secretaries...

During the next 17 days the letter columns of *The Times* were filled, not surprisingly, with different reactions to this appeal. Conder was the first to reply. His own excavations of the tomb in 1873 revealed that it had been used as a Crusader tomb. There were many bones in it and he claimed that there were two red Latin crosses on the east wall. So conceivably it had originally been carved by Greek Christians in the ninth century. (Later he reverted to a twelfth-century date, linking it to the Crusaders' hostelry or *asnerie* on the site, and suggesting that the many bones found in the tomb were the result of the Kharezmian massacre in AD 1244.)[16] He warned against repeating 'the errors of the fourth century', giving to the world 'two false and impossible sites for the Holy Sepulchre'.

Haskett Smith responded by rehearsing several of his already published arguments (see above). He correctly pointed out that the subsequent use of the tomb by Crusaders did not in any way determine the date of its original construction. Underneath the 'Crusader' bones there was in fact much accumulated debris, suggesting many centuries of disuse. Although the garden and the tomb were, he believed, 'fraught with the most sacred and hallowed associations of Christianity', there was no intention of 'converting them into shrines of superstitious adoration, nor of elevating them even to the position of undoubted "holy sites"'. Nevertheless, 'the very possibility that the garden and tomb are those mentioned by the Sacred Evangelists should surely arouse the devout interest of Christians and lead them to take measures for securing their immunity from desecration'. In any case, because of its close proximity to Skull Hill, this tomb was far more likely to be the correct one than that proposed by Conder himself. Henry Tristam argued in similar terms on the Monday.

The next day Thomas Chaplin raised some doubts concerning the identification of Golgotha with Skull Hill, suggesting that if the Holy Sepulchre were ever proved inauthentic, then a better alternative would instead be the little knoll adjacent to Conder's tomb. However, since the whole matter simply could not be proved, he thought it undesirable for people in modern times to repeat the credulity of the Middle Ages and to 'pay six or eight times its value' for this tomb which could never be proved to be that of Jesus.

This last point was repeated on Saturday, 1 October, by Charles Wilson, who had conducted the survey of Jerusalem for the Palestine

Exploration Fund. He accepted the tradition that 'Skull Hill' was a traditional Jewish 'place of stoning'. But he reckoned that this told *against*
this being the place of the crucifixion – because Jesus was executed by
Roman authorities. After conversations with Bishop Gobat in 1864–5,
he had sensed the force of the argument that Jesus' sacrificial death
might have occurred directly to the north of the Temple (just as the
sin-offerings in the Old Testament); but Skull Hill lay more to the
north-*west*. He had been informed that open-air services had been held
on Skull Hill during the previous year and that one lady had actually
slept all night in the tomb. So he was becoming concerned that in the
next 50 years the history and errors of the fourth century would be
repeated all over again.

Influenced by the apparent weight of such scholars as Wilson and
Conder, the editors one week later concluded their editorial by stating
their opinion that the advocates of the tomb had shown 'no adequate
grounds for their appeal for public aid' (8 October). But many others
thought differently.

The deeds at last

There was a generous response to the appeal. Over 160 people gave sums
in excess of one pound, including the biblical scholar B. F. Westcott (later
Bishop of Durham) and Randall Davidson (later Archbishop of Canterbury). As a result the purchase agreement was signed in May 1894.

Not all, however, was then 'plain sailing'. Prior to 1908 land in
Jerusalem could not be bought by committees, because Turkish law
stated that the purchaser needed to be an individual who appeared in
person. This was solved when a local CMS missionary, the Revd
Charles T. Wilson (no relation to Charles Wilson the scholar!), agreed
to be the named purchaser, making out a separate trust deed in favour
of the Committee.

The Turkish authorities then made it a condition of the sale that a
thick wall be built between the Garden and the Muslim cemetery. This
too was done. Most of the cost of this and some other walls (some
£360) was met through the generosity of Louisa Hope (pictured as a
child in Plate 28).

Next, Frutiger's bank went into liquidation and those appointed to
complete the transaction for the final 'third' of the property started to

increase the price and to suggest a redrawing of the original bound-
aries. In July 1898 an appeal was sent out to raise the outstanding
£200 which was required to pay off the balance.

Finally, there was great controversy as to whether the original
deeds included the tomb itself, or whether this belonged to the person
who owned the ground some 25 feet immediately above it! This again
was probably linked to the sensitivities aroused by the proximity of the
site to the Muslim cemetery. This issue involved numerous communi-
cations between the British Consul in Jerusalem (John Dickson) and
the British Ambassador in Constantinople (Philip Currie). It was not
finally settled until 1898, when it was agreed that, although the
'grotto' (i.e. the tomb) had for some reason not been listed in the
archives of the Land Registry Department, it nevertheless *had* been in
the original deeds. The Consul was pleased to report in one of his letters that 'An *Ilam* has been issued by the Court of the Sheri confirming
the fact that the grotto forms part of Miss Hope's ground, and is her
exclusive property.'

Even then the final deeds got lost between Jerusalem and England,
and they had to persuade the authorities that an Arabic copy could legit-
imately be taken as adequate proof. In the end, however, the matter was
settled. But it had taken years of negotiation followed by high-level,
almost 'gun-boat' diplomacy! Louisa Hope, without whose determination and generosity this cherished dream could never have become a
reality, died a few years later (2 February 1901) at the age of 60.

So the tomb which was so important for so many was at last safely
and surely acquired. The first trustees of the Garden Tomb Fund were
the Duke of Argyll, the Marquis of Northampton, the Earl of Aberdeen,
the Revd Charles T. Wilson (CMS) and Louisa Hope. The original Trust
Deed stated that their purpose was to ensure that the Garden and Tomb
be 'kept sacred as a quiet spot, and preserved on the one hand from
desecration, and on the other hand from superstitious uses'.

So it was that, in the teeth of some quite extensive opposition,
there appeared on the Jerusalem map a second site, putting forward its
claim to be the possible setting for the greatest event in Christian history. Compared to the Holy Sepulchre, with its long history spanning
over 1,600 years, it was very much a new arrival. Many would never
come to terms with the arrival of this new child, so it was not
promised an easy life. In fact, it would often find itself, whether it liked

it or not, at the centre of controversy. But in the following decades it would also come to be treasured by many thousands, and would develop in ways far beyond the wildest dreams of those involved in its original purchase.

After this intriguing start in life, what happened next?

THE SUBSEQUENT HISTORY OF THE GARDEN (1894–1967)

Turkish rule (1894–1917)

In the course of the next 100 years the Garden Tomb would experience no less than four changes of governmental administration and would be within firing-range of four local wars and numerous disturbances. We will concentrate here on the first three of these periods (looking briefly at the period since 1967 in Chapter 10).

In 1894 Jerusalem was still under the rule of the Ottoman Turks in Constantinople (modern Istanbul). The distance between Jerusalem and Constantinople had some advantages, allowing for a certain freedom of development in late nineteenth-century Jerusalem. But it also had grave disadvantages when it came to matters of diplomacy. So when the controversy over the title deeds flared up again after the death of Louisa Hope in 1901, the result was a vast amount of correspondence between London, Jerusalem and the ambassador in Constantinople. Matters were not fully resolved on this score till 1906.

Charlotte Hussey and the Great Dane

If Louisa Hope was a leading force behind the Garden Tomb's promotion in England, then her female equivalent in Jerusalem during this period was Charlotte Hussey. Hussey had arrived in Jerusalem in 1892 and soon became involved in the purchase of the Tomb. There were occasions in those early years when she had to deal almost single-handed with the Garden's affairs. We learn of this and about other events in those early years from a handwritten memo penned by Hussey many years later (in December 1919), which was witnessed by another female champion of the Tomb in the early 1900s, Mabel Bent.

It was Hussey who invited Conrad Schick to survey the property and who, with him, discovered the anchor/cross figure now clearly visible on the front of the Tomb (see Plate 44). Some critics had also suggested that the ground level was probably 20 feet below the entrance of the Tomb. This was proved quite wrong when she arranged for the area in front of the Tomb to be cleared. She discovered the flat rock floor, the 'groove' which seemed to be 'similar to those along which rolling-stones were moved' and the niches (which appeared to 'support the spring of arches'). She arranged for a wall to be built on the 'north-west boundary of the garden, dividing it from the road', and she ensured that the cistern was repaired.

She also replaced the native caretaker with an 'elderly Danish carpenter and his wife who remained there several years – from the week they were installed receipts increased very largely' (visitors were being charged half a pence each). This was Peder Beckholdt (1845–1934) who was caretaker from 1896 until his return to Denmark around 1912. This adventuresome Dane had worked in Alaska and North and South America, and was present when Stanley met Livingstone at the Victoria Falls. After working as a cabinetmaker in Portugal, Alexandria, Beirut, Jaffa and Bethlehem, he was eventually appointed to work at the Garden Tomb because he was fluent in 13 languages! To begin with, Peder and his wife lived in a small, decrepit Crusader dwelling close to Skull Hill, but they soon built a cottage (which to this day serves as a chapel). It has been suggested that he completed much of the remaining walls around the entire site with his own hands. He was also meticulous with money, as can be seen from his accounts book. Nevertheless, it was well known that any Danish visitors to the Tomb were allowed in free (apparently some 60 Danes took advantage of this free offer in the winter of 1908/9 alone)!

Controversy and concern

In her account Hussey also records that Protestants had tended to gather on the site on Good Friday and Easter Day for joint services even before the purchase of the site. This continued, and in 1898 General William Booth preached on Skull Hill under a Salvationist flag (see Plate 32). However, unlike Moody six years previously, he refrained from using one of the Muslim graves as a pulpit! This latter activity had not unnaturally infuriated the Muslims, who thereafter required Christian visitors to have a permit before entering the cemetery and soon denied them access altogether, encircling the hill with a wall. Even so, it seems that a World Sunday School Convention was held in the vicinity of Calvary in 1904.

Although the full purchase amount had been found, not surprisingly there were still several financial concerns. So in 1911 the honorary secretary of the Association, A. W. Crawley-Boevey, produced a book entitled *The Jerusalem Garden Tomb*, as part of an appeal for a permanent endowment fund 'to complete the objects of the original purchase, and secure the preservation of the property'. The book was also intended in part as a riposte to Sir Charles Wilson's important book *Golgotha and the Holy Sepulchre* (1906), which took a far more negative view of the new Calvary than had his colleague in the Palestine Exploration Fund, Sir Walter Besant in his book *Thirty Years Work in the Holy Land* (1895). Wilson argued that the area in front of Skull Hill had only been quarried in the Crusader period; he had also come to be sceptical about the reliability of the 'place of stoning' tradition and uncertain about the direction of the roads in Jesus' day. Wilson's book had clearly affected the tide of public opinion – as had the various articles by Canon Malcolm McColl written in a decidedly trenchant style between 1893 and 1901. Some kind of response was necessary.

In *The Jerusalem Garden Tomb* Crawley-Boevey continued to emphasize the tradition associating Skull Hill with the 'place of stoning', suggesting that this might have been the place of Stephen's death. He also noted the wide variety of dates proposed by the 'experts' for the Tomb (Macalister had recently suggested AD 300), and the fact that the line of the second wall still favoured the Garden Tomb. He did not, however, take up an intriguing suggestion made in 1905 by Scholfield in support of the site: namely that at Passover time only the northern side of the city would have been free from tents and caravans because it was reserved for the Samaritans, who in the time of Jesus never attended this Jewish feast. In fact, Crawley-Boevey's book was more a compilation of the arguments used 20 years previously, which had led up to the purchase of the site. And, despite his evident desire to put the best possible case for the Tomb, he also gave ample space for disagreement. Several extended quotations of those who denied the Tomb's authenticity were quoted without comment so that readers could assess the different arguments for themselves. This eirenic and non-dogmatic attitude would continue to be cultivated in future decades, especially by the Home Committee.

The First World War

The peace of the Garden, however, was soon to be disturbed. At the outbreak of the First World War the Garden was under the supervision of a Major Fielding. When Turkey entered the war as Germany's ally British residents in Palestine had to leave. Friends at the American consulate undertook to look after the Garden, whilst Fielding's Jewish servant-girl stayed on site. But then America entered the war, and the Americans also had to leave in haste. The Jewish girl was suddenly left quite alone. The next day some Turkish soldiers started to make their way down Skull Hill towards the site. But just then a Turkish colonel banged on the gate. This quiet spot was just what he needed for a comfortable billet! So he dismissed the soldiers and adopted the Jewish girl as his cook!

Then at Christmas 1917 Jerusalem fell to the British under General Allenby. The Turkish colonel had scarcely left in retreat when a Lieutenant Charles Robertson from the front line of Allenby's advance reached the site. He was in fact a cousin of Louisa Hope and therefore had obtained special leave to ensure the Tomb's safety. The Jewish girl was still at her post. Events happened so fast that the site was spared any pillaging – either by the Turkish or British soldiers.

So it was that, just 25 years after that letter in *The Times*, the piece of land which must have seemed so far away from Victorian Britain now found itself under the rule of London in the era of the British 'Mandate'.

British rule (1917–48)

The arrival of British administration would clearly make life easier for the Garden Tomb in many ways. Yet, if it was thought that the British would take this opportunity strongly to promote the cause of the Garden Tomb within Jerusalem, this was quite mistaken. If anything, the British desire not to upset the status quo played in the opposite direction.

The Anglican connection

The Garden Tomb Association had been set up on a non-denominational basis. Yet at the outset it had received the backing of some leading figures within the Church of England and throughout its history it would continue to have close links with that church. In these circumstances it might be supposed that the Anglican Church in Jerusalem would have been tempted during the Mandate to promote the Garden Tomb as its own 'holy place'.

Instead the bishops continued their established policy of seeking to maintain good relationships with the historic churches within the city. This meant any such promotion of the Garden was out of the question. Instead the Anglican Church came to see its lack of any 'holy places' as something of a blessing, giving it a respected neutrality in the city's ecclesiastical debates. Perhaps with hindsight this also worked out to the long-term advantage of the Garden Tomb, allowing it to preserve its own non-denominational atmosphere for the benefit of all its visitors.

Thus, as far as we can tell, Bishop Blyth (the Anglican bishop in Jerusalem from 1887 to 1914) never gave any official support to the Garden Tomb. However, his successor, Rennie MacInnes (1914–31), was 'patron' of the Garden Tomb for at least four years and his successor, Graham Brown (until his tragic death in a car accident in 1942), agreed to be a 'vice-patron' – though only when he had been given due assurances that 'the Association desired to avoid all controversy as to the authenticity of the site'. The next bishop, Weston Henry Stewart (1943–57), was also invited to take up this position, but declined for various reasons. He believed that, despite some claims to the contrary, a great emphasis *was* in fact given in the Garden itself to the issue of authenticity. As a result the formal recognition of the Tomb by the local Anglican Church was withdrawn – a situation which continues to the present, though individual relationships have often been good.

This state of affairs is a fascinating window into the much larger question of British involvement in Palestine. How neutral could the Anglican Church be in the midst of all the other denominations present? But it also reveals the delicate path that had to be trodden by the Garden Tomb Association. How neutral could it be on the question of authenticity in the midst of so many who were thoroughly convinced of the Tomb's genuineness? These issues would continue to be unresolved long after the end of the British Mandate.

The Venus-stone

In one important sense Bishop Stewart was quite right. The argument as to the site's authenticity was still very much a hot topic – as is made clear from two episodes in this period.

The first of these concerns the discovery of a wine-press in the Garden in the early 1920s. Together with the existence of the large cisterns nearby, this suggested to many that the area near the Tomb had indeed been cultivated in ancient times – and therefore was the 'garden' referred to in John's Gospel (19:41). However, more of a stir was caused by Charlotte Hussey's discovery in 1923 of the 'Venus-stone' (see Plate 34). Unless there were two such objects, this was almost certainly a rediscovery, since Beckholdt had much earlier made a clay copy of it. In any event Hussey gained the impression from a visiting German, Dr Brandenburg (though he later denied it), that this was the shrine-stone of a Venus temple. Mention of this immediately made her wonder if this proved that a temple of Venus had stood in front of the Tomb. If so, could this be the Venus temple which, according to Eusebius and others, had been built by Hadrian over Jesus' tomb? Was this the proof that was needed?

Pére Vincent of the Ecole Biblique responded with a forthright critique (1925), but a member of the Committee, Cyril Dobson, began to see this as a vital piece of evidence in favour of the Tomb's authenticity. The weakness of his position should be apparent, however. A hundred years before, when there was still some hesitancy in some quarters as to whether the Crusader Church of the Holy Sepulchre was truly on the site of Constantine's church, the Venus-stone might have helped; was *this* perhaps where Constantine had built his church? Once, however, it was firmly established by the Madaba map that Constantine's church was on the site of the present Holy Sepulchre, then no amount of such Venus-stones could avail. For it was quite clear that Constantine's church was itself built on the same site as the Venus temple, which had to be destroyed before his building could commence. Dobson, however, responded by claiming that *two* such Venus temples were built by Hadrian, and that in the fourth century Bishop Macarius had chosen the wrong one.

The base of the Skull

This issue of authenticity led to a second, slightly different episode in the 1930s. In 1934 there were signs that the land at the foot of Skull Hill might soon be coming up for sale. Till now visitors had been able to walk out through a little iron gate and stand at the foot of the quarry. Now it might be possible for the Association to own this land for itself. Lord Lee of Fareham (the Association's chairman) despatched the treasurer, A. R. Heaver, to Jerusalem to see if he could negotiate the purchase. Meanwhile, back in England, Dobson was pursuing his researches for a book about the Garden Tomb when he suddenly came to a startling new conclusion. For the previous 90 years everyone (both those who identified Skull Hill as 'Golgotha' and those opposed to it) had been assuming that Jesus would have been crucified on *top* of the hill. Dobson now concluded that Jesus was almost certainly crucified instead at the *foot* of the escarpment – a position which is now readily accepted amongst advocates of this position. The Gospels never in fact speak of a 'hill', only the 'place' called Golgotha. Yet this was precisely the piece of land which was currently under negotiation for purchase!

Dobson wrote of his findings to Lord Lee who, sensitive as to how this would affect the negotiations in Jerusalem, bound him to secrecy for the time being (though he and Lady Lee privately decided that they themselves would pay the whole price for the land anonymously, if need be). At that stage only one more signature was required for the purchase to be complete. Yet there was a hitch. Although the Grand Mufti had given his provisional assent to the sale, obstacles were now raised, and it never came to pass – despite a further 10 years of careful negotiations. The British may have been in overall authority, but even the High Commissioner was no match for the local city authorities!

Some time later (in 1956) this strip of land would in fact become the site of the East Jerusalem bus depot. Although there was a city plan in the 1980s which proposed the moving of the depot to a position north-*west* of the Damascus Gate, this too never came to pass. As a result, those who believe this was the place where Jesus was crucified are forced to come to terms with this less-than-ideal situation. No doubt they will feel a proper sense of gratitude towards Lord Lee for what he sought in vain to accomplish on their behalf in a previous generation.

Important visitors

So the question of authenticity continued to be of vital importance. At the same time there was an increased realization during the 1930s of the Garden's incredible potential to reach international visitors with the Christian message. In 1937 Maxwell Hall was therefore appointed as warden with the express task of being a 'resident evangelistic missionary'. Even so, one of his first responsibilities had more to do with the archaeological debate – to welcome the famous archaeologist, Flinders Petrie, and carefully record his opinions.

On the crucial issue of dating, Petrie acknowledged that the Tomb 'might be of the date of Herod the Great'. He was influenced by the excavations of Sukenik and Meyer in the late 1920s which suggested that the 'third' wall (built by Herod Agrippa in AD 44) lay further north of the site (see Figure 31, p. 147).

Any tomb, therefore, which was to the south of that line was presumably built before that time. Petrie was inclined, however, to see the trough in front of the Tomb as being a Crusader 'manger'. He drew attention to the grooves surrounding the three grave *loculi*; these indicated that there had been side-slabs supporting three horizontal shelves (such that any bodies would have then been placed either inside or on top). Though puzzled by the Venus-stone, he did not see the niches in the rock-face as an integral feature of a Venus temple; instead they were for supporting some wooden beams of a later construction (whether for pagan, Christian or secular use, he could not say). Finally, he gave his opinion that the heart-shaped formation in the bedrock was not evidence for a baptistery, but simply a cutting out of rough stone so that even-levelled flagstones could then be paved on top.

A few years later another archaeologist, Sir Charles Marston, gave his opinions to the Garden Tomb's Annual General Meeting (1939). He focused chiefly on the line of the walls. Sukenik's 'maximalist' 'third' wall was accepted and the Damascus Gate appeared to be on the top of Herodian walls (despite Hamilton's excavations in 1937, which suggested that they were in fact Hadrianic). For Marston, therefore, the Holy Sepulchre was most unlikely to have been outside the walls. He conjectured that if the Byzantines were wrong in their location of Mount 'Zion', they could easily have been wrong about Golgotha. He also considered that in all the cities of the world there was nothing quite comparable in appearance to Skull Hill.

The Second World War

Within a few years the ministry of the Garden would experience yet another dramatic change. The start of the Second World War brought tourism to a sudden halt. During those years, however, thousands of men and women in the armed forces were on leave in Jerusalem. Visiting the Garden, they were helped by the padres who acted as guides and chaplains. The War ended in Europe, but things continued to be tense in Jerusalem as the British prepared to leave Palestine. When they did so in May 1948, there was fierce fighting between Jews and Arabs around the Garden, resulting in the complete destruction of some neighbouring areas (such as the Jewish quarter a little to the west). The Warden's house suffered some damage, but the Tomb and Garden were comparatively unscathed.

When the fighting was over, the Garden found itself close to the border of a divided city. The hills of West Jerusalem in Israel were but 400 yards away, but the Garden was now in Jordan, whose government was across the River in Amman.

Jordanian rule (1948–67)

A devoted warden

This third period of the Garden's history will forever be linked with the name of one man – Solomon Mattar. He was a Christian Arab who, after the departure of Mr and Mrs May (wardens since 1946), was the warden until his death in 1967 (see Plate 30). To this day Mattar is remembered by many as a devoted Christian servant who touched many lives. He was a passionate believer in the authenticity of the Tomb and evidently took great pride in his position. Thus, when telling the Resurrection story of Mary supposing Jesus to be the 'gardener', he would frequently comment: 'Hearing a voice behind her, she thought it to be my predecessor!'

It is generally agreed now that on at least one occasion this enthusiasm took him a little too far. He jumped to the conclusion that the massive cistern (which needed some urgent repair soon after his appointment) might have been a place where the early Christian believers gathered for worship – not least because of the giant cross on one of its walls (see Plate 43). This 'discovery' caused quite a sensation in some quarters at the time, and some archaeological work was done to see if there was any stairway down to the cistern or any connecting passage to the Tomb. But the matter soon subsided, with supporters of the Garden Tomb becoming concerned that Mattar's lack of archaeological expertise might bring the whole ministry of the Garden into unnecessary disrepute. When commenting on this episode, Bill White (the Association's secretary in the 1980s) rightly noted that 'such unrestrained flights of pious fancy have brought unwarranted ridicule upon the Garden Tomb, so that open-minded analysis of the site has often been suppressed'.[17]

Ever since then, the Garden Tomb authorities have generally refrained from conducting any independent archaeological work of their own and, if anything, have been wary of the overly enthusiastic. It is salutary too to remember that in the nineteenth century Protestant critics of the traditional 'holy places' claimed to elevate the dispassionate 'science' of archaeology above the over-enthusiastic and incredulous assumptions of their Byzantine forebears; they argued that the emotional desire to find suitable holy places caused them to leave the facts behind. Sometimes in the twentieth century, it has to be said, the 'boot has been on the other foot'!

Death in the Garden

Putting this episode behind him, Mattar continued in post for a further 12 years, a period during which the number of visitors increased dramatically (from 10,000 in 1954 to 38,000 in 1964). Then came the Six-Day War (June 1967). Given its location, the Garden was bound to be a dangerous place. Mattar, however, loyal to the end, refused to leave. It would cost him his life. As one of his staff said afterwards:

> In a true sense it was Mr Mattar's faithfulness to the Garden Tomb that cost him his life. In the days just before the 1967 war when things looked more and more serious, it was suggested that Mr Mattar should lock up the Garden and move to a safer place (than being right beside the border zone), until threatened hostility ceased. Mr Mattar's reply was 'No. We have enjoyed the blessing of this place and seen its good times. Now, when there is trouble, why should I neglect the Garden and leave it?'[18]

During the night of 5 June Skull Hill became the last-ditch stand for the Jordanian artillery. Mr and Mrs Mattar and a staff member called Sigfrid Proft took shelter day and night in the Tomb. Eventually Israeli paratroopers were sent in. But at just that moment Mr Mattar was going across to the house to get some refreshment for the others. When they broke down the gate, he greeted them with a 'good morning'. But he was killed instantly by the troops, who believed they had broken in on a pocket of enemy resistance. The whole Garden was then raked with machine-gun fire. One bullet penetrated the Tomb, narrowly missing Mrs Mattar. Thinking they had killed her, Sigfrid for some reason emerged from the Tomb – only to be confronted by an Israeli soldier reloading his gun. She survived, it seems, because of her fair skin and long, blonde hair – unlike Mattar, she was quite clearly not an Arab. So Skull Hill was captured by the Israelis and the next day the fighting was over. On the Friday Mr Mattar was buried in the Garden by the Anglican Archbishop in Jerusalem, Campbell MacInnes (1957–68).

So an important era in the history of the Garden Tomb came to a sudden and tragic end. It was time now for the Garden to brace itself for another change of circumstances – it was no longer on the border of a divided city, but was near the centre of a reunified city, with Palestinians on one side and Israelis on the other. In under 75 years the Garden Tomb had experienced first Turkish, then British, then Jordanian rule. Now Arab Jerusalem was to be administered by the Israelis. It would mark the beginning of yet another, quite different episode – extending up to the present day.

What the original purchasers of this tranquil plot of land would have made of this subsequent history is hard to imagine! But if they were aware (as surely they were) of the important claims which they were making for its Tomb, and if they were also aware of some of the controversy which the city of Jerusalem might come to provoke in the modern world, perhaps they would not be so surprised after all. Indeed, some of them might have sensed that, amidst all these stormy issues, there would be the need for just such a Garden of peace and profound remembrance – a Garden focused on the most important message the world will ever know.

An Ongoing Debate

Where Did It Happen?

So the visitor to Jerusalem today is presented with two different sites for the most important event within Christian history – the Crucifixion and Resurrection of Jesus Christ. For some visitors these rival claims only confirm their growing agnosticism caused by the puzzling nature of modern Jerusalem, with its complex layers of history and many competing traditions. Others find themselves preferring one of the two sites at the expense of the other, instinctively siding either with the long-established tradition of the Holy Sepulchre or with the natural and aesthetic appeal of the Garden Tomb. Still others may come to value both sites and see them as in some senses complementary: both witness in their very different ways to the centrality of the Resurrection for Christians ancient and modern.

Of course, those who hold to the last position are fully aware that in historical point of fact only *one* of the two sites can be the right one! If one is authentic, the other must be false. It might be nice to opt for both, but if the question of authenticity is to be pursued, a choice ultimately needs to be made. Jesus only died in one place. It remains perfectly possible, however, that neither site is correct. After all, there is ample biblical precedent in the story of Moses (Deuteronomy 34:6) for the believing community to be ignorant of the precise burial-place of one of its greatest leaders – an ignorance which some have seen as helpfully preventing subsequent disputes or an undue focus on one particular place or hero (cf. Jude 9).

Nevertheless, this chapter will lay out in summary form the strengths and weaknesses of the claims made for the authenticity of both sites, leaving readers free to come to their own conclusions. Much has been written on this subject in the last hundred years. The following is intended to give some understanding of how the argument stands at the present time, as well as some awareness of the ebb and flow of the debate through the last century.

THE MOUNT OF OLIVES

At this point, however, we need to highlight the fact that the situation is even more complex still. For there are various other sites around Jerusalem that have also been suggested! In recent years one in particular has begun to catch the popular imagination.

A new suggestion

Ernest Martin, in his self-published book *Secrets of Golgotha*, has argued strongly that the Holy Sepulchre and the Garden Tomb are both inauthentic: instead Jesus was crucified on the Mount of Olives. The true site of Golgotha, he argues, is the summit of the Mount (currently marked by the Muslim building on the traditional site of the Ascension). Joseph's tomb would have been a little way to the south (possibly in the area of the cave underneath the Paternoster Church). The principal arguments which he uses are as follows:

1. The confession of the Roman centurion ('This man was God's Son' [Mark 15:39]) was inspired, Martin argues, not just by the manner of Jesus' death but also by his being able to see the rending of the Temple veil (15:38). Yet this Temple curtain could only be seen *from the east* – on the upper slopes of the Mount of Olives.
2. Hebrews 13:10–12 reads:

    We have an altar from which those who officiate in the tent
    have no right to eat. For the bodies of those animals whose
    blood is brought into the sanctuary by the high priest as a

sacrifice for sin are burned outside the camp. Therefore Jesus also suffered outside the city gate in order to sanctify the people by his own blood.

This cultic burning of the animal bodies, so Martin claims, took place at an altar on the Mount of Olives, an altar which he associates with that of the Red Heifer. The author of Hebrews is therefore referring to a literal 'altar' and suggesting that this is precisely where Jesus died. In this way the closest of parallels emerges between Jesus' sacrificial death and the earlier Levitical sacrifices. They can be linked not just typologically but geographically as well.

3. According to his reading of the Old Testament, special significance was given to the area to the east of the Temple. The Holy of Holies, the place associated with the divine presence, faced eastwards; so this area was effectively 'before the Lord' and was the place of his judgement.

4. There is evidence that the city of Jerusalem and its environs were understood in cultic terms as the continuation of the wilderness 'camp' and that there were stipulations that executions and burials had to take place 'outside' this camp area. This required a distance of at least 3,000 feet from the Holy of Holies. Both the Holy Sepulchre and the Garden Tomb are closer to the Temple than that, not so the summit of the Mount of Olives.

5. Since the word 'place' (*topos*) was sometimes used as a shorthand for the Temple (see Acts 6:13; 21:28; John 4:20; 11:48), the text of John 19:20 should more properly be translated, 'Nearby was *the Place of the City* where Jesus was crucified.'

Examining the evidence

What are we to make of this? Back in the late nineteenth century a couple of people (S. Manning and N. Hutchinson) speculated that the Mount of Olives was a possible site.[1] This is the first time in recent decades, however, that the Mount of Olives has been championed so strongly as a possible site.

Possibly the most illuminating point that Martin has brought into the debate is his emphasis on the cultic and practical significance given to the 'east' – though we note that the biblical texts which he cites (e.g. Numbers 5:16–31; 16:41–50; Leviticus 10:1–7; Psalm 96:13) do not *explicitly* make this point at all.

So too his understanding of the centurion's reaction helpfully sends one back to reread the Passion narrative more carefully. Nevertheless, the traditional interpretation seems far preferable. Even if this Temple incident was only reported subsequently (and was not therefore visible to those standing round the Cross), the reason why the Evangelists link it to the moment of Jesus' death is because it made a vital theological point about what was achieved at that moment – the new way of entering God's holy presence through the blood of Christ (cf. Hebrews 10:19ff.). In any case, there must be some question as to whether *anyone* on the Mount of Olives could actually have seen what was happening to this *inner* curtain within the Temple precincts.

Martin's whole approach, however, is marked by the conviction that the Old Testament types and the Jewish regulations must have been fulfilled *literally* in the details of Jesus' crucifixion. Even if the points concerning the cultic significance of the 'east' have some validity, it does not follow that this essentially Roman execution obligingly conformed to this Jewish notion. The Roman authorities are much more likely to have wanted the deed to be done as quickly as possible and to have made use of a location much nearer to hand. Nor is there any positive evidence of a Jewish execution-site on the Mount of Olives. In the case of Stephen's stoning, the only necessity was to move him 'out of the city' (Acts 7:58).

Clearly the writer of Hebrews was convinced that Jesus' death *did* fulfil the cultic sacrifices associated with the Temple (hence his whole argument in chapters 7–10). There is nothing, however, to suggest that this fulfilment could only be valid if the crucifixion occurred in exactly the self-same spot. For the author of Hebrews Jesus' death also fulfils the cultic sacrifice of animals *within* the Temple precincts, and his exaltation into heaven encapsulates the Day of Atonement ritual when the High Priest had entered the Holy of Holies (Hebrews 9:12, 24; 10:12 etc.). Yet it would be quite absurd to suggest that Jesus also died (or indeed ascended into heaven!) whilst *within* the Temple precincts. Theological parallels can be quite valid, regardless of precise geographical identity.

Instead almost all commentators uniformly understand the 'altar' of Hebrews 13:10 to be a graphic but symbolic means of summarizing the author's whole argument concerning Jesus' death as the ultimate sacrifice. The whole point of his letter is to persuade the Jewish Christians to whom he is writing (possibly in Rome?) that through Jesus they have a complete access to God, which is not dependent in some way on Jerusalem. To emphasize the literal Mount of Olives at this point would effectively undercut the entire purpose of his letter.[2]

Concerning the Red Heifer, it is worth noting that according to the Mishnah (*Parah* 3–4) this was burnt not on an altar but in a pit. Moreover, those in the nineteenth century who were similarly struck by this argument from typology pointed instead to some ash-heaps to the *north* of the city (not far from the present-day St George's). They reckoned that these ash-heaps were the result of the Temple sacrifices.[3] If correct, then this particular argument would point our investigation towards the north of the city, not to the east.

Martin's other arguments also raise many questions. The translation of John 19:20 is very strained. In the other verses which he cites, the context makes it quite clear that a reference is being made to the Temple; not so here. His several arguments concerning early Christian tradition are similarly slight. In particular it needs to be emphasized that, contrary to Martin's claim, Eusebius of Caesarea never refers to the Mount of Olives as 'Mount Zion'.[4] Instead he consistently uses that term either to describe the Temple Mount or the Western Hill (now called Mount Zion). Thus when he says that 'Christ was crucified near Mount Zion',[5] he is *not* referring to the Mount of Olives. He is quite clearly speaking of the recently uncovered Holy Sepulchre (located at the northern end of the same hill-formation as Mount Zion). Eusebius' other writings make it quite clear that in his day there was no Christian tradition of Jesus' death on the Mount of Olives; Christians went there instead to remember the Ascension and Jesus' prophetic words against Jerusalem.[6] This does not mean that everything Eusebius says is necessarily correct. But it does mean that his writings cannot be used to support the idea that Jesus was crucified on the Mount of Olives.

Conclusion

Martin has raised some interesting questions, but the overwhelming likelihood is that the site of the crucifixion is to be found much nearer to the city walls of Jerusalem. The Evangelists refer to the Mount of Olives quite frequently, often including elements of geographical detail (see Luke 19:37; 21:37; 22:39). So they would surely have made it clear that Golgotha was located somewhere upon its slopes – if it was. They relate that the Mount of Olives was the scene of the Triumphal Entry, the Apocalyptic Discourse and the Ascension. Why did they not indicate that it was also the scene of the most important event of all? Instead they simply say, 'they led him out to crucify him ... and brought him to the place called Golgotha' (Mark 15:21–2). Where is that Golgotha?

THE GARDEN TOMB

Outside a city wall

In comparison with the Mount of Olives, the Garden Tomb site has the great advantage of being close to the city, whilst at the same time being quite clearly outside the so-called city wall of Jesus' day (what Josephus refers to as the 'second wall'). The traditional site of the Holy Sepulchre has consistently been vulnerable to the charge that it might perhaps lie inside the line of this 'second wall'. If this could be proved, its claim to authenticity would have to be dismissed immediately. For the one fixed point in this debate is that Jesus was crucified *outside* the city wall (Mark 15:20; Hebrews 13:12). So far, however, nobody has ever suggested that the area of the Garden Tomb was inside the city of Jesus' day. It lay just outside the city wall, not far from an important gate, and close to the roads leading to the north and east.

Most scholars believe that the northernmost point of the 'second wall' would have been roughly along the line of the current Turkish walls – at least for the section going eastward from the Damascus gate. (The gate that is now visible beneath the Damascus Gate is Hadrianic, dating from the second century, but this probably was built on the line of the earlier 'second' wall.) Others argue that the wall would have come no further north than the level of the Antonia Fortress (see Figure 1, p. 2). Even so, everyone agrees that at the time of Jesus the Garden Tomb and Skull Hill were outside the walls.

Within 15 years of Jesus' death, however, a 'third' wall was built. This was during the reign of Herod Agrippa (AD 41–4). Many archaeologists, especially Israelis, have advocated that some large ashlars to the north of the Garden Tomb (close to the American Consulate) mark the line of this third wall (see Figure 31). This is often named the Meyer-Sukenik wall after the scholars who were responsible for the excavations there in the late 1920s. If so, the Garden Tomb would have been brought within the city walls for the short period leading up to the fall of Jerusalem in AD 70. What happened after the time of Jesus may be interesting on other grounds, but of course none of this affects the possible authenticity of the Garden Tomb, which is determined by the line of the city wall in Jesus' own day.

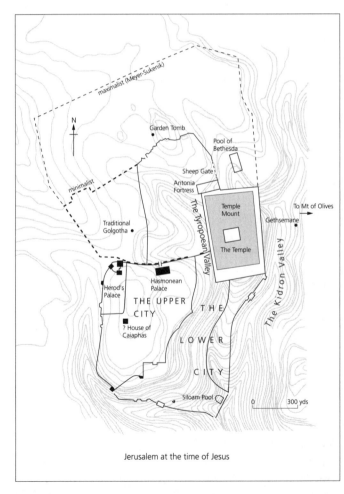

Jerusalem at the time of Jesus

Fig. 31. Alternative suggestions for the line of the 'third' wall. The 'Meyer-Sukenik' wall (named after the archaeologists who excavated it in 1929) is favoured by scholars such as Metzer, Avi-Yonah and Bahat. The 'minimalist' alternative is advocated by scholars such as Hennessy, Wightman, and Murphy O'Connor.

Visitors to the model of Jerusalem at the Holy Land Hotel will be familiar with this understanding of how the city looked in the years leading up to AD 70. For there the rock of Skull Hill can clearly be seen encompassed well within the city (see Plate 19). A number of scholars, however, dispute this 'maximalist' interpretation. The stones of the Meyer-Sukenik wall, they argue, may instead be the remains of a temporary barrier-wall erected hastily in the First Jewish Revolt to prevent the Roman *ballistae* from getting too close to the city.[7] Some coinage discovered in the 1960s near the present Damascus Gate dates to the era of Herod Agrippa.[8] If so, the 'third wall' would have been roughly along the lines of the present Old City walls. The great difference between this 'third' wall and its predecessor would then be that it went much further to the north-west (as do the Old City walls today), bringing within the city the area of the modern Christian Quarter.[9]

This whole debate about the line of the 'third' wall leaves the Garden Tomb unaffected. But it does have possible repercussions for the Holy Sepulchre. For a start it means that this traditional site *was* brought within the city walls very soon after the crucifixion. The tomb was probably left visible and intact, but it would have required emptying and ritual cleansing; it may gradually have been surrounded by new housing developments. Secondly, the increasing preference amongst scholars for the minimalist position suggests that throughout the Herodian period Jerusalem may have been much smaller than was earlier imagined. If so, this only increases the possibility that the area of the Holy Sepulchre may also have been outside the 'second' wall.

The reason for this is as follows. If the *third* wall were indeed much further to the north (on the Meyer-Sukenik line), then there would be a strong presumption that the *second* wall must also have reached out much further to the north-west. Otherwise Herod Agrippa's expansion of the city would have effectively doubled the size of the city. Although we know that the Romans were alarmed by Agrippa's work, and that it was therefore never completed,[10] it seems most unlikely that he dared to expand the city by quite such a vast extent. If, as is more likely, the third wall ran roughly along the lines of the present Turkish walls, then the second wall will have been that much further to the south, probably leaving the Holy Sepulchre outside the city.

A great advantage of the Garden Tomb site, by contrast, is that it is left unscathed by all these debates concerning the line of the wall in

Jesus' day! There is no doubt that it was outside the city on that fateful April weekend.

A disused quarry

It is also fairly likely that the area in front of Skull Hill had for some time been a disused quarry. Geologically, Skull Hill (which is 110 feet higher than the rock in the Temple area) is the continuation of the seam of rock which starts with the Temple and continues right up to the present Turkish wall (see Plate 24). It has been separated from that seam, however, by quarrying. So at some point in the past the area now covered by the modern bus-station was a quarry. But when was the quarrying done?

Although some date this to the Hasmonean period (second century BC) and some think the quarrying would have continued well after the time of Jesus, one of the most likely dates for this quarrying is the era of Herod the Great (40–4 BC). More building and construction work was done in those years than perhaps in any other comparable period in Jerusalem's history. This was the time when Herod expanded the Temple platform, built himself a new palace and probably ordered the construction of a theatre and hippodrome. All this required a phenomenal amount of stone. If so, this area to the north of the Temple enclosure was a logical place to quarry.

The quarrying did not proceed further to the north, however, because the rock of Skull Hill was unsuitable for use. At this distance in time, of course, we cannot know what this unquarried rock would have looked like – it may or may not have had the 'skull' features which it bears today – but it is quite likely that the area below Skull Hill had been substantially quarried out by the time of Jesus. As such it was a comparatively useless patch of ground. Perhaps, then, an ideal area for a place of execution?

Within the literary sources there is strictly no evidence as to where the Jewish execution site was during this period (only 25 years previously, in AD 6, the Jewish authorities had lost their right to inflict capital punishment – the so-called *ius gladii*). But there is an interesting passage dating from the second century AD in the Mishnah (*Sanhedrin* 6:1–4) which talks about the 'place of stoning' (*Beth-has-sekilah*) outside the city. This seems to have been a cliff 'twice the height of a man', over which the condemned was thrown by the first of his two accusers; the second then threw stones down on him (compare the attempts on Jesus' life in Luke 4:29). Could this have been the spot?

Certainly, in the mid-nineteenth century Conder and others encountered Jewish residents in Jerusalem who preserved a tradition that 'Skull Hill' was indeed this 'place of Stoning'.[11] Its geographical contours would certainly fit well. This was one of the arguments that convinced Hanauer.[12] He also was impressed by the area's association with Jeremiah – the prophet who not only wept over the destruction of the city but who, according to later tradition, was also stoned to death (see the *Rest of the Words of Baruch* and possibly Hebrews 11:37).

Readers of the Book of Acts are familiar with the story of just such a stoning which took place outside Jerusalem's walls within a few years of Jesus' own death – namely the martyrdom of Stephen. 'They dragged him out of the city and began to stone him' (Acts 7:58). This was a hastily contrived event and there is nothing to suggest that Stephen was necessarily taken to an already established place of execution. They may simply have taken him to the nearest convenient location outside the city. Yet the area around Skull Hill remains a serious possibility.

Certainly this general area has been associated with Stephen's memory ever since the fifth century, when the great Church of St Stephen was built on the site now covered by the church in the Dominican Ecole Biblique (just to the north of the Garden Tomb). Possibly this area was chosen at that time simply because it was one of the few remaining locations which were not covered with a basilica of some kind. Yet they may have been following some earlier tradition. And, if not, their choice may be the result of some intelligent guesswork, inspired by the same geographical considerations that we witness today. The area *does* make sense as a place of execution.

This does not, of course, prove that it was. Nor does it prove that Jesus too must have been put to death in this spot (despite Luke's interest in the parallels between Stephen and his Master, there is nothing in Acts to suggest that they were both put to death in the same spot). Yet it does raise the interesting question: would it not make eminent sense for the Romans to perform their crucifixions on a site which had already been used as an execution-site by the Jews?

Roman crucifixions in Jerusalem were comparatively rare during this period. This was a punishment reserved chiefly for political rebels, and the Roman political centre was Caesarea, not Jerusalem. So there may not have been an established procedure or regular location used by the Roman authorities. In these circumstances, what would they do? Would they not then have opted to use an existing site, previously used by the Jewish authorities? Or did they simply treat each case on its merits (anywhere reasonably public would do)?

Intriguingly, the area of the Holy Sepulchre is also now known to have been a disused quarry area, with 'traditional Golgotha' being a rock left unquarried because it was flawed. At this point there are several close parallels between the Garden Tomb and the Holy Sepulchre. In both cases the name 'Golgotha' ('the place of the skull') could have originated because of the association with executions and/or because the protruding rock bore some general resemblance to a skull. In both cases this resemblance, if it existed, might have been based on various facial features (the eye-sockets etc.) but more probably was simply the result of the overall shape of the rock as a whole. Finally, in both cases, it is only popular tradition which suggests that the crucifixion must have occurred on the top of this skull-shaped 'hill'; it could quite easily have taken place at the bottom, or indeed anywhere in the general vicinity, all of which was called the 'place of the skull'.

The parallels here suggest that the instincts that caused people in the last century to focus on the Skull Hill north of the Damascus Gate were perfectly reasonable. The whole area makes perfect sense as the 'place of the skull' known to us from the Gospels. The fact that the escarpment resembled a skull only confirmed this.

'There was a garden in the place where he was crucified'

Thirdly, the area of the Garden Tomb brings together what otherwise a Gospel reader might find it hard to imagine: namely the close proximity of an execution-site to a garden and a tomb. There continue to be debates about the date of the major cistern to the south-east of the tomb (see Plate 42); but the wine-press seems to give some support to the idea that this was a cultivated area at the time of Jesus (see Plate 46). Remarkably, this 'garden' area is very close to Skull Hill and yet largely tucked out of sight (see Figure 32, p. 152).

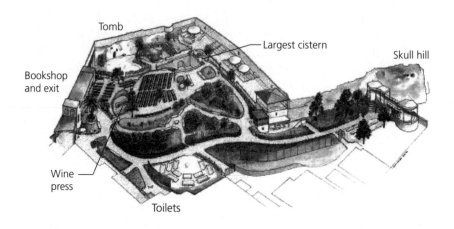

Tomb

Largest cistern

Skull hill

Bookshop
and exit

Wine
press

Toilets

Fig. 32. Aerial plan of the Garden Tomb enclosure, showing the relation between Skull Hill, the garden and the tomb.

The dovetailing with the Gospel accounts at this point is striking and indeed compares favourably with the Holy Sepulchre, where the distance between 'traditional Golgotha' and the Sepulchre is that much less (just under 30 metres). This does not disprove the authenticity of the Holy Sepulchre. After all, it is not impossible for a cultivated area to have been so close to an execution-site or for some of the quarried area gradually to have become covered with vegetation. Nevertheless, the layout of the Garden Tomb enclosure certainly has some distinct advantages on this score, with its garden area being tucked round to one side of Skull Hill.

'And in the garden there was a new tomb'

Throughout the last hundred years, much work has been done by people trying to reconstruct in some detail the events of that first Easter morning and also to glean as much as possible from the scriptural account as to the size and nature of Joseph's tomb. No doubt, other configurations are quite possible, but it remains significant that the internal appearance of the Garden Tomb does not overtly contradict the biblical record in any detail. Conder, though in favour of Skull Hill, continued to favour a tomb he had earlier found some 500 feet to the west, but it was not surprising that the present Garden Tomb became the focus of such interest. For by comparison both with Conder's tomb and with many others roundabout, it matched the scriptural requirements in a particularly close way.

The Gospel accounts indicate that the inside of the Tomb had at least two features: the place where Jesus was laid was visible to a person peering in from outside (John 20:5). There was also enough space for the angelic visitor to be seen 'sitting on the right side' (Mark 16:5). In both these respects the Garden Tomb fits the required specification extremely well.

The Bible also requires a tomb with a rolling-stone. Some have thought that the trough in front of the Tomb may date from a later period – possibly a Crusader trough or water-system.[13] Yet there is nothing to suggest that the original Tomb could not have had a rolling-stone. A close examination of the doorway suggests that the original entrance may well have been much smaller (perhaps three feet at most). Quite probably too the ground level would have been somewhat higher than it is at present.[14] As a result, the entrance might have been partially beneath ground level, being approached perhaps by a few steps down. There are other examples of this arrangement in the Jerusalem area (for example, Herod's family tomb to the west of the Old City and the tomb in the grounds of the church in Bethphage). If the small window was part of the original (for ventilation purposes?) then this would explain how the tomb's interior was still visible even when a visitor was blocking out the light from the entrance-way.

So a Skull Hill, a cultivated area and an appropriate tomb – all just outside the city wall of Jesus' day! The Garden Tomb site offers the visitor this combination, which makes a deep impression. The cumulative effect is striking. No wonder those who first discovered the site began to get excited!

Some questions: the absence of any tradition?

So it is hardly surprising that they wanted to acquire the site and to preserve it for posterity. Then (as now) it offered a brilliant visual aid – in a way that the Holy Sepulchre never could. Moreover, for all the above reasons, there were many who believed it was more than that: not just a visual aid but possibly the original site.

Inevitably, however, the Garden Tomb has been the subject of immense controversy, especially in the early years after its discovery and purchase. Ever since then some important questions have been raised on the whole issue of its possible authenticity. These have fallen in two main areas.

First, in comparison with the Holy Sepulchre, the Garden Tomb is clearly vulnerable on the issue of *tradition*. The 300 years which separate the first Easter from the uncovering of Constantine's Sepulchre may seem long to some, but they are short in comparison with the 1,850 years which elapsed before the uncovering of the Garden Tomb. Effectively, we need to assume that the memory of the Tomb's location was forgotten quite quickly and lost to Christian tradition until the advent of modern archaeology. This, of course, is by no means impossible, but it does make the Garden Tomb vulnerable to the charge of being a modern idea without the backing of history or tradition.

In seeking to bridge this gap, some have argued that there is indeed some early tradition in support of the Garden Tomb. Some have suggested that the archaeological features in front of the Tomb are indicative of a Byzantine church. Why would this have been built if it was not to commemorate some event associated with the Tomb? Others have wondered if the Venus-stone discovered by Charlotte Hussey in 1923 might indicate that this was the area of the Hadrian's Venus temple, which (so Eusebius claims) covered Jesus' tomb until the time of Constantine. Are then those archaeological features in front of the Tomb signs, not of a Byzantine chapel, but instead of Hadrian's pagan temple?

The latter suggestion (as noted in Chapter 6, p. 135) is strange indeed. After the discovery of the Madaba map in 1884 there could no longer be any serious doubt that the present Holy Sepulchre, not the Garden Tomb, was the site built on by Constantine. No amount of

Venus artefacts found at the Garden Tomb could change that. For, even if there had been some worship of Venus here, this was clearly *not* the site that Eusebius and others were talking about.

The alternative suggestion, that perhaps Byzantine Christians venerated the Tomb as a possible site of the Resurrection, is also most unlikely. For from 325 onwards there was no doubt as to where that great event was believed to have taken place – namely the Holy Sepulchre. Possibly that belief was wrong. Yet there is no literary or historical evidence that there was any dispute thereafter on this matter, or any rival claim. The tomb inscription found in the neighbouring Ecole Biblique (see Figure 30, p. 125) which referred to the church of the 'Holy Resurrection' simply means that the man buried there, while being a monk in the monastery attached to the church of St Stephen, was also a deacon at the church of the Resurrection (that is, the Holy Sepulchre). Despite some rumours put about soon after the inscription's discovery in 1889, it did not speak of the tomb being 'close to the place where lay the body of the Lord'. This inscription does not therefore constitute evidence for an alternative Byzantine tradition as to the possible site of Jesus' burial.

There is no such evidence. If the Byzantines were interested in this site, it was not because in their minds it was a possible alternative to the Holy Sepulchre. Instead it appears that they simply re-used it as a tomb – something which as Christians they presumably would not have done if they were really convinced that it was Jesus' tomb. This re-use of the Tomb in the Byzantine period is the simplest explanation for the beautiful cross on the right-hand inner wall, dated to the fifth or sixth centuries AD (see Figure 29, p. 123). As for the markings in front of the Tomb, these may come not from the Byzantine period but rather from the Crusader period, when this area was probably part of a hospice known as the Asnerie.[15]

The Garden Tomb therefore cannot really rely on any tradition in support of its claim to authenticity. This does not mean that it is a mistaken identification; only that its case has to be tried on its own merits.

• The date of the Tomb?

This then leads to the second major question that has been raised, namely the date of the Tomb. Many different dates have been offered. Macalister suggested the twelfth century AD, Conder the ninth. Reputable scholars such as Petrie, Marston and, not least, Kathleen Kenyon all believed that it could be a Herodian tomb, thus dating it to the era of Jesus. More recently however, Gabriel Barkay has published an article in which he argues for its being an Iron-Age tomb – that is, from the eighth or seventh century BC. Originally, he argues, the three *loculi* would have been slabbed benches, but these were 'troughed out' during the Byzantine period when the tomb was re-used.[16]

Barkay's argument is not based on any artefacts found within the Tomb that can be dated to the Iron-Age period. Nothing has survived after it was cleared in 1867. He does draw attention, however, to some artefacts found by Beckholdt in 1904 near the Tomb, a photograph of which later appeared in the *Quarterly Statement* of the Palestine Exploration Fund[17] (see Plate 35). Already in the 1920s these had been lost, but from the photographs Barkay is convinced that they resemble other artefacts known from the archaeological period 'Iron Age II'. If it could be confirmed that the artefacts really had been found near the tomb, this might be significant evidence. However, some now reckon that they were brought to the Garden Tomb from elsewhere.

Barkay also argues that the shape of the Tomb is quite different from the many other Herodian tombs since excavated in the Jerusalem area. The Garden Tomb is unusual both in having a flat roof and in having two chambers side by side (rather than set *behind* each other). He also asserts that the cutters' marks reflect the cutting techniques of that earlier era, not the comb chisel of the Second Temple period. He therefore sees the Garden Tomb as part of an Iron-Age necropolis which includes several other tombs in the area – one now buried under the main road by the Damascus Gate, Conder's tomb in the White Sisters, some others in Schmidt's School, and the tombs in the gardens of the Ecole Biblique. These tombs in the Ecole Biblique, though in some respects quite different in style, are just two metres away from the Garden Tomb (see Figure 33).

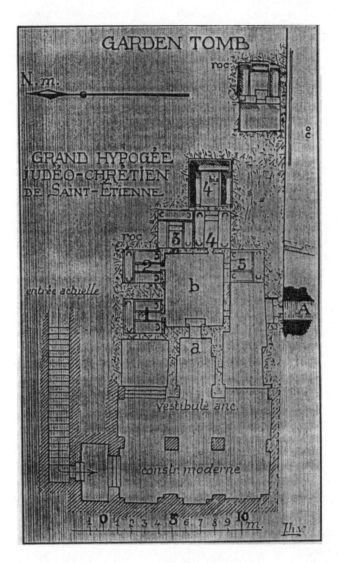

Fig. 33. Plan of the tombs in the neighbouring Dominican property (from Vincent [1925], p. 407). This large cave complex of tombs is only two metres away from the Garden Tomb (depicted in the top right-hand corner). Vincent's labelling shows that he believed the tomb complex was built after the New Testament period by Jewish Christians.

Barkay's arguments naturally caused quite a stir. They overturned the previous assumptions about the tombs in this area. Many archaeologists, however, have come to accept them. To be sure, the scholarly opinions of one generation have been known to be overturned by the next. So it is not impossible that some years from now advocates of a later date will re-emerge within archaeological circles. As yet, however, they have not done so.

Some readers will be persuaded by these archaeological arguments. Others will chose to be more sceptical, remembering that with archaeology we are rarely dealing with certainties, only patterns and probabilities. Nevertheless, at the moment the dating of the Tomb remains the single greatest question that affects the authenticity of the site as a whole.

It is possible, of course, that Joseph's tomb had its own distinctive style quite unlike other tombs of its time – brought about perhaps by its never being properly completed. But then there would still be the issue of assessing the cutters' marks which, so it is currently argued, belong to an earlier period. It is also possible that Joseph's tomb had indeed been cut many centuries before; it was 'new' to him only in the sense that he had recently acquired it. Yet this would seem to run counter to the plain sense of the Gospels which speak of a 'new tomb in which no one had ever been laid' (John 19:41).

Nevertheless, there remains the intriguing possibility that this is a mistranslation of John's Gospel. For there is a minor variant in the Greek manuscript tradition, where the word *kainon* (translated 'new') is replaced by the word *kenon* (meaning 'empty'). If this reading were accepted (though it is considerably less well attested), then John is not teaching us about the age of the tomb, only that it was empty. In which case, those who want to identify the tomb in which Jesus was buried are not necessarily looking for a first-century tomb after all! Any tomb existing at the time of Jesus would be a possibility, including the Garden Tomb.

So the case for the authenticity of the Garden Tomb has both its strengths and its weaknesses. The same also is true, as we shall now see, in the case of the Holy Sepulchre.

THE HOLY SEPULCHRE

The strongest argument in favour of the church of the Holy Sepulchre has always been its claim to ancient tradition. The argument runs as follows. The present church is essentially a Crusader church that was built on the site of Constantine's basilica. And Constantine's church will have been on the site of Jesus' crucifixion because his advisers in the early fourth century were following a reliable, local tradition.

Tradition or legend?

For some this claim to ancient tradition does not lend any real credibility to the site; they would see this dependence on tradition as the church's major weakness, not as one of its strengths. For others it is the reverse: the presence of this tradition gives the Holy Sepulchre a great advantage over the Garden Tomb. It is worth our investigating this tradition in more detail.

There is no doubt that by the end of the fourth century various legends had begun to be circulated concerning Queen Helena and the ways in which she was thought to have discovered the 'true cross' in collaboration with Bishop Macarius of Jerusalem. Despite some important variations, the gist of them all is that three crosses were found during the excavation work in 325 and that the 'true' one was then detected by supposedly miraculous means. After 400 the story of this miracle was increasingly used as a confirmation of the authenticity of the site as a whole. It is hardly surprising if modern Christians find themselves somewhat sceptical about this legend. If this is the reason why the church of the Holy Sepulchre is supposed to be authentic, they conclude, then it is a very flimsy tradition indeed.

However, we saw above (Chapter 5, p. 96) that Eusebius of Caesarea (our chief source for this whole episode) was equally sceptical. He never mentioned Helena in connection with the Holy Sepulchre. And, even though there is good evidence that he knew about it, he never explicitly spoke of this 'wood of the cross' – almost certainly because he doubted its authenticity. At best it was misguided enthusiasm, at worst it was a dangerous hoax. Eusebius evidently had not abandoned his critical faculties!

This means, however, that when he speaks so positively about the tomb, we would do well to take him seriously. There may well have been good evidence to support its identification as the tomb of Jesus. At the least, it must have matched the accounts found in the Gospels. Some have wondered if there might have been some graffiti marks left on it by first-century Christians, which helped the excavators to identify it; but Eusebius and Cyril make no mention of this. Of course, just as in the 1880s with the Garden Tomb, so in 325 there was always the danger that enthusiasm would result in people reaching a wrong conclusion. But in both cases we can charitably presume that those who discovered the respective tombs were not given over to mere credulity.

Part of Eusebius' enthusiasm no doubt resulted from the excitement at having found *anything at all* (see Chapter 5, p. 90). Searching for something that has not been seen for nearly 300 years is a risky venture at the best of times. So, when they discovered not just one tomb but several, we may rightly imagine their excitement, as well as their sense of relief! The tradition that they had been following seemed after all to have been a good one.

But were they following a tradition? Some have suggested that Constantine and the Jerusalem Christians chose the site for quite other reasons. Perhaps they were just wanting to remove the 'blot' of this pagan temple in the middle of Jerusalem. Or perhaps they were wanting to take possession of this high point near the city centre that conveniently overlooked the destroyed Jewish Temple. Was it not the ideal place for an impressive church?

These may well have contributed to the appeal of the site. But would Constantine have so readily granted Bishop Macarius' request if he had not been given good reasons for believing that this was the true site? After all, Macarius was asking him to spend imperial funds and to destroy a temple built by his revered predecessor, Hadrian. There was also the obvious truth that Jesus' death had occurred *outside* the city. This location which Macarius was suggesting must have seemed absurd! It was buried so far within the city, as Hadrian had redesigned it. So anyone who made this suggestion would need to be very confident that there was indeed a long-standing tradition which could justify such an anomaly. After all, it was not as though they had the advantages of modern archaeological methods to help them prove their case! Evidently Macarius convinced Constantine that there *was* a strong tradition. This was the place, he assured him, which had been preserved in the memory of Christians in Jerusalem.

Three early indications

There are several factors that indicate that just such a tradition may have existed. First, Melito of Sardis, who visited Jerusalem around AD 170, speaks on three occasions in his *Paschal Homily* of Jesus being crucified 'in the middle of the city'. He also in the same passage speaks of Jesus being crucified in the middle of the *plateia*, a word which may be translated as 'plaza' or 'square'.[18] Do these strange statements, which clearly contradict the Gospel record, reflect his recent travels in Palestine? Had his guides pointed out to him the probable scene of the Crucifixion – now located in the heart of Aelia Capitolina and under Hadrian's forum and temple precinct? If so, this would indicate that the traditional identification was well established by the latter half of the second century.

Christians at the time of Eusebius were convinced that this identification was also public knowledge a little earlier than that – back in the 130s. They presumed that Hadrian's building over the site in 135 was an act of anti-Christian malice – the Emperor's vindictive response when he heard of this Christian tradition. In fact this was probably not the case (see Chapter 5, p. 97). Hadrian's choice of this site was for quite other reasons. So this cannot be used as a secure argument for the existence of this tradition at that time. But within Eusebius' writings there is another factor that probably *does* suggest the early nature of this tradition.

Eusebius says that quite a number of Christians came to Jerusalem before 325 to investigate the Gospel sites, but the two chief places on their itinerary were Bethlehem and the Mount of Olives (see p. 84). They remembered Jesus' birth, his Apocalyptic Discourse and his Ascension. But why did their itinerary not include the most important event of all, the site of the Crucifixion and Resurrection? Given their natural interest in this site, one could almost imagine the willing guides inventing a suitable place for them! The fact that no such site was visited suggests that there was a strong tradition locating it in a place which was currently inaccessible. If it was already well established that the tomb had been covered by the Venus temple, this

Fig. 34. Artist's impression of the boat graffito, as discovered in 1971 underneath the Holy Sepulchre.

would readily explain why no one thought to visit it – and also why no one invented another, more accessible location! Instead Eusebius simply states that Golgotha was 'pointed out in Aelia to the north of Mount Zion'.[19] The general location was remembered, but there was nothing as such to *visit* (see Chapter 5, p. 84) – though some have recently suggested that the top of the rock of Golgotha might have been visible, protruding into the court of the pagan temple.[20]

In recent years a third factor has sometimes been introduced into the debate. In 1971 a stone was discovered underneath the Armenian 'crypt of St Helena' (within the Church of the Holy Sepulchre) on which there is a sizeable graffito of a boat (see Figure 34).

Underneath there is some writing which some have deciphered as 'DOMINE IVIMUS' (Latin for 'Lord, we have come'). Is this the work of some devoted Christian pilgrims? Were they perhaps reflecting on the words of Psalm 122:2, and wanting to leave a suitable record of their visit to Jerusalem and this holy site?

It is an intriguing possibility. The stone is actually an integral part of the foundation structures. As such it would only have been accessible when those foundations were temporarily exposed – either in AD 135 or else in 325. Was this when the pilgrims left their mark? If so, this would give us a fascinating window into Christian devotion during that far-distant era – especially if it could be dated to the second century. Was the site an object of pilgrimage even at that early date?

Major questions, however, have been raised which bring this interpretation into serious doubt. One scholar has deciphered the words quite differently (e.g. 'D.D. NOMINUS'), and others think it has been slightly altered since its first discovery.[21] In fact it is now thought likely that the stone already bore the graffito when it was brought in from another place to serve this purpose. So this may not support the argument for an early tradition at all.

The other factors mentioned, however, *do* point in that direction. Many therefore are convinced that the site may after all be the correct one.

Back to the first century?

But our arguments have only taken us back to the second century. Those who believe in the site's authenticity have to assume that the tradition was successfully passed on from the time of Jesus through to the time of Melito.

Others think this most unlikely. After all, the Jewish Christians fled the city during the First Jewish Revolt (AD 66–70) and had their places taken by Gentile Christians in the aftermath of the Second Jewish Revolt (AD 135). Would the tradition really have survived these upheavals?

And what if the first generations of Christians did not make very much of the actual tomb? 'The early church was making history not writing it,' comments White; 'they did not publicise a redundant tomb; they proclaimed a risen Lord.'[22] If so, then even in the first century the location of the site might have been forgotten. This seems a little unlikely, given both the general Jewish interest in the tombs of their prophets and also the references to the empty tomb in the Gospels (probably composed just before and after the fall of Jerusalem in AD 70). Yet it does alert us to yet another hurdle which needs to be crossed by those who assert that the tradition continued unbroken from that first Easter day through to the second century.

If the tradition did not survive throughout this period, then the tradition that we have identified in the second century is comparatively worthless. Christians in second-century Jerusalem, it could then be argued, simply invented a particular site as a matter of convenience in order to fill the vacuum. If so, we have a tradition which is undeniably ancient, but it still does not take us back far enough.

Amongst those on the other side, who reckon the tradition *does* have its roots back in the first century, there are inevitably those who go further and argue that both the Sepulchre and 'traditional Golgotha' are exactly correct. Others, while accepting the correctness of the general vicinity, want to ask some questions about the precise locations. What if the real tomb was a further 30 metres to the south, in an area just missed by the Constantinian excavators? Or what if the tomb is correct, but not Golgotha?

Is there then any archaeological evidence from the site that can help us?

Recent archaeology

During the last 30 years the necessary work of restoring the church has given the opportunity for some archaeological work to take place which previously was impossible. This has confirmed that the area was a disused quarry (like that in front of Skull Hill) and that the rock of 'Golgotha' was a flawed piece of rock which was left to stand up some five metres above the surrounding bedrock. There is also evidence of some red soil which is frequently associated with areas of cultivation near limestone rock. On the basis of this Corbo believes that in the first century the area would have been a market garden given over to the cultivation of vines, figs, carobs and olive trees.[23] But there are no botanical remains to support this conclusion. More significant perhaps is the fact that the nearby gate was known as the 'Gennath' or 'Garden' Gate – suggesting that this region was given over to vegetation of one kind or another.[24] So, in general terms, there is nothing that has been discovered during this archaeological excavation which has served to question the site's general plausibility.

Archaeological work on the tomb itself is naturally difficult. The surrounds of the original tomb were cut away by the Constantinian builders; and most of the remains of the tomb were destroyed at the order of Caliph Hakim in 1009. Very little of the original remains. Nevertheless (as noted above, p. 102) recent photogrammetric tests suggest that more of the original rock may have survived than was previously thought. In the aftermath of the devastating fire in 1808 and before the edicule was rebuilt, there was apparently a substantial amount of native rock still visible on the north and south sides. But even if it becomes possible in the future to investigate this portion in more detail, it is most unlikely that it will provide any conclusive evidence as to the tomb's authenticity.

If this unsatisfactory situation does not particularly endorse the tomb's authenticity, some important endorsement may come from the existence of the tombs just 10 metres to the west (see Chapter 5, p. 91, and Plate 22). It is now commonly agreed that these *kokhim* tombs were only in use in Palestine from c. 100 BC to c. 100 AD. If correct, then the presence of these tombs indicates that this area was outside the city walls during some of this period. (There are also two other tombs in the vicinity: one under the Coptic monastery, the other under the entrance court.) This is important evidence in favour of the site's general authenticity. However, it remains possible that these tombs were only outside the walls during the *earliest* part of this period and that they were then incorporated within the limits of the city when the 'second' wall was built shortly before the reign of Herod the Great. If so, there is still no firm archaeological proof that this site was indeed outside the walls at the time of Jesus. The existence of these tombs makes it very likely, but we cannot be certain.

Some questions: the line of the 'second' wall

So the major question-mark against the Holy Sepulchre remains the thorny issue of whether or not it was outside the city walls of Jesus' day. The evidence of the *kokhim* tombs is significant. It is also likely that the Jerusalem of Jesus' day was smaller than many have imagined (see p. 148). Nevertheless, many would still dispute the claim that Herod's 'second' wall really kept itself to the east of this area.

At the moment it is customary for maps of Jerusalem in Jesus' day to be drawn in such a way that the second wall comes out at 90 degrees from the first wall in the area of the Gennath Gate (some 35 metres to the south-east of 'Golgotha'). It then proceeds in a northerly direction (leaving Golgotha some 15 metres to the west) before turning eastwards in the area of the modern Damascus Gate (see Figure 35, p. 166).

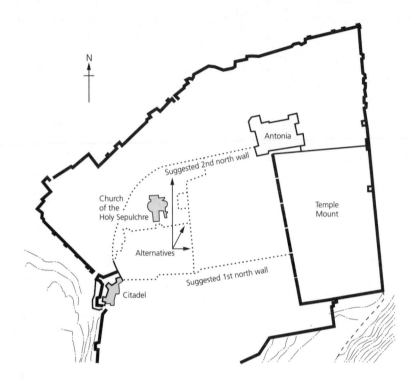

Fig. 35. Alternative lines recently suggested for Jerusalem's 'second' wall (after Kenyon [1974], p. 233).

This reconstruction may well be right, but to this day no part of this 'second' wall has yet been identified with certainty. And even the existence and location of the Gennath Gate cannot be fully established – because the archaeologists had too little time before the builders wanted to move in.[25]

The reconstruction is based chiefly upon an interpretation of Josephus' description of the walls in his *Jewish War*: 'The second wall started at the Gennath, a gate in the first wall. It enclosed the northern quarter only and went up as far as the Antonia.'[26] Those who question this reconstruction of the 'second wall' do so for a variety of reasons. Some think that Josephus' language of 'enclosing' (or more literally, 'encircling') does not fit very well with the more indented appearance of what is normally suggested. Others,

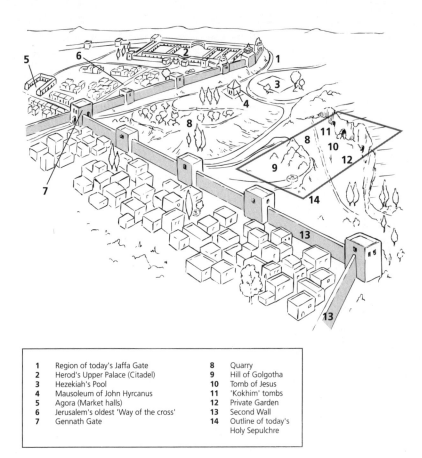

1	Region of today's Jaffa Gate	8	Quarry
2	Herod's Upper Palace (Citadel)	9	Hill of Golgotha
3	Hezekiah's Pool	10	Tomb of Jesus
4	Mausoleum of John Hyrcanus	11	'Kokhim' tombs
5	Agora (Market halls)	12	Private Garden
6	Jerusalem's oldest 'Way of the cross'	13	Second Wall
7	Gennath Gate	14	Outline of today's Holy Sepulchre

Fig. 36. The area of traditional Golgotha, as it might have appeared at the time of Jesus (according to Pixner). This view is taken from the north-east and assumes that the 'second' wall was indented.

since at least the time of Conder,[27] have wondered if this would really have been a sensible course for the wall from a strategic-defence point of view. Jerusalem has always been most vulnerable from its northern side. Yet this reconstruction of the wall would effectively leave the higher ground (of today's Christian Quarter) outside the wall – giving a potential advantage to the enemy. Certainly it is not surprising if Herod Agrippa, in building the 'third'

168 The Weekend that Changed the World

wall, ensured that this higher ground *was* brought within the city. On the other hand, it could be argued that the evident quarrying in this area reflects just such a concern for defence and that there was a small fosse created between the wall and the higher ground to the north.

Yet others wish to question the proposed line of the second wall on demographic grounds. Estimates for the population of Jerusalem in Jesus' day vary from 30,000 to 120,000.[28] Would the area enclosed within this wall have been sufficient for such a population, especially in the light of the number of workmen who were brought into the city to work on the construction of the Temple? And even if this was the line of the 'second' wall, the fact that Agrippa, so soon after Jesus' crucifixion, chose to expand the city quite sizeably towards the north-west might suggest that there was an overcrowding problem (as indeed Josephus explicitly states.[29] In which case, were some people beginning to take up residence outside the city walls? If so, this would mean that the traditional site of Golgotha was surrounded by new dwellings. Is this a likely place, it is asked, for an execution-site?

Finally, some have also questioned whether the Romans would have used an area which was quite close to the aristocratic quarter of the city and not far from Herod's palace (where Pontius Pilate was staying). As a possible corroboration of this, it is noted that there are comparatively few tombs on the western side of the city. Was this similarly because the wealthy residents of the upper city did not want to be disturbed by the smell of death, borne on the prevailing westerly winds? Yet there clearly were *some* tombs in this area, and even if there are fewer tombs on this western side, that may have more to do with the hardness of the limestone rock. It was also an area which received more rain and which therefore was needed for agriculture.

Nevertheless, some archaeological work has been done near to the Holy Sepulchre which seems to suggest that the area was indeed outside the city walls. Kenyon dug in the Muristan area (her site 'C') and more recently Lux was working under the Lutheran church.[30] In both excavations there was no evidence of the area being inhabited in the time of Jesus – indeed at any time between the second century BC and AD 135. In that later period, however, a vast amount of earth and other material was evidently brought in to 'fill' the area. This would be in keeping with what we know of Hadrian's new building in this vicinity.

Again this is an argument from comparative silence, but it does suggest that the area experienced its most dramatic alterations in the century *after* Jesus' crucifixion.

As with the Garden Tomb, therefore, there are strengths and weaknesses in the case for the Holy Sepulchre. It has an ancient tradition, going back almost certainly to the second century, but does it go back far enough? The excavations of Lux and Kenyon suggest it may have been outside the city wall in Jesus' day, so do the nearby *kokhim* tombs; but the exact line of the 'second' wall still gives cause for some uncertainty. Above all, even if the general vicinity were established as correct, there would be no way of knowing for sure that the fourth-century excavators were correct in identifying *that* particular tomb and *that* particular rock. Many are convinced they were. Others are not so sure. Eusebius, as we saw, never identified the rock with Golgotha. So some scholars, even if they favour the authenticity of the tomb, believe that Golgotha lay elsewhere – perhaps further south towards the Gennath Gate.[31] Ultimately, whatever conclusion one comes to, it is a matter of weighing up a string of probabilities.

CONCLUSION

And so the debate continues! It is hoped that the above gives a sufficient overview of the arguments for readers to be able to come to their own conclusions. Some will give extra weight to tradition, others to the various archaeological questions. Some will become fairly convinced of their position, others will continue to be hesitant or to prefer to keep an 'open mind'.

Still others will conclude that there will never be such a thing as complete certainty on this issue and that perhaps, after all, this really does not matter! What is important is not so much the *place where* these historic events happened but the *fact that* they happened.

In general terms this is the perspective from which this book is written. The various arguments from tradition and archaeology have been given, and some of them are clearly stronger than others. Yet ultimately the important thing to stress is the Resurrection *itself* as an event within history – not so much its precise location on a map. To put it simply, history is more important than geography. In our modern climate, however, it is this historical aspect of Jesus' Resurrection that so frequently has come under attack. *This* is the issue, therefore, on which we need to stand firm. We can choose to keep an open mind on the whereabouts of that Easter garden. But if the Resurrection itself is a fable and 'if Christ has not been raised', then, as Paul said, 'your faith has been in vain' (1 Corinthians 15:14). No Resurrection, no Christianity!

To be sure, the precise manner of Jesus' Resurrection and the precise details concerning those first Easter events may still give grounds for healthy discussion (see Part I). But, as far as believing Christians are concerned, the historic reality of the Resurrection itself is a fixed point in their faith. Without it, they would not be Christians. It is an essential part of what it means to be called by that name. They fail to see how yet another failed messiah (as Jesus would have been if he had not been raised from death) would have been of any use to anyone. And they can think of no reason why this new message about a Risen Lord would ever have been concocted by the apostles (or indeed welcomed by their hearers) if Jesus' body were really still in the tomb.

So Christians feel called to certainty when it comes to the issue of the Resurrection as a historic event. Did God raise Jesus bodily from the grave? Answer: yes! But as for its precise location, they are prepared to live with uncertainty. If ever the exact spot could be determined beyond any shadow of doubt, that would cause them no problem. In the meantime, however, they sense that this uncertainty may perhaps serve an important providential purpose.

For within the New Testament a much greater priority is clearly given to the *person* of Jesus, compared to any particular *place*. Jesus counsels the Samaritan woman to be less concerned with issues of place and more concerned with 'worshipping God in spirit and in truth' (John 4:18–24). And the women on that first Easter morning, despite being invited to 'come see the place', are quite clearly told that this Jesus 'is not here, for he has been raised!' (Matthew 28:6). They are to go from that place with a life-changing message for their friends, and indeed for the world.

So, at the end of the day what is important is not the venue, but the fact – not the Place, but the Person. Indeed, 'He is not here, for he has been raised!'

PART III

The Significance

Jesus said:
'I am the Way, and the Truth and the Life.'
(JOHN 14:6)

THE OLD CITY TODAY

Pl.36: A 'bird's eye view' showing how Hadrian's street lines (AD 135) have survived to this day (cf. Fig.17). The Garden Tomb enclosure lies outside the city's northern wall (top middle); the Holy Sepulchre is well within the Old City (middle left).

Pl.37 (inset): taken in front of the Damascus Gate, this shows how the grey dome of the Holy Sepulchre is on a slightly higher hill than the golden Dome of the Rock. Did this influence the choice of the site for the Holy Sepulchre? Was it outside the wall in AD 33?

SKULL HILL VIEWED FROM THE CITY WALL (1890 AND 1990)

Pl.38 (top): A tinted photograph showing Skull Hill as observed by General Gordon and others. Note also Jeremiah's Grotto (right) and the former 'slaughter-house' (upper left) recently converted by the Dominicans.

Pl.39 (bottom): The site, now a bus station for Arab East Jerusalem, is surmounted by a Muslim cemetery. The skull 'sockets' (right) appear much the same, but the ground level below the skull has been raised by over 6 metres, thereby obliterating what some identified as the skull's 'mouth'.

SKULL HILL TODAY

Pls.40–41: As seen late afternoon from the Garden Tomb's viewing platform.

AROUND THE GARDEN TOMB ENCLOSURE

Pl.42 (main picture): The vast cistern near the tomb (during re-plastering, 1977).

Pl.43 (top inset): One of two Crusader crosses cut into the lower side-walls of the cistern.

Pl.44 (middle inset): The anchor/cross in the rock-face outside the tomb, probably carved by Byzantine Christians.

Pl.45 (bottom inset): The ancient wine-press, suggesting the importance of cultivation in the area.

Pl.46: An example of what a first-century rolling-stone would have looked like.

Pl.47: The international nature of the Garden Tomb, which welcomes each day visitors from all round the world.

Pl.48 (above): The tomb
immediately after its discovery
in 1867.

Pl.49 (above right): A few
months later, when the front of
the tomb had been bricked in.

Pl.50 (below): Much later
(c. 1905), after Hussey's
excavation in front of the tomb.

Pl.51 (below right): Peder
Beckholdt, the first warden
(1896–1912), outside the tomb.

**THE GARDEN TOMB IN
ITS EARLY YEARS**

THE GARDEN TOMB TODAY

Pl.52 (above): As seen since 1998, with the vegetation above the tomb now removed.

Pl.53 (left): The author inside the tomb (Easter 1998).

Pl.54 (below): The inner chamber, showing the three 'loculi'; the largest one, on the north wall, appears to have a sloping head-rest and an extra section cut out for the feet.

MEMORIES OF A VISIT

Pl.55 (above): A cross-shaped tree in front of the tomb.

Pls.56–57 (right and below): Two important New Testament texts (Mark 16:6; Rom. 1:4), proclaiming the truth and real significance of Jesus' Resurrection.

Truth for the World

The Resurrection in the New Testament

In Part I we examined the *story* of that first Easter weekend – what exactly happened? In Part II we looked at the various debates as to the site of those events – where do we think it actually happened? But all this would be quite incomplete if we did not go on to consider the *significance* of all this for ourselves and for the world. What difference does it make? What does it all mean? Do those strange events outside Jerusalem 2,000 years ago have any relevance for us today? What, if any, are the consequences?

For the disciples, it has to be said, there were immediate consequences. Even amidst the joy and excitement of that first Easter evening, when they were suddenly reunited with Jesus, they were given a solemn charge: 'as the Father has sent me,' said Jesus, 'so I send you' (John 20:21). Jesus would not allow them to keep this good news for themselves. No, it was for the world outside – a world which would never hear of it so long as those few disciples, gathered fearfully in that Jerusalem upper room, decided to keep silent. In that instant, the disciples must have realized that they could never be the same again. Jesus appeared to be giving them, and indeed he was, the awesome responsibility of making what he had done in Jerusalem to be known throughout the world. The Resurrection changed their lives forever. It can do exactly the same today.

What was turned upside down, however, was not just their lifestyle (a life now committed to passing on this message) but also their mindset. Everything they had previously thought had to be melted down and reconfigured around this single, unexpected event. Or, to use a different picture, the Resurrection triggered off profound shock waves which inevitably had a ripple effect on every part of their thinking.

The New Testament is the result of those dramatic ripple effects – the fruit of their considered reflection. So in this chapter we will examine those New Testament writings in order to learn from them on this important subject. What did Jesus' own apostles decide were the implications of his Resurrection? It turned their thinking upside down. It can do the same for us. As we learn from their conclusions we will gain a whole new way of understanding not just Jesus, but the very heart of God and his future purposes for his world. At the same time the Resurrection is also an event which has important, unavoidable repercussions for us as individuals. These will be the focus of Chapter 9.

THE VINDICATION OF JESUS

First, and most obviously, the Resurrection gave those disciples a new understanding of Jesus himself – who he was and what he came to do. To put it mildly, if the God of Israel had chosen to raise this Galilean prophet from death, it suggested the stamp of divine approval! During his ministry there had been those who were opposed to Jesus and his ministry, but it was clear now that God himself thought quite differently. At the time of his crucifixion it had looked as though Jesus were a complete failure. Now that he had been raised from the dead, however, he had evidently received divine vindication.

This cast a whole new light on Jesus' ministry. It led the disciples to think the unthinkable as to who he really was, and also to look more deeply at the enigma of the crucifixion. Who was that person dying on a Roman cross and what exactly was he doing there?

Jesus' life and teaching affirmed

As the disciples looked back over the three years of Jesus' ministry, it was evident that all along he had said and done some rather surprising things. He had overturned their expectations as to what a godly prophet would do and what kind of company he would keep (Mark 2:16; Luke 7:39). He had claimed the ability to forgive people their sins (Mark 2:10). He had sat loose to some of the traditions which had grown up concerning the observance of the Sabbath and the proper food to be eaten (Mark 2:18–3:6; 7:1–23). In some ways he seemed to have been redefining the Law and, in calling 12 disciples, he gave a clear hint that he was reconstituting Israel around himself. Above all, in his elusive references to himself as the 'Son of Man' (Mark 8:31 etc.) and as the Suffering Servant (Mark 10:45), he had been giving a whole new twist to the role of the long-awaited Messiah.

Now this Jesus had been raised from death. So the God of Israel was effectively saying 'yes' to all these shocking activities and claims. Although they had not understood his words at the time, Jesus had also predicted that he would be raised again from death (Mark 8:31; 9:9, 31; 10:34). The Resurrection proved him right. He was God's true prophet.

Jesus' prophetic call to Israel, warning like Jonah of judgement to come if there was no repentance, had been a true call (Luke 13:5). His interpretation of the Scriptures, which was marked both by deep loyalty and radical re-evaluation (e.g. Luke 4:21), was a true interpretation. His miracles, which some could only explain by invoking the name of Beelzebul, had truly been accomplished through the 'finger of God' (Luke 11:20). And his teaching, which to his followers had all along possessed a unique authority (Mark 1:27), was now confirmed as possessing an authority that came from God himself. Jesus himself had said that human beings 'live by every word that comes from the mouth of God' (Matthew 4:4). Not surprising, then, if Jesus' disciples now treasured in their memory every word that had proceeded from the mouth of *Jesus*.

Everything about Jesus' ministry, what he said and what he did, was seen in a sharp new way in the light of the Resurrection – indeed as embodying the very words and works of God himself.

Jesus' identity revealed

Yet it was not only Jesus' words and actions that needed re-examination from this new vantage point. It was Jesus himself! Who exactly was this person?

Obviously this had been a hot topic in the minds of many people throughout the preceding three years (Mark 1:27; 2:12; Luke 7:16). Jesus himself once asked his disciples for their private opinion on the matter (Mark 8:27). On that occasion Peter found himself uttering the word 'Messiah' and Jesus confirmed his verdict. But he immediately made it clear to both Peter and the other disciples that their thinking still had a long way to go: *this* Messiah would not do what the political activists wanted, but strangely would suffer and die in Jerusalem (Mark 8:31). Now, in the light of that death and Resurrection in Jerusalem, it was confirmed that Jesus really was the Messiah – even if a very different one from what was expected. As Peter said in his first public address on the subject, the Resurrection revealed that God had made Jesus to be 'both Lord and Messiah' (Acts 2:36).

This is stranger than it appears. In the popular religion of the time there were various tasks that the Messiah might perform. He was expected to restore the independent sovereignty of the Jewish people in their own land, to bring an end to pagan domination, to establish peace, to rebuild the Temple and to reform its worship. Yet on the surface of things, *this* Messiah had not apparently fulfilled any of these expectations. On what basis then could Peter (and eventually all the writers of the New Testament) make this bold assertion that Jesus *was* after all the Jewish Messiah?

The claim would have been a non-starter, but for one thing: the Resurrection. Certainly a vague sentimental notion that Jesus' spirit somehow 'lived on' would not have been sufficient to justify this radical new way of thinking. Jesus' bodily Resurrection, however, gave them the evidence they needed. God *had* vindicated Jesus. He had thereby endorsed Jesus as the true Messiah. Jesus' redefinition of messiahship must therefore be correct. So if this was what Israel's Messiah truly looked like, they had to look again at those messianic expectations. Even if it was in unexpected ways, Jesus *had* fulfilled the messianic tasks.

Peter's speech also broke startling new ground in declaring in public that through the Resurrection God had vindicated Jesus as 'Lord'. This represents the Greek word *kurios*, a word which at one level can simply mean a 'master' (Luke 5:5). But it also had a far more staggering meaning (see, e.g., Mark 11:3; John 20:28). For this same word *kurios* was the regular word used in the Greek version of the Bible (known as the Septuagint) to translate the Hebrew word for God himself. In using this word as a title for Jesus (it occurs over 300 times in the epistles alone) the New Testament writers were making a startling claim – namely that Jesus was in some mysterious way to be identified with the God of Israel himself.

Previously the watchword of Jewish faith was the *Shema* ('Hear, O Israel: the LORD is our God, the LORD alone' [Deuteronomy 6:4]). Now within 25 years of the Resurrection a thoroughly Jewish writer like Saul of Tarsus could dare to say instead: 'There is one God ... and one Lord, Jesus Christ' (1 Corinthians 8:6). Jesus has somehow been placed right up there within the very being of God himself! Later in the same letter (1 Corinthians 16:22) he also quotes the Aramaic tag *Maranatha* ('O Lord, come') – a clear sign that the first Aramaic-speaking believers in Jerusalem and Galilee had thought of Jesus as 'Lord'. So from the earliest days Jesus' followers dared to take for themselves a watchword which was quite different from that of their Jewish contemporaries: '*Jesus* is Lord' (Romans 10:9; Philippians 2:11).

Given the Old Testament resonances of this word, this was an extraordinary move. It was also a courageous move. For it would, of course, provoke opposition – not just from their fellow Jews but also in time from the Roman authorities for whom it was quite clear that Caesar, not Jesus, was 'Lord'.

What made them do it? Only one thing. The Resurrection.

For Paul the Resurrection also validates the use of another great title for Jesus – not just 'Messiah' and 'Lord', but also 'Son of God'. Jesus, he states, is 'declared to be Son of God ... by resurrection from the dead' (Romans 1:4). This too is a title used throughout the New Testament of Jesus (just over 50 times in the epistles). It was a phrase which had been used in a looser sense of the people of Israel as a whole (Hosea 11:1). Now, however, it was used of one specific individual with the clear intention of ascribing to him a unique and definitive status. Once again it suggested that Jesus in some way shared in the very being of God himself.

By and large the New Testament writers were simply content to proclaim their startling conviction, leaving the Christian Church of the next 400 years the task of unravelling the vast implications! Yet this striking claim was again based on one supreme event: the Resurrection. Jesus, they now could see, had always been the 'Son of God' even before the Resurrection – what he was now, was what he had always been (cf. Hebrews 13:8). Yet it was the Resurrection which 'declared' this truth in a public way. The Resurrection was God's way of revealing to the world what had previously been not fully clear – Jesus' unique identity. On seeing the Risen Lord, Thomas declared the unthinkable: 'My *Lord* and my *God*!' (John 20:28).

Jesus' death given meaning

Jesus' death had made everything seem so pointless. Great hopes had been raised only to be dashed on the cruel anvil of history. Jesus' life, which seemed to promise so much, had now been brought to a tragic end. By a strange sequence of events, which Jesus himself seemed unconcerned to alter, the festival visit to Jerusalem had gone horribly wrong. How could they now celebrate the feast when they were coming to terms with their Master's death – crucified just as if he were a common criminal on an ugly Roman cross? No wonder those two disciples leaving Jerusalem for Emmaus were feeling miserable and 'looking sad', as they made their weary way home (Luke 24:17–24).

All that was changed by the Resurrection! It put a smile back on the faces of those Emmaus disciples, and sent them back up to Jerusalem to tell their friends. The death of Jesus had appeared a cruel accident of history. In the light of the Resurrection, it looked completely different.

The New Testament writers would come to describe Jesus' death in numerous ways: as an example of patient suffering, as a victorious wrestling with the forces of evil, and as a sacrifice or atonement for sin (see, e.g., 1 Peter 2:21–4; Hebrews 10; Romans 3:23–5; Colossians 2:15). Through them all, however, there runs one abiding conviction – that Jesus' death was no accident but was instead the climax of a long-intended divine purpose. As Peter says in that same Pentecost speech, Jesus was 'handed over according to the definite plan and foreknowledge of God' (Acts 2:23). What caused this change of view? What helped them to see that Jesus' death was not pointless, but rather a key part of God's loving purposes? Answer – the Resurrection.

Some people still think that the Resurrection was just a 'spiritual' event – all part of the disciples' fertile imagination. We saw in Chapter 4 how this fails to account for their being willing to die for this imaginary event. Yet it also fails to explain how they ever came to see Jesus' death in such a positive light. Only the vindication of Jesus in bodily Resurrection could turn the crucifixion from a disaster into a victory, from a cause for mourning into a cause for endless rejoicing. In other words, the events of that Sunday morning gave a whole new meaning to the events of the previous Friday.

The Resurrection is a divine affirmation of all that Jesus intended to accomplish through his death. He had spoken of 'giving his life as a ransom for many' (Mark 10:45). He had spoken at the Last Supper of his body being broken and his blood poured out 'for the forgiveness of sins' (Matthew 26:28). In Gethsemane he had intimated that in his death he was effectively drinking the 'cup' of God's wrath (Mark 14:36; cf. Isaiah 51:17–22; Jeremiah 25:15–28; Psalm 75:8). These were cryptic sayings, which at the time may have been quite puzzling. The Resurrection, however, made the purposes both of Jesus and of God himself far clearer. It also indicated that Jesus had been successful in what he sought to achieve.

Paul put it in black and white to the Corinthian Christians: 'If Christ has not been raised ... you are still in your sins' (1 Corinthians 15:17). No Resurrection, no forgiveness. All the subsequent references in the New Testament to the divine gift of forgiveness through the death of Jesus are meaningless without the Resurrection. For only through this divine act of vindication could it be made clear that Jesus' sacrifice of himself had indeed been acceptable and that human sin had indeed been fully dealt with. A death without Resurrection would have achieved nothing. Thus if the New Testament sometimes focuses simply on Jesus' death and not on his Resurrection, it is crystal clear that the various writers were simply taking the Resurrection as a given. Without it Jesus' death was meaningless.

With it, however, Jesus' death could be seen to have been effective. His 'blood' had been shed for the 'forgiveness of sins' (Ephesians 1:7). Christ had 'suffered for sins once for all, the righteous for the unrighteous, in order to bring us to God' (1 Peter 3:18). Through the 'new and living way opened up for us' by Jesus' sacrifice, believers could indeed enter into God's presence with 'full assurance of faith' (Hebrews 10:20–2).

So the Resurrection assured the disciples that Jesus' death had purpose. In other words, the Resurrection not only revealed Jesus' unique self-identity, it also confirmed his unique self-sacrifice. It vindicated his life's ministry, his whole Person and his final Work. Have we followed their lead? Do we too acknowledge that this Jesus is unique, the one whom God has sent to us – to reveal himself and also to die for us? The Resurrection forced the disciples to think very seriously about Jesus. It should do the same for us.

THE VALIDATION OF HOPE

Inevitably the Resurrection forces us to consider very carefully the character of the one who was raised. Yet it also gives us, secondly, some clear indications of God's intention for the world, and the direction in which his divine purposes are moving. It is a matter not just of past history, but of future hope.

A promise to Israel

Those two Emmaus disciples expressed the matter bluntly: 'we had *hoped* that he was the one to *redeem Israel*' (Luke 24:21). Behind this statement there lies a host of assumptions which the modern reader of the Gospels can all too easily miss. The Jewish people in Jesus' day were longing that God would one day act to visit and vindicate his people, Israel.

We have already noted some of the hopes that clustered around the notion of the coming Messiah (see p. 176). Fuelling all of these hopes were the promises in the Old Testament that God had something better in store for his people. They had experienced the trauma of exile and, although there had been a partial return to their homeland, there was a profound sense in which they were *still* experiencing the anguish of exile – even *within* their own land (cf. Nehemiah 9:36). The people of God in subsequent centuries continued to sense this ambiguity – this tension between the promise in Scripture and the reality on the ground. It gave rise to a string of 'apocalyptic' writings which set forth in colourful terms the eventual victory of God's people and the vindication of his promises. When would God come and do something?

It also gave rise in time to the revolt of the Jewish people against their Greek overlords in the time of the Maccabees (167 BC). This political activity makes it quite clear that Israel's 'hope' was not merely 'spiritual' but had everything to do with this world. They were not looking for 'pie in the sky', nor for the end of this space-time universe. No, they were looking for the vindication of Israel's God and his people in this world – the world of the here and now.

This is important to grasp. Often when we hear this hope described in terms of a longing for 'the age to come' or for the 'resurrection of the just', we hear this as a longing for escape from this world. Instead these were regular Jewish ways of referring to that time when God would restore the fortunes of his people *in this world*. This would indeed be the longed-for 'end of the ages'. But that 'end' would not be some final, cosmic meltdown (such as the word 'apocalyptic' might now conjure up in our minds). No, it was the *beginning* of God's kingdom fully established at last on this earth. 'Your kingdom come – on earth' (Matthew 6:10).

These hopes continued to have a powerful effect on the popular imagination. Luke, for example, carefully sets the scene for his Gospel by showing the various hopes at the time of Jesus' birth: Zechariah was longing for Israel to be 'saved from our enemies and from the hand of all who hate us' (Luke 1:71); Simeon was looking for the 'consolation of Israel' and Anna for the 'redemption of Jerusalem' (Luke 2:25, 38). In other words, they were waiting for God to act to bring in that longed-for time when his kingdom would be established, Jerusalem redeemed, the exile would be over, and Israel fully 'comforted' (cf. Isaiah 40:1). So when the Emmaus disciples later express their hope that Jesus was the one to 'redeem Israel', it is quite clear what Luke at least had in mind.

It is also equally clear that Luke believed *Jesus had fulfilled that hope*. The whole Emmaus episode is built around the irony that these two disciples are actually talking to the one who had indeed 'redeemed Israel'. Luke expects his readers to see for themselves what at that precise moment the two on the road could not see – until their 'eyes were opened' (Luke 24:31). If this is Luke's meaning, then we can safely assume that once again it is the Resurrection which has given rise to this new conviction. Through the Resurrection God has acted to fulfil his promises to his people and to give them hope. Once again it might not be quite in the manner currently expected, but the Resurrection was indeed 'in accordance with the scriptures' (as Paul says in 1 Corinthians 15:4). Scriptural promises and hopes had been fulfilled.

A helpful insight comes from noting how within Jewish thought this longed-for 'end of the ages' was also called the 'resurrection of the just'. But now, in or around AD 30, God had suddenly raised from death a man whom his followers sometimes referred to as the 'just one' or God's 'holy servant' (see, e.g., Acts 4:27, 30). In other words, contrary to all expectation, God had done for *one individual in the midst of the ages* what it was expected he would do for *all God's faithful people at the end of the ages.*

This then gives rise to the New Testament idea that Christians live in the 'end-times'. We are those, says Paul, 'on whom the ends of the ages have come' (1 Corinthians 10:11; cf. Acts 2:17; Hebrews 1:1). This is because the Resurrection, once understood against its true backdrop of Jewish hope, was itself *the* end-time event. It is true that the first Christians were taught to look for a day when Christ would return (see, e.g., John 21:22; 1 Corinthians 16:22; 1 Thessalonians 4:13ff.). But their emphasis on the end-times sprang not so much from their conviction about what God would one day do at the Christ's Second Coming as from their conviction about what God *had already* done in his First Coming – namely raising him from the dead. As far as the biblical writers are concerned, every day of the last 2,000 years has been lived in the 'end-times'. The first Easter Day marked the beginning of the 'end-times'. The biblical 'new age', the long-awaited 'age to come', had arrived!

The Resurrection therefore needs to be seen not in isolation but very much against the backdrop of this Old Testament hope. It was a stunningly new event, which took everyone by surprise. Nevertheless, once it was acknowledged as truly the work of Israel's God, it was clear that it had been 'in accordance with the scriptures' – fully in keeping with God's promises revealed to the prophets. They had longed for the time when God would truly be King. Jesus in his ministry had then begun to proclaim exactly that – the nearness of the kingdom of God. Now through his Resurrection that kingdom had at last arrived.

So the Risen Jesus is God's appointed King. Wherever he rules, there is the kingdom of God. And one day he will usher in the final, completed kingdom. We need to ensure that we are part of that kingdom by recognizing Jesus as our King. The Resurrection not only tells us who the King is. It is also a promise that one day his kingdom will come in power.

A pledge to creation

Yet the world continues to be full of evil. This Kingdom of God, decisively established through the Resurrection of Jesus, is still only a foretaste. A bridgehead has been created, but the final victory is still awaited. The kingdom of God has come, but yet, in another sense, it is still to come. In emphasizing what has already come to pass as a result of the Resurrection, we must not fall into the trap of forgetting what still lies in store.

In other words the prophetic hope of the Old Testament was broken into two parts in the New – one part fulfilled in Christ already, the other part awaiting that final day. Christians live necessarily in the 'interim' period, experiencing simultaneously both the 'now' and the 'not yet'.

Within the New Testament we learn of some who failed to get this balance right and who fell into the trap of thinking that the final Resurrection had 'already taken place' (2 Timothy 2:18). Everything was 'now'; there was nothing that was 'not yet'. They clearly needed correction. They needed to learn to wait. Yet the fact that they could make such a mistake is a measure of the incredible emphasis which the apostles gave to what God had *already* done in Jesus. The Christian Church truly was a Resurrection-people.

Some in the Corinthian church made the same mistake – hence Paul's teaching in 1 Corinthians 15. Against those who denied that Christ was ever raised bodily from death, he simply repeated the most primitive 'tradition' from the Jerusalem apostles (vv. 1–7). On the other hand, against those who thought Christians had already experienced the Resurrection in full, he taught that Jesus' Resurrection was only the 'first-fruits' (v. 20). Yes, it was a solid, guaranteed down payment. But there was much more in store – when Christ's kingdom would be fully established and death, the last enemy, finally conquered (vv. 23–8).

This language of 'first-fruits' flows directly from what we noticed just above: Jesus' Resurrection is a bringing forward into time of what God will ultimately do at the end of time. It gives us a 'peep' into the future. God is moving history towards the ultimate goal of Resurrection. His raising of Jesus from the dead is thus his way of giving humanity an advanced warning or (more positively) a solemn pledge. The Risen Jesus is a 'prototype' of God's 'new creation'.

We will look in a moment at what this means for individual human beings. It is worth noting at this point, however, that the Resurrection also has implications for creation as a whole. Paul saw creation as being in a state of groaning, longing for the freedom that God alone could bring (Romans 8:9–27). Many in this situation might be tempted to despair of the material world and to postulate a purely 'spiritual' future in God's purposes. Biblical hope, however, remained far more earthy, believing that God had purposes for the 'renewal' of his creation. No, insisted Paul, 'the creation itself will be set free from its bondage to decay' (v. 21). The Resurrection is God's pledge of a new creation, an assurance that this physical realm will one day be rid of evil and infused with the glory of God.

The way the Gospel writers talk of the Risen Jesus is fully in keeping with this. The Risen Lord had a physical body, but it was also transformed by the power of the Spirit. Although it is a puzzle for all who like to pin things down scientifically, Easter is an event which brings together what we so often separate – what we call the 'physical' and the 'spiritual'. It is an act of God which assures us that matter is not inherently evil, and that God has good purposes for this material world. We are presented with the *Resurrection* of a *body*. It was not just a mere resuscitation (the material of Jesus' body being simply revived). Nor was it a purely spiritual reconstitution (leaving the material of Jesus' body behind). No, it was neither. It was what the Jews called 'resurrection'. And as such it was a sure sign that God was serious about the business of renewing his created order.

God's purposes, therefore, are not purely 'spiritual' – whether now or at the end of time. God's purposes are for the whole person and indeed for the whole of creation. The Resurrection corrects all other false notions. It is a solemn pledge by God to his creation. It is a sign of what he has in store.

So the Christian, biblical hope is that one day God will renew this earth. God's creation is not junk. Though marred by the Fall, it will one day be restored. So what we do with our bodies and what we do with creation are vitally important. They cannot be jettisoned or dismissed. No, the Resurrection assures us that they count for much in God's purposes, and we should treat them accordingly.

A pattern for believers

So the Resurrection is God's pledge to renew the whole of his creation. It is a glorious and expansive hope, which helps us to look beyond our own individual concerns. Yet there is no denying that the Resurrection can also have, and indeed does have, vital implications for us as individuals.

Ever since that first Easter day the followers of Jesus have been convinced that Jesus' Resurrection is also a pledge of what God particularly intends for his own people – for those individuals who commit themselves to him. In that same passage in Romans, Paul tells us that we are to be people who not only expect the renewal of this earth but also the 'redemption of our bodies' (Romans 8:23). Individual believers have something great to look forward to!

The ancient world was gripped by the fear of death. Think, for example, of the burial practices of Egypt or the many mythical stories about the 'underworld' designed to comfort people as they faced this ultimate journey. The Old Testament itself, for all its trust in God's faithfulness, rarely speaks of the after-life (but see Job 19:25; Psalms 49:11; 73:24). So it was only natural for the apostles to make Jesus' Resurrection the major focus of their preaching (e.g. Acts 17:18; 24:21). In the first-century world, as now, this was good news indeed. As the writer of the Epistle to the Hebrews put it, Jesus had come to 'destroy the one who has the power of death, that is, the devil, and free those who all their lives were held in slavery by the fear of death' (Hebrews 2:14–15).

The other apostles were similarly excited about Christ's victory over death for believers. Paul wrote to assure his converts that they need not mourn 'as others do, who have no hope' (1 Thessalonians 4:13). Peter promised his readers that the Resurrection had brought them into a 'living hope' and into an 'inheritance that is imperishable, undefiled, and unfading, kept in heaven for you' (1 Peter 1:3–4). And John recorded Jesus' promise that, although his disciples could not at this moment go where he was going, he nevertheless was going to 'prepare a place' for them (John 14:3).

Thus the New Testament writers were all convinced that the Resurrection of Jesus had set a pattern which his followers could confidently follow. They too could pass though death into new life. 'I know the one in whom I have put my trust,' said Paul, 'and I am sure that he is able to guard until that day what I have entrusted to him' (2 Timothy 1:12). They looked forward to being 'with Christ' and experiencing the joys of life with God in heaven (Philippians 1:23; Hebrews 12:22; 1 John 3:2; Revelation 7:9).

Once again the key passage which expressly develops this theme is 1 Corinthians 15. In describing the future life of believers after death Paul speaks of their being raised with 'spiritual bodies' (v. 44). A better translation would be 'bodies animated by the Holy Spirit'. The combination is deliberately paradoxical. It brings together the material and spiritual realm – precisely because (as noted just above) this was what had been seen in the Resurrection of Jesus. He writes to assure the believers that, because Jesus was raised from the dead, they too can be sure of their own resurrection: 'We will not all die, but we will all be changed, in a moment, in the twinkling of an eye, at the last trumpet. When this perishable body puts on imperishability, then the saying that is written will be fulfilled: "Death has been swallowed up in victory"' (vv. 51, 54). In the meantime, with this sure hope set before them, Christians were free to give themselves to the work of God's kingdom, knowing that in the Lord their labour was not in vain (v. 58).

The New Testament therefore resounds on almost every page with hope. In English the word 'hope' suggests some kind of vague wishful thinking; in the New Testament it speaks of a solid assurance. The future is unseen but not uncertain (Hebrews 11:1ff.; Ephesians 1:18; Romans 8:24–5; 1 John 3:2–3). So the first Christians had something exciting to look forward to. As Paul said, 'we are expecting a Saviour, the Lord Jesus Christ. He will transform the body of our humiliation that it may be conformed to the body of his glory' (Philippians 3:20–1).

And when we enquire what are the grounds of this early Christian confidence in the face of personal death, we are thrown back once more to that garden in Jerusalem – the place where death was defeated. 'We *know*,' said Paul, 'that the one who raised the Lord Jesus will raise us also with Jesus' (2 Corinthians 4:14). 'We know that Christ, being raised from the dead, will never die again,' he told the Christians in Rome; so 'we believe that we will also live with him' (Romans 6:8–9).

By taking Jesus' Resurrection as their sure fixed point in the past, the New Testament Christians were able then to look forwards, and to plot a sure trajectory for God's purposes in the future. The Resurrection caused them to gain a new realization not just of who Jesus was but also of what lay round the corner. And it gave them great confidence. For in the Resurrection they sensed that God had not only been at work to fulfil the hopes of his people in previous times, but also to reveal more clearly his will for the future – both for creation as a whole and for those who in Christ had themselves already become a 'new creation' (2 Corinthians 5:17).

They were excited about the Scriptures and their story, because they now knew what the God of Israel had been planning all along; he had acted dramatically in the world, faithfully fulfilling his ancient promises. They were excited about life, because they knew their Creator and they knew what he was doing with the world. They were excited about the future, even in the face of death, because they knew where they themselves were going. Do we?

THE VICTORY OF GOD

Finally, the Resurrection did not just teach the disciples about Jesus, or about the future. It also taught them about God. It was the supreme moment of his revelation. In particular the Resurrection could be seen as *the* great moment when God had demonstrated his power and overcome evil. It was his moment of victory.

In raising Jesus to life God clearly had revealed once and for all his capacity to work in the realm of nature and human life. He was a God of power and had 'put this power to work in Christ when he raised him from the dead' (Ephesians 1:20).

Yet it was more than this, too. Because the Resurrection was an event integrally involved with the pain and evil of the Cross, it also spoke of God's judgement upon evil. It spoke too of his loving and creative capacity to absorb human evil and to turn it into the means of divine blessing.

The Resurrection therefore shows us three great attributes of God: his power, his judgement, and his love. Each of these needs to be affirmed if we are to do justice to the riches of the biblical teaching. We will now look at each in turn.

The power of God

In a sceptical world the Resurrection may seem to some a scientific or historical impossibility. People often divide the world up into the 'natural' and the 'supernatural' realms. They often go on to say that the supernatural world does not exist, and, even if it does, God certainly cannot work in our 'natural' world. The 'natural' world is the only real world, so they say. What cannot be analysed scientifically or tied down rationally must be dismissed 'out of court'.

All this would have been quite alien to the biblical writers. For them nature was itself an expression of divine creativity and life. There was no great divide. But it is the Resurrection which, above all, blows apart this humanly constructed game. It demonstrates that we cannot divide off the physical from the spiritual, nor the 'natural' from the 'supernatural'. No, all these things which we tend to separate are brought together in Jesus' Resurrection.

The Resurrection is therefore a very awkward customer. It demands to be placed at the centre of the stage, not dismissed to one side. All our constructions of reality must take this as their only safe starting-point, because this is where God has supremely revealed himself. It cannot be fitted into other frameworks. Instead it has to be made the central piece of a quite new framework.

Once this is conceded then the Resurrection becomes a vital piece of evidence for the existence of a powerful and creative God. He is well able to be at work in his world. For the New Testament writers the Resurrection indicated the 'immeasurable greatness of his power' (Ephesians 1:19). The word they used was *dunamis*, from which we derive the modern word 'dynamite'. God's power is 'dynamic'. To be sure, such evidences are not given every day, but on this one historic occasion that divine power was indeed revealed. In the language of Isaiah, God has indeed 'bared his holy arm before the eyes of all the nations' (Isaiah 52:10). In modern terminology, he has 'rolled up his sleeves', and set to work. The Resurrection reveals that our God is a God of power. He has created the world, worked in history, and now has raised his Son from the clutches of death.

The judgement of God

Yet the Resurrection also reveals God's judgement. Judgement is an unpopular category today. And, if it is ever mentioned, it tends to be associated with the Cross, not with the Resurrection. To associate judgement with the Cross is entirely correct. For the Cross is the place where Jesus 'bore our sins' (1 Peter 2:24). There is indeed a sense in which we see God's judgement *revealed* at the Cross, whereas his judgement is *removed* at the Resurrection. Hence Paul can say that Jesus was 'handed over to death for our trespasses but was raised for our justification' (Romans 4:25). Nevertheless, there is at least one important New Testament verse which links judgement, not to the Cross, but expressly to the Resurrection.

In Acts 17:31 Paul warns his Athenian audience that God 'has fixed a day on which he will have the world judged by a man whom he has appointed, and of this he has given assurance to all by raising him from the dead'. In other words, Jesus' Resurrection is the pledge not only, as we saw above, of a restored creation; it is also the pledge that this Jesus is the one whom God has appointed to be the judge of humankind. The Resurrection gives us advance warning of who it is that we can expect to meet on that day.

There is also a hint of this earlier in Acts when Peter warns his audience to repent; for God has raised to life, he asserts, him whom 'you crucified' (Acts 2:23; 4:10). In other words, God has overturned the human verdict which led to Jesus' crucifixion and has announced his divine opposition to those opposed to Jesus. Later in his life Peter in fact makes it quite clear that *all* of us are effectively opposed to Jesus. It is not as though Jesus was rejected only by those on that particular day in Jerusalem. No, he was rejected by *all* humankind – he was the 'stone rejected by mortals' (1 Peter 2:4). If so, the Resurrection is then a warning to all of us that we need to quit our opposition to Jesus. Those who continue to reject him, Peter dares to claim, will find that he is the 'stone' over which they one day will 'stumble' (v. 8). The Resurrection warns us, while there is still time, to take Jesus' side.

As a result it is a dangerous half-truth to say that the Resurrection indicates the removal of divine judgement. It *does* for anyone who repents and believes in Jesus, who acknowledges God's work of judgement on the Cross; such a person 'does not come under judgement, but has passed from death to life' (John 6:24). But this is not the case for any who effectively continue to take a stance of opposition to Jesus. God does not vindicate everyone. His vindication of Jesus tells us quite plainly where his vindication now lies and how it is that we can find it. It is to be found in Jesus and by identifying with him. That alone is the one sure place of refuge. The Resurrection makes it clear that God will one day judge his world through Jesus, the one whom he raised from the dead. Are we ready?

The love of God

It is only fitting, however, that the final word about the Resurrection should be a strong declaration that this is the event which supremely reveals God's victorious love.

Throughout this chapter we have seen what follows from believing that God himself was at work in the death and Resurrection of Jesus. Yet if this is so, it is strange indeed. For it reveals a God who in Jesus was willing and able both to suffer and to die. It introduces us to a God who was prepared to enter into the darkest places of human sin and depravity. It suggests that God in some mysterious way was able to absorb the hostility that was thrown at him by those whom he had created, and turn it into a means of blessing them. The whole drama therefore smacks of divine mystery and mercy – of divine love in powerful but costly action.

So the Resurrection cannot be glibly focused upon in isolation from the Cross. Indeed without the Cross, it would be quite impossible to see the Resurrection as an act of divine love. When, however, it is set in the closest of relations to the Cross, it becomes the moment when divine love is seen to conquer, when evil has done its worst, and when divine forgiveness and healing are offered in their place.

Peter himself is a good example of this. Yes, as we have just seen, he warned people of what it meant to reject Jesus, but that was partly because he knew from his own bitter experience what it meant to reject Jesus in his hour of need. Three times he had denied that he even knew him (Mark 14:66–72). So three days later, when the women returned with the story that Jesus had been raised from the dead, we can imagine something of what Peter might have felt: certainly a little anxious about what the Risen Jesus would say to him when they first met. But he need not have feared. They indeed met. They had time alone together, and Peter found out that Jesus had truly forgiven him; he was even recommissioned for service (John 21:15–21; Luke 24:34). In other words, whatever evil had been thrown at Jesus was now absorbed and forgiven. Love had indeed covered over a multitude of sins; good had overcome evil.

The Resurrection, then, is an announcement that although human beings may do their worst, God's love and grace go deeper still. Humankind may spurn the love of God, but the offer of divine love remains forever open. When Paul told Christians not to repay 'evil for evil' but rather to 'overcome evil with good' (Romans 12:17, 21), he was probably thinking of God's love shown in the Cross and Resurrection – a love which itself did not repay evil with evil but rather overcame evil with good. And Paul himself, like Peter, had experienced this in his own life – the man who had received love and forgiveness from the Jesus he had persecuted. In the face of evil the Resurrection is the victory of divine love.

In all of this we note how God was mysteriously able to turn evil into a means of blessing. In Romans Paul also declares that 'we know that all things work together for good, for those who love God, who are called according to his purpose' (Romans 8:28). Again this is a conviction shaped by the Cross and Resurrection. Jesus was the person who *par excellence* had been 'called' according to the divine purpose, and God was able to cause even the agony of the Cross to 'work together for good'. Evil did its worst, but God took it as the raw material by which to bless his people.

This, then, becomes a fundamental part of Christian hope and experience: to trust in this God is to trust in someone who can bring us through suffering to glory, through difficulty to joy. He is the God both of the Cross *and* of the Resurrection, the God who constantly weaves this pattern through the heartbeat of the universe. Those who trust in him, even though they may experience 'death' in many ways, are confident that through the power of this love he will bring about in the lives of his people that Resurrection victory. To live with this conviction is indeed to live with hope.

As Paul concluded that same chapter in Romans, so we can conclude ours – with a declaration of God's unbreakable, unbeatable love:

Who will separate us from the love of Christ? Will hardship, or distress, or persecution, or famine, or nakedness, or peril, or sword? As it is written, 'For your sake we are being killed all day long; we are accounted as sheep to be slaughtered.' No, in all these things we are more than conquerors, through him who loved us. For I am convinced that neither death, nor life, nor angels, nor rulers, nor things present, nor things to come, nor powers, nor height, nor depth, nor anything else in all creation, will be able to separate us from the love of God in Christ Jesus our Lord.

ROMANS 8:35–9

The Resurrection reveals that the God of all power and the God of solemn judgement is also the God of unbeatable love. However much we may have rejected him or spurned his love, he can always welcome us back. Whatever circumstances we may go through, we can always trust in his goodness, power and love. Do we know this unbeatable, unbreakable love for ourselves?

Life for the Dead

The Resurrection Today

No wonder, then, that Christians become excited when it comes to the Resurrection! No wonder a visit to a garden in Jerusalem is for many of them a very powerful experience. For regardless of the precise historical and archaeological details, the Resurrection *itself* is the source of their joy.

It is the basis for their *faith* in Jesus – the one whom God vindicated as Messiah and Lord, and as his own Son.

It is the grounds for their *hope* in a world of suffering and death.

And it is the event which enables them to experience the powerful *love* of God, which can overcome the evil in their own hearts and in the world.

The Resurrection is a divine bombshell dropped into the heart of the world, loaded with truth, and utterly transforming in its effects. It is a sure sign that there is a powerful God, that he can and must be approached through Jesus Christ, and that there is a life beyond the grave when one day we shall meet him.

But we have forgotten one important thing – a consequence of the Resurrection which, if we fail to grasp it, makes all we have said so far completely useless.

THE FORGOTTEN FACTOR?

The story goes of a Christian academic in the 1930s who was writing a book on the Resurrection. Suddenly one day, as he was working in his study, this most important truth dawned on him afresh and he started to pace up and down the length of his study reciting slowly four very simple words: 'Christ is alive today, Christ is alive today!'

It is so easy to lose sight of this most basic truth. Over and above everything else, the Resurrection is the event that establishes that *Jesus is still alive*. As two writers in the New Testament put it: 'Christ, being raised from the dead, will never die again; death no longer has dominion over him; the life he lives, *he lives* to God' (Paul in Romans 6:9–10); 'he *always lives* to make intercession' for us, for he is 'the same, yesterday and today and forever' (Hebrews 7:25; 13:8).

Of course, for the disciples who experienced that very first Easter in Jerusalem this was not the *last* thing that they discovered, but the very first! The Jesus whom they had known in the hills of Galilee was gloriously alive. Their previous relationship with him could in some mysterious way be restarted. It was time to be friends once more.

Within a few weeks, however, Jesus was taken from them when he returned into God's presence (Acts 1:9). Was *this* then to be the end of their relationship with him?

No, not at all. In fact Jesus himself had expressly told them that his leaving them would be to their advantage: if he did not leave them, he would not be able to send them the Holy Spirit (John 16:7). This Holy Spirit was in effect to be 'another Jesus': 'the Father will send you *another* Advocate, to be with you for ever' (John 14:15). And what Jesus promised soon proved true. After they had received the gift of the Spirit at Pentecost, the disciples sensed that Jesus was indeed with them – even though in physical terms he was now absent.

Yet there was something even more remarkable. Those to whom they preached, most of whom had never met Jesus in a physical sense, were able to meet with this Risen Lord as well. They too were able to enter into a relationship of love with him. So later in his life Peter could write – perhaps still with some degree of amazement – to believers living far away: 'Although you have not seen him, you love him; and even though you do not see him now, you believe in him and rejoice with an indescribable and glorious joy' (1 Peter 1:8). These

Christians, even though they were in the middle of what is now modern Turkey, had met personally with Jesus of Nazareth – that tiny village in Galilee. Incredible! How could this be? Only because this Jesus was now alive!

The Christians we encounter in the New Testament were people who had met Christ for themselves. No doubt they came to meet him in many different ways. But they had all had an encounter with the Risen Lord which was transforming their lives. The same can be true today. If Christ was alive then, he is alive now. If they could meet him then, we too can meet him today.

CHRISTIANITY IS CHRIST

Yes, it is possible to meet with Christ for ourselves. Sometimes, however, this seems to be one of the 'best-kept secrets' within the Church! All sorts of impressions are given as to what will help people come to faith or what will make them a true Christian. People are encouraged to read books or study theology, to attend church regularly or do good to their neighbour. All of these are indeed strongly to be encouraged! But not one of them actually makes a person into a Christian. They are a means to an end, not the end itself. What makes a person a Christian is, at it was for the disciples, an encounter with the Risen Christ himself.

For some people the Christian faith may seem very complicated; 'I'll never be able to understand it all!' they say. Others may view themselves in a negative light; 'God would never be interested in me!' they think. But the Good News is that anyone can meet with this Jesus. No one is 'beyond the pale'. And when people do so, Jesus automatically takes them right into the very heart of the Christian faith. It all then begins to make sense. Why? Because they themselves know in a personal way the One who is at the very centre of it all – the very one around whom the rest of the Christian faith is built. Christianity, before it is ever a system of doctrines, is first and foremost a relationship with a person. As in other walks of life, it is not *what* you know, but *who* you know!

So the most important truth which derives from the Resurrection is that we ourselves, whatever our age or nationality, can meet with the one who on that first Easter day was raised from death. The Risen

Christ is alive and he longs to meet with us. We are invited by God to an encounter with his Son: meet Jesus – '"This is my Son, the Beloved; listen to him!"' (Mark 9:7).

DIFFERENT RESPONSES

It is important to stress at this point that no two individuals are identical. For countless thousands of people throughout the last 2,000 years this experience of meeting with Christ has occurred almost unconsciously or gradually, without any great drama or soul-searching. The important thing is that, regardless of the precise mechanics, they have indeed come to know Christ – what Paul calls the 'surpassing value of knowing Christ Jesus my Lord' (Philippians 3:8). Many people today have met with Christ – some in a sudden conversion experience, others gradually over a period of years, perhaps through being brought up in a Christian home. The great thing is to know Christ personally – and to know that we know him! 'I am the good shepherd; I know my own sheep and my own sheep *know me*,' said Jesus (John 10:14).

For any readers in this category it is hoped that the focus in this book on the Resurrection has been a reassuring experience, confirming them in the things of the faith and giving them a new joy in this great Easter message from Jerusalem.

To be sure, such people may occasionally feel that despite their being Christians their lives are marked more by death than by Resurrection (cf. 2 Corinthians 4:12). Sometimes great shadows may cross their paths. Yet it is in those moments that a renewed trust in God can be found – the God who in all circumstances can bring good from evil and Resurrection-possibilities out of the jaws of death: 'Even though I walk through the valley of the shadow of death, I will fear no evil, for you are with me' (Psalm 23:4). So the Christian life is sometimes covered not with roses but with thorns – as of course it was for Jesus himself. Jesus' disciples are called 'to take up their cross daily' (Luke 9:23), but they are also those who, even as they share in Jesus' 'sufferings', can also 'know the power of his Resurrection' (Philippians 3:10). Christians are ultimately an 'Easter people' – those who come through death into Resurrection life.

Other readers, however, know that there are some decisions to be made. Earlier chapters, which focused on historical and archaeological matters, may have been illuminating. But this present discussion on the Resurrection's implications is more unsettling. What if it is true? What if it really did happen? How does one make an appropriate response?

EXAMPLES FROM THE PAST

For such people the following true stories may be of some help. They are simply a selection of examples which indicate that this challenge of meeting with Christ is not an experience which was confined to the first century. It has been a profound reality for many ever since.

One of the most famous encounters with Christ is that of Augustine of Hippo (AD 354–430). Augustine has been described by some scholars as simply the most intelligent man alive in his generation. Fortunately for posterity he subsequently wrote a very personal and moving account of his life and of how eventually he was forced to acknowledge the claims of Christ (the *Confessions*). For Augustine the whole process took an extremely long time, and by the time readers find themselves in the eighth book, they too are on tenterhooks, wondering if Augustine will ever finally make a decision! His quest took many turns, through many different philosophies, and from Africa to Rome; until one day, when the mental anguish and torture was almost too great to bear, he was sitting near his friend Alypius in a garden in Milan. He continues:

> A mighty tempest arose bearing a great storm of tears... I flung myself carelessly down under some fig-tree, and let the reins of weeping go. I said to you: 'And you, O Lord, how long, how long? Will you be angry for ever? Remember not past iniquities.' Such were my words and I wept in the bitter contrition of my heart.
>
> And, see, I heard a voice from a neighbour's house chanting repeatedly, whether a boy's or a girl's I do not know: 'Pick it up and read it, pick it up and read it'... Restraining a rush of tears, I got up, concluding that I was bidden of heaven to open the book and read the first chapter I should come upon... Excitedly then I went back to the place where Alypius was sitting, for there I had put down the apostle's book when I got up. I seized it, opened it and immediately read in silence the paragraph on which my eyes

first fell: '... not in the ways of banqueting and drunkenness, in immoral living and sensualities, passion and rivalry, but clothe yourself in the Lord Jesus Christ...' I did not want to read on. There was no need. Instantly at the end of the sentence, as if a light of confidence had been poured into my heart, all the darkness of my doubt fled away.[1]

In that moment Augustine finally met with Christ. And he went on to be an unrivalled theologian – the dominant figure in Christian thought for the next thousand years.

Move now across over 1,500 years to hear from someone who also was one of the leading academic thinkers of his day. This man too later wrote a book to describe how he eventually came to a personal faith in Christ. This time, however, the scene is not an Italian garden but the 'dreaming spires' of Oxford in England.

C. S. Lewis was later to become Professor of Medieval and Renaissance Literature at Cambridge University as well as one of the most famous modern Christian thinkers. Back in the 1920s, however, he was a convinced atheist. He was also regarded as having read more books than any other person in England. He had a keen philosophical mind and gradually adopted the position of the Idealists, believing in absolutes but definitely not believing in any personal God. Gradually, however, this changed. One important episode took place as he was returning home on the bus:

I became aware that I was holding something at bay, or shutting something out. Or if you like, that I was wearing some stiff clothing, or even a suit of armour. I felt myself being, there and then, given a free choice. I could open the door or keep it shut; I could unbuckle the armour or keep it on. The choice appeared to be momentous but it was also strangely unemotional. I chose to open, to unbuckle, to loosen the rein. Then came the repercussion on the imaginative level. I felt as if I were a man of snow at long last beginning to melt. I rather disliked the feeling.

The process gradually continued, with Lewis increasingly realizing how much his interest in philosophy had been a secret attempt to avoid meeting with a personal God. 'Amiable agnostics,' he noted, 'talk cheerfully about "man's search for God". To me, as I then was, they might as well have talked about the mouse's search for the cat.' Things came to a head a few months later:

> You must picture me alone in that room at Magdalen, night after night, feeling the steady, unrelenting approach of Him whom I so earnestly desired not to meet. That which I greatly feared had at last come upon me. In the Trinity Term of 1929 I gave in, and admitted that God was God, and knelt and prayed: perhaps, that night, the most dejected and reluctant convert in all England.[2]

Here was someone who honestly did not desire to meet with God, but found himself meeting him all the same. In his own words, he was 'surprised by joy'. The 'hound of heaven' had found him.

CHRIST TODAY

It is not just brilliant thinkers, however, who can meet with Christ. People in all walks of life, from all over the globe, and in vastly different circumstances, can testify to the difference which he can bring. Perhaps some of the most impressive testimonies in recent years of Christ's life-changing power have come from those in the midst of real adversity. The following true stories have been selected from *Man Alive*, an inspiring book by Michael Green on the power and relevance of the Resurrection today.[3]

Consider this letter, for example, written in the 1960s by 15 prisoners in Pulau Senang prison, Singapore, just hours before they were led out to execution. In the months since the passing of their death sentence a Methodist minister (Rev Khoo Siaw Wah) had introduced them to Jesus Christ. They wrote to express their thanks:

> We thank you from the bottom of our hearts. You were the beacon that guided us to the haven of Jesus Christ ... during these long agonising months of mental torture. Now we stand at the very brink of death, at the very edge of eternity. We know that in three and a half hours' time, when we pass from off this earth, our Lord and Saviour Jesus Christ will be waiting with open arms to lead us to our new home. With our dying breath we once again

affirm our undying gratitude – gratitude that will transcend even death itself.

Or consider the testimony of Gikita, one of the Auca Indians (a tribe in the heart of Ecuador living a Stone-Age lifestyle) who had been responsible for spearing to death some missionaries in 1956. Ten years later, after the missionaries' widows had gone to live amongst their husbands' murderers, many had come to a personal faith in the Risen Christ: 'I used to hate and kill,' said Gikita, 'but now the Lord has healed my heart.'

Meanwhile in Russia a well-known story recounts how a member of the communist party addressed a packed audience on the Resurrection of Christ. He spoke at great length, seeking to discredit it. At the end an Orthodox priest rose and asked if he might reply. He was warned that he was only allowed five minutes. 'Five seconds is all that I require!' He turned to the audience and gave the traditional Orthodox Easter greeting: *'Kristos vahskryes!'* ('Christ is risen!'). Back with a deafening roar came the traditional reply: *'Vahistinu vahskryes!'* ('He is risen indeed!'). Decades of atheistic training could not dislodge this deeply engrained conviction: there was more to life than mere secularism, and more to Jesus than the lecturer could see.

So the Resurrection is a truth which belongs to the whole Church – not just one part of it. And it has been powerful in its effect not just in the first century but ever since. Many other examples could be given, but these may be sufficient to show that all sorts of people have continued to experience the Risen Christ. This then becomes further evidence to support the New Testament claim that Jesus was indeed raised from the dead on that first Easter Day in Jerusalem. If he were not raised, then such encounters would be impossible. The fact that so many testify to the solid reality of this encounter begins to suggest there may be some truth in that original claim after all. Jesus really is alive today!

THE RESURRECTION: CHALLENGE AND OPPORTUNITY

This message of Jesus being alive was so central in the apostles' preaching that, when Paul spoke in Athens, his audience initially misunderstood him to be talking about two new gods – one called Jesus, the other called 'Resurrection' (Acts 17:18). It would be good if modern Christian preachers so emphasized the Resurrection that they made a similar impression!

The Resurrection is so important. Without it, the whole Christian message ceases to make any sense. However, the brief account of Paul's speech on that occasion also includes (as we saw above, p. 189) an important warning which is also an integral part of this Resurrection message:

> God commands all people everywhere to repent, because he has set a day on which he will have the world judged by a man whom he has appointed, and of this he has given assurance to all by raising him from the dead.
>
> ACTS 17:31

For all its positive aspects, the truth of Jesus' Resurrection also includes this solemn note. It is a past event *within* history, but it also points forward to another event *beyond* history – for which we need to be prepared. Through raising Jesus from that Jerusalem grave, God has declared that his divine standards were fully met in the life of Jesus. So Jesus alone now has the authority to act on God's behalf as our divine judge. We are invited to meet with Christ as our Saviour now because there will come a time when, even if we do not wish it, we will be required to meet him in the future as our Judge.

This is an invitation we dare not refuse – because it is an encounter which ultimately is unavoidable. Jesus cannot be by-passed or side-stepped. Through the Resurrection God has confirmed Jesus' words: '"I am the way, and the truth and the life; no one comes to the Father except through me"' (John 14:6). There is no escaping from God and the road to God goes via Jesus.

So, whether we are conscious of our need or not, it is vital that we respond to this Resurrection message:

- *accepting* the uniqueness of who Jesus is and what he has done,
- *acknowledging* the ways in which we have turned from his ways, and
- *asking* that we might now meet with him who is powerfully alive today.

Such a prayer will not go unanswered. It is a request that will never be turned down. 'Ask,' said Jesus, 'and it will be given to you; search and you will find' (Matthew 7:7).

Initially we may be fairly reluctant, as was C. S. Lewis, but we will meet with Christ all the same.

Many, on the other hand, are only too well aware of their failings before God. To them the Risen Christ offers forgiveness on the basis of his own sacrificial death 'for our sins'.

There are many in the world who are conscious of feeling alone or lost; to them the Risen Christ offers friendship and direction on the basis of his powerful and authoritative life.

And there are many who feel anxious about the challenge of death or are inadequate to face the challenges of life; to them the Risen Christ offers his peace and his power.

Jesus offers to everyone a new life – his own eternal life, starting now and going on into eternity.

FINDING 'ETERNAL LIFE' – NOW!

As we seek to respond to this challenge and invitation it is good to focus in closing on three brief extracts from the Gospel associated with John – that 'disciple whom Jesus loved'. He was the one who stooped into that empty tomb, saw the grave-clothes and immediately began to understand what it all meant.

Writing many years later, after a lifetime of reflection, John recounts two statements by Jesus which are as relevant today as when they were first recorded:

Anyone who comes to me, I will never drive away.

JOHN 6:37

I am the Resurrection and the life. Those who believe in me, even though they die, will live, and everyone who lives and believes in me will never die.

JOHN 11:25

He also concludes his chapter on the Resurrection with this famous episode:

Jesus said to Thomas, 'Put your finger here and see my hands...
Do not doubt but believe.' Thomas answered him, 'My Lord and
my God!' Jesus said to him, 'Have you believed because you have
seen me? Blessed are those who have not seen and yet have come
to believe.'

Jesus did many other signs in the presence of his disciples
which are not written in this book. But these are written that you
may come to believe that Jesus is the Messiah the Son of God, and
that through believing you may have life in his name.

JOHN 20:27–31

In these passages John teaches us that Jesus is the Son of God who can
give us life. Even though we have not seen him in the same way that
John did, we can experience God's blessing as we believe in him. And
even if we feel unworthy, Jesus never turns away anyone who sin-
cerely comes to him. If anyone opens the door to him, the Risen Christ
promises, 'I will come in' (Revelation 3:20).

All we have to do is to open that door – to ask him to come in. He
will do the rest! And our responsibility is then simply to rely on his
promise (not on our feelings which so easily change) and to draw our
strength from his risen life and power – through prayer, through reading the words of Scripture and through sharing with other Christians
in worship and practical service.

Once we have been joined by faith to Christ in this way, then the
overwhelming promise of the Bible is that we are truly an adopted
'child of God' (John 1:12); God is our Father, his Spirit is within us,
and we are truly members of the people of God (see, e.g., Romans
8:9–17). Moreover, we can look forward to 'sharing the glory of God';
for 'there is now no condemnation for those who are in Christ Jesus'
(Romans 5:2; 8:1).

In John's Gospel Jesus is also portrayed as his disciples' 'friend'
(John 15:14). So long as we do not forget that Jesus is also described
in the New Testament as our Lord and Judge, this idea of Jesus being
our friend can be really helpful. For then the first step of faith can be
seen as really just the start of a personal friendship with Jesus – the
Jesus whom the hymn-writers have described as 'our Saviour,
Brother, Friend', and 'our friend indeed who at our need his life did
spend'. The question then becomes: do we have such a friendship

with Christ? Do we know him? Or will he one day sadly say to us: 'I never *knew* you; away from me' (Matthew 7:23)? Either we know him or we don't.

Christ is alive today. Let us be sure that we meet with him as our friend, Lord and Saviour – both now and for the future.

Way for the Future

The Resurrection Garden in Jerusalem

The Resurrection of Jesus is as important today as it has ever been. It is the foundation of the Christian Church and the basis of all Christian experience. Inevitably, then, a garden in Jerusalem which is set aside for the sole purpose of proclaiming this unique message will always have a special place in the hearts of Christian people. The Garden Tomb depends on the Resurrection of Jesus for its very existence and seeks to ensure that, amidst all the business of the modern world and the confusion of the contemporary city of Jerusalem, this message at the centre of the New Testament is clearly heard.

Since 1967 the Garden Tomb has been surrounded by a bewildering amount of change. In that year it came under Israeli rule. Instead of being at the extreme edge of a Jordanian city administered from Amman, it now found itself in the middle of a city comprising both Jews and Arabs. Its focus on the Resurrection began to gain a whole new importance within the context of contemporary Jerusalem. For in this message there lies a word of reconciliation to those who are currently divided, both in terms of politics or religion. In this concentration on the Resurrection there is also a call to the differing expressions of the Christian faith within Jerusalem to unite around that which is of central importance, putting to one side other concerns and emphases which, however

legitimate, nevertheless have the tendency to divide. As Paul said to
the Jews and Gentiles of his day:

> He is our peace; he has made both groups into one and broken
> down the dividing wall, that is, the hostility between us... So he
> came and proclaimed peace to those who were far off and peace to
> those who were near.
>
> EPHESIANS 2:14, 17

In the face of those who might wish to foster their own distinctive
messages, the central purpose of the Garden remains simply to promote this centrality of the Risen Christ – both to those who live nearby
and to those who come from afar.

The years since 1967 have also seen a vast increase in the number
of those who are able to travel from long distances to Jerusalem and to
visit the Garden. The reunification of the city and the development of
international tourism have brought hundreds of thousands through its
gates each year (see Figure 37).

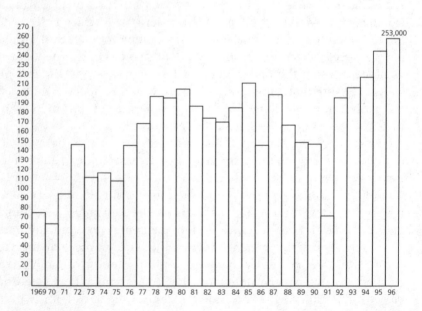

*Fig. 37. Annual number of visitors to the Garden Tomb since 1969 (in thou-
sands). Note the effect of the Gulf War in 1991.*

In 1995, for example, this reached 250,000 and groups are now required to specify in advance the time of their visit. Peder Beckholdt, the warden in 1900, would be amazed if he could see the Garden 100 years on! The regular Sunday morning service, only introduced in 1955, now continues in all weathers. And on Easter Day there are services in five different languages, attracting sometimes up to 3,300 worshippers in a single morning. Yet, in a sense, any Sunday in the Garden is an Easter Sunday.

The concentrated focus on the message of the Resurrection is important for another reason. For, as is only to be expected, the controversy over the issue of authenticity has continued to rage. In this regard perhaps the two most important writings to appear are *The Search for the Authentic Tomb of Jesus* by W. S. McBirnie[1] and 'The Garden Tomb: Was Jesus Buried Here?' by Gabriel Barkay.[2] McBirnie favoured the Garden Tomb not least because of the demographic arguments; he thought it unlikely that Jerusalem at the time of Jesus could really have been contained within the 'traditional' line of the 'second wall'. Meanwhile Barkay swung the pendulum on the dating of the Tomb. Sceptics had previously opted for a Byzantine date, but now it was argued that the Tomb dated to the Iron Age.

Given these archaeological uncertainties, the focus of the Garden has increasingly been instead to meet the spiritual needs of the thousands of visitors. To be sure, visitors are presented with the salient facts and many come away thoroughly convinced of the site's probable authenticity. But there is no intention to foster again any sense of rivalry with the church of the Holy Sepulchre (or indeed with any other proposed site). It is recognized that people will give different weight to various historical arguments and will have their own personal preferences. The intention is rather to focus single-mindedly on the Resurrection itself.

Moreover, for people surrounded by a noisy city and often moving quickly through a packed tourist itinerary, it is hard to deny the value of a place which offers space for reflection. Many have come to Jerusalem with the desire to think through the implications of Jesus' life for themselves. Yet the realities of modern Jerusalem can make this hard. Some may find that Galilee offers them the space which they need. For many, however, at least when in Jerusalem, it is the Garden which best provides for their needs. This becomes the place where, within reasonably familiar surroundings, they can focus on the One who was crucified outside the city's walls and was raised on the third day.

At the same time, the very number of visitors to the Garden at any one time, coming as they do from all over the world, only testifies to the spread of that Resurrection message far from Jerusalem 'to the ends of the earth'. Indeed it points forward to the day when matters of history and archaeology will have passed away and the vision of Revelation will at last be fulfilled:

> There was an enormous crowd – no one could count all the people! They were from every race, tribe, nation, and language, and they stood in front of the throne and of the Lamb. They called out in a loud voice: 'Salvation comes from our God who sits on the thone, and from the Lamb.'
>
> REVELATION 7:9–10

This is the hope, the vision for the future which is held out to us in the Bible. It is also the hope and vision which inspires those involved with this Resurrection Garden in Jerusalem. The Garden's ministry is to point to the Risen Christ, and in the Risen Christ there is indeed a bright hope for the future.

As a fitting conclusion, it is appropriate to quote some extended extracts from the final address given at the Garden's centenary celebrations (in May 1994) by the Association's President, John Taylor (at that time the Anglican Bishop of St Albans in England). In their own right they serve as a memento of a significant occasion within the history of the Garden. Yet they also make an important statement about how the Garden Tomb saw its ministry at the dawn of a new century.

Previous speakers had focused (as we have done in this book) on the nature of the *place* and of the *person* who is proclaimed there. It was appropriate therefore to focus in conclusion on the *purpose* of the Garden Tomb – not so much the purpose of those who first acquired the property in 1894, but the purpose of those who now found themselves as its custodians for the future. The bishop summarized this under four brief headings:

1. *To preserve a quiet place for prayer in Jerusalem where there are no distractions.* Time and again visitors to the Holy Land say that it was in the Garden that they could pray best – there and in Galilee.

    To some extent this reflects our Christian Protestant heritage. We are not Christians who are greatly helped by religious artefacts and we do not find ourselves uplifted, as some others do, by being surrounded by the furnishings of an historic church building, with its smoke-stained walls, its ancient icons and its religious art and symbols. Those suit some cultures, but they are foreign to our tradition and do not resonate for us in the same way as the peace of a garden in the sun with overshadowing trees and treasured associations.

    This is where we feel at home and can pray. It suits our biblical and meditative tradition, and without looking down on other ways we want to preserve it at all costs. And we have to work to preserve it – because Western Protestant Christianity also has a strand that is noisy and preaching and intrusive, and if we allow this too much freedom we shall lose the very thing we are committed to preserve.

2. *To demonstrate that the truth of the Resurrection is not dependent on precise locations.* When you have done all your arguing and proving or disproving, what do you have in the end? Nothing but a grid-reference on a map! Some may believe that they have precise locations, historical evidence, archaeological criteria all on their side, but if there is no love and hope and inspiration to believe and to follow, then (to use the words of St Paul in 1 Corinthians 13) they profit nothing.

    The Garden Tomb says 'It does not matter' where he was laid. Where precisely he died is not an article of the faith. No one can ever know for sure. But he did die – and he died here in this city – and he did rise from the dead – and it was here in this city. And it could have been here – or at least in a garden like this. So let your memory feed your spirit and draw from this place and its surroundings all the blessing that comes from the historical truth of that Cross and Empty Tomb, and leave the location to others to argue over. The facts and their meaning are more important than mere places on the ground.

3. *To use the Garden as an ideal setting for the preaching of the gospel.* The staff of the Garden Tomb do not have to be for ever talking, but

they do have to be forever pointing – pointing people to the Risen
Christ by the love on their faces, the helpfulness of their assistance
to harassed pilgrims and tour guides, their green-fingered care
of the grounds and gardens, their judicious encouragement of
Christian literature or memorabilia, their patient explanation of
what the Garden stands for, their unobtrusive witness to New
Testament teaching, their rejection of the high-pressure sales
talk that others prefer, their transparent sincerity and joyful
Christian faith.

This makes up their ministry, their preaching and
commending of the gospel, and they need our constant prayers
just as other Christian workers do. They are front-line evangelists:
and we know that there are many people for whom a visit to the
Garden while touring in the Holy Land has brought that deep
saving faith that eluded them elsewhere in their journey.

This can only come about when prayer is offered and the
channels are open and God's Spirit is at work. Please never forget
that we are maintaining it primarily to enable others to find the
Christ, the Son of the living God – and that believing they may
find life through his Name (John 20:31).

4. *To be 'a light to lighten the Gentiles and to be the glory of my people
   Israel' (cf. Luke 2:32).* The relationship between Jews and Arabs
   (both Christian and Moslem) continues to be a matter of
   controversy. Jerusalem is at the centre of that ferment and I
   suspect always will be. At the Garden we are daily rubbing
   shoulders with Israelis and Palestinians, as well as ministering to
   tens of thousands who visit from every part of the world. To listen
   to the variety of languages spoken in the bookshop can be quite
   bewildering. To stand at the gate after an Easter Sunrise service
   and to ask people where they were from is a mind-blowing
   experience. Everywhere is represented, East and West, 'down
   under' and 'up over', Europe, Africa, the Americas, Asia, the
   Antipodes. The ancients were right to regard Jerusalem as the
   centre of the whole world, just as it is the focal point of the three
   great monotheistic religions of the world.

And there, bearing witness to the light of Christ is the Garden
– a place where Christ, I pray, will always be honoured, revered
and proclaimed – a place to which the nations flow and from

which they go with, please God, a better picture of the world's Saviour, discovered in a place of peace and love and Resurrection wonder.

It is not a temple with a shrine; it is a Garden with a Tomb. But we must always remember that when the Lord came to his Temple, there were things that had to be overturned and people who had to be driven out. It is our duty, as stewards of this 'sanctuary', to ensure that such unholy influences are kept at bay, and that the Garden will never cease to be a place of prayer for 'all the nations' (Mark 11:17) – both for those who live near and find peace so hard to find, and also for those who come from afar with faith needing to grow and to be fed on all the benefits that this little tract of 'holy territory' can supply.

May that always be our aim, our vision, our prayer for the Garden and all who work in it.

Notes

CHAPTER 1

1. See B. Pixner, 'Church of the Apostles found on Mt. Zion', *Biblical Archaeological Review* 16.3 (May 1990), pp. 16–36; and P. W. L. Walker, *Holy City, Holy Places? Christian Attitudes to Jerusalem and the Holy Land in the Fourth Century* (OUP, 1990), ch. 9.
2. Epiphanius, *De Mensuris* 14.
3. B. Pixner, *With Jesus in Jerusalem: His First and Last Days in Judea* (Corazin, 1996).
4. C. J. Humphreys and W. G. Waddington, 'The Jewish Calendar, a Lunar Eclipse and the Date of Christ's Crucifixion', *Tyndale Bulletin* 43.2 (1992), pp. 331–52.
5. Eusebius, *Onomastikon* 74.

CHAPTER 2

1. B. Pixner, *With Jesus in Jerusalem: His First and Last Days in Judea* (Corazin, 1996).
2. See A. Millard, *Discoveries from Bible Times* (Lion, 1997), p. 293.
3. Cicero, pro Rabirio 16.
4. See M. Hengel, *Crucifixion* (SCM, 1977); and P. Connolly, *Living in the Time of Jesus of Nazareth*, revised edn (OUP, 1994).

CHAPTER 3

1. Josephus, *Jewish War* 7:217.

CHAPTER 4

1. A. Millard, *Discoveries from Bible Times* (Lion, 1997), pp. 293–4.
2. D. F. Strauss, *New Life of Jesus*, (Williams & Norgate, 1865), vol. I, p. 412.

CHAPTER 5

1. Josephus, *Jewish War* 2:224–7.
2. As reconstructed in M. Avi-Yonah, *The Jews of Palestine* (Blackwells, 1976), p. 50.
3. Josephus, *Antiquities* 20:200.
4. Eusebius, *Ecclesiastical History* 2:1, 23.
5. Ibid. 4:5.
6. Ibid. 3:11; 4:5; 5:12.
7. Ibid. 3:19–20.
8. Ibid. 4:8.
9. Ibid. 5:12.
10. Ibid. 4:26.
11. Ibid. 6:11.
12. Cf. Origen, *Against Celsus* 1:51.
13. See P. W. L. Walker, *Holy City, Holy Places?* (OUP, 1990), p. 10.
14. H. Chadwick, 'The Circle and the Ellipse', inaugural lecture (Oxford, 1959), p. 7.
15. Eusebius, *Demonstration of the Gospel* 6:18:23 (Mount of Olives).
16. Ibid. 1:1; 3:2; 7:2. (Bethlehem)
17. Eusebius, *Ecclesiastical History* 7:19.
18. Eusebius, *Onomastikon* 74:19–21.
19. Council of Nicaea, Canon 7.
20. Eusebius, *Life of Constantine* 2:72.
21. Ibid. 4:62.
22. Ibid. 3:25–40.
23. Ibid. 3:41–3.
24. See further P. W. L. Walker, op. cit., chs. 5, 7.
25. Cyril, *Catechetical Lectures* 4:10; 10:19; 13:4, 39.
26. See Jerome, *Commentary on Zephaniah* 1:14–16.
27. Walker, op. cit., pp. 114–16.
28. J. Wilkinson, *Egeria's Travels to the Holy Land*, revised edn (Aris & Phillips, 1981).
29. Cf. Jerome's fascinating description of Paula's pilgrimage around the 'holy places' of the Land in the early 400s in his *Epistle* 114.
30. Cyril, op. cit. 14:9.
31. Eusebius, *Theophany* 3:61.
32. M. Biddle, *The Tomb of Christ* (Sutton Publications, 1999), p. 72.
33. Cyril, op. cit. 14:5.
34. Egeria, 37:2.
35. Bordeaux Pilgrim, 593–4.
36. Eusebius, *In Praise of Constantine*, 11–18.

CHAPTER 6

1. S. Kochav, 'The Search for a Protestant Holy Sepulchre in Nineteenth Century Jerusalem', *Journal of Ecclesiastical History* 46 (1995), pp. 281ff.
2. Edward Robinson, *Biblical Researches in Palestine*, (London, 1841), vol. II, pp. 13–14, 64–5.
3. Josephus, *Jewish War* 5:146.
4. See E. L. Wilson, *In Scripture Lands* (London, 1891), pp. 223ff.

5. See Gordon's note on 'Eden and Golgotha' in the April 1885 issue of the *Quarterly Statement* of the Palestine Exploration Fund (abbreviated as *PEQ* [*Palestine Exploration Quarterly*] below), pp. 78–81.
6. *PEQ* 17 (April 1885), p. 81.
7. 8 March 1883.
8. In G. R. Elton, *General Gordon* (Collins, 1954), p. 313.
9. B. Spafford Vesper, *Our Jerusalem* (The American Colony, Jerusalem, 1950), pp. 102–3.
10. See Kochav, op. cit., p. 294.
11. *PEQ* 15 (1883), pp. 69–78.
12. C. R. Conder, *The City of Jerusalem* (Murray, 1909), p. 154.
13. A. W. Crawley-Boevey, *The Jerusalem Garden Tomb* (Garden Tomb Association, 1911), p. 30.
14. *PEQ* 22 (1890), pp. 11–12.
15. *PEQ* 24 (1892), pp. 120–4.
16. Conder, op. cit., p. 155.
17. W. L. White, *A Special Place* (Stanborough Press, 1989), p. 92.
18. Unnamed source in White, op. cit., p. 47.

CHAPTER 7
1. *PEQ* 24 (1892), p. 299.
2. See further P. W. L. Walker, *Jesus and the Holy City* (Eerdmans, 1996), ch. 6.
3. See *PEQ* 24 (1892), p. 299.
4. See P. W. L. Walker, *Holy City, Holy Places?* (OUP, 1990), ch. 9.
5. Eusebius, *Commentary on Isaiah* 2:1–4.
6. Eusebius, *Demonstration of the Gospel* 6:18.
7. See E. W. Hamrick, 'Northern Barrier Wall in Site T', in A. D. Tushingham (ed.), *Excavations in Jerusalem 1961–1967*, (1985), vol. I, pp. 215–32.
8. A. Millard, *Discoveries from Bible Times* (Lion, 1997), p. 129; J. B. Hennessy, 'Preliminary Report on Excavations at the Damascus Gate Jerusalem, 1964–6', *Levant* 2 (1970), p. 23.
9. See G. J. Wightman, *The Walls of Jerusalem: From the Canaanites to the Mamluks* (Mediterranean Archaeology Supplement 4, 1993).
10. Tacitus, *Histories* 5:12:2.
11. *PEQ* 15 (1883), p. 70.
12. *PEQ* 24 (1892), p. 199.
13. See C. C. Dobson, *The Garden Tomb, Jerusalem, and the Resurrection* (Garden Tomb Association, 1958), noting that this was the opinion of Rider Haggard in the nineteenth century; and see G. Barkay, 'The Garden Tomb: Was Jesus Buried Here?', *Biblical Archaeological Review* 12.2 (April 1986), p. 57.
14. Again, see Dobson, op. cit., and Barkay, op. cit.
15. See, e.g., *PEQ* 9 (1877), pp. 143–4.
16. Barkay, op. cit., pp. 40–57.
17. *PEQ* 56 (1924).
18. See M. Biddle, *The Tomb of Christ* (Sutton Publications, 1999), p. 61, who notes a similar phrase in Revelation 11:8.
19. Eusebius, *Onomastikon* 74:19–21.
20. D. Bahat and C. T. Rubinstein, *The Illustrated Atlas of Jerusalem* (Simon & Schuster, 1990), p. 66.

21. See J. Wilkinson, 'The Inscription on the Jerusalem Ship Drawing', *PEQ* 127 (1995), pp. 159–60; S. Gibson and J. E. Taylor, *Beneath the Church of the Holy Sepulchre: The Archaeology and Early History of the Traditional Golgotha* (Palestine Exploration Fund, 1994), pp. 31ff.
22. W. L. White, *A Special Place* (Stanborough Press, 1989), p. 55.
23. V. C. Corbo, *Il Santo Sepulchro di Gerusalemme*, (3 vols., Publications of the Studium Biblicum Franciscanum 29, 1981), vol. I, p. 29.
24. See Gibson and Taylor, op. cit., p. 61.
25. See N. Avigad, *Discovering Jerusalem* (OUP, 1984).
26. Josephus, *Jewish War* 5:146.
27. *PEQ* 15 (1883), p. 73.
28. See J. Jeremias, *Jerusalem in the Time of Jesus* (SCM, 1969), p. 84; M. Broshi, 'Estimating the Population of Ancient Jerusalem', *Biblical Archeological Review* 4.3 (June 1978), pp. 10–15; J. Wilkinson, 'Ancient Jerusalem, Its Water Supply and Population', *PEQ* 106 (1974), pp. 33–51; W. Reinhardt, 'The Population Size of Jerusalem and the Numerical Growth of the Jerusalem Church', in R. J. Bauckham (ed.), *The Book of Acts in Its First Century Setting*, (Eerdmans and Paternoster, 1995), vol. IV, pp. 237–65.
29. Josephus, *Jewish War* 2:148.
30. See K. Kenyon, *Jerusalem: Excavating 3000 years of history* (Thames & Hudson, 1967) and *Digging up Jerusalem* (Benn, 1974); K. J. H. Vriezen, *Die Ausgrabungen unter der Erlöserkirche im Muristan, Jerusalem, 1970–1974* (Harrassowitz Verlag, 1994).
31. See, e.g., J. E. Taylor, 'Golgotha: A Reconsideration of the Evidence for the Sites of Jesus' Crucifixion and Burial', *New Testament Studies* 44 (1998), pp. 180–233.

CHAPTER 9

1. Augustine, *Confessions*, bk. 8, translated by E. M. Blaiklock (Hodder & Stoughton, 1983), pp. 203–5.
2. C. S. Lewis, *Surprised by Joy* (Geoffrey Bles, 1955), pp. 179–82.
3. Michael Green, *Man Alive* (IVP, 1967).

CHAPTER 10

1. W. S. McBirnie, *The Search for the Authentic Tomb of Jesus* (Acclaimed Books, 1975).
2. G. Barkay, 'The Garden Tomb: Was Jesus Buried here?', Biblical Archaeological Review 12.2 (April 1986), pp. 40–57.

Bibliography

Anderson, J. N. D., *The Evidence for the Resurrection* (IVP, 1950)

Augustine of Hippo, *Confessions*, translated by E. M. Blaiklock (Hodder & Stoughton, 1983)

Avi-Yonah, M., *The Jews of Palestine: A Political History from the Bar Kokhba War to the Arab Conquest* (Blackwells, 1976)

Avigad, N., *Discovering Jerusalem* (OUP, 1984)

Bahat, D., 'Does the Holy Sepulchre Church Mark the Burial of Jesus?', *Biblical Archaeological Review* 12.3 (June 1986), pp. 26–45

Bahat, D. and Rubinstein, C. T., *The Illustrated Atlas of Jerusalem* (Simon & Schuster, 1990)

Barkay, G., 'The Garden Tomb: Was Jesus Buried Here?', *Biblical Archaeological Review* 12.2 (April 1986), pp. 40–57

Besant, Sir W., *Thirty Years Work in the Holy Land* (Palestine Exploration Fund, 1895)

Biddle, M., 'The Tomb of Christ: Sources, Methods and a New Approach', in K. Painter (ed.), *Churches Built in Ancient Times*, (Societies of Antiquaries of London Occasional Papers 16, 1994), pp. 73–147
   —*The Tomb of Christ* (Sutton Publications, 1999)

Broshi, M. and Barkay, G., 'Excavations in the Church of St Vartan in the Holy Sepulchre', *Israel Exploration Journal* 35 (1985), pp. 108–28

Broshi, M., 'Estimating the Population of Ancient Jerusalem', *Biblical Archaeological Review* 4.3 (June 1978), pp. 10–15

Brown, R. E., *The Death of the Messiah* (Doubleday, 1994)

Bruce, F. F., 'The Church of Jerusalem in the Acts of the Apostles', *Bulletin of the John Rylands Library* 76 (1985), pp. 641–61

Chadwick, H., 'The Circle and the Ellipse', inaugural lecture (Oxford, 1959)

Conant, J., 'The Original Buildings at the Holy Sepulchre in Jerusalem', *Speculum* 31 (1956), 1–48.

Conder, C. R., *Tentwork in Palestine* (Bentley, 1878)
    —*The City of Jerusalem* (Murray, 1909)

Connolly, P., *Living in the Time of Jesus of Nazareth,* revised edn (OUP, 1994)

Corbo, V. C., *Il Santo Sepulchro di Gerusalemme* (3 vols., Publications of the Studium Biblicum Franciscanum 29, 1981)

Couasnon, C., *The Church of the Holy Sepulchre in Jerusalem* (Schweich Lectures of the British Academy, 1972)

Crawley-Boevey, A. W., *The Jerusalem Garden Tomb* (Garden Tomb Association, 1911)

Dobson, C. C., *The Garden Tomb, Jerusalem, and the Resurrection* (Garden Tomb Association, 1958)

Drake, H. A., 'Eusebius on the True Cross', *Journal of Ecclesiastical History* 36 (1985), pp. 1–22

Elton, G. R. *General Gordon* (Collins, 1954)

France, R. T., *The Man They Crucified* (IVP, 1975)

Geva, H. (ed.), *Ancient Jerusalem Revealed* (Israel Exploration Society, 1994)

Gibson, S. and Taylor, J. E., *Beneath the Church of the Holy Sepulchre: The Archaeology and Early History of the Traditional Golgotha* (Palestine Exploration Fund, 1994)

Gordon, C. G., *Reflections in Palestine 1883* (Macmillan, 1885)
    — *General Gordon's Letters to his Sister* (Macmillan, 1888)

Green, E. M. B., *Man Alive* (IVP, 1967)
    —*The Empty Cross of Jesus* (Hodder & Stoughton, 1984)
    —*The Dawn of the New Age* (DLT, 1993)

Hamrick, E. W., 'Northern Barrier Wall in Site T', in A. D. Tushingham (ed.), *Excavations in Jerusalem 1961–1967,* (1985), vol. I, pp. 215–32

Hengel, M., *Crucifixion* (SCM, 1977)

Hennessy, J. B., 'Preliminary Report on Excavations at the Damascus Gate Jerusalem, 1964–6', *Levant* 2 (1970), pp. 22–7

Humphreys, C. J. and Waddington, W. G., 'The Jewish Calendar, a Lunar Eclipse and the Date of Christ's Crucifixion', *Tyndale Bulletin* 43.2 (1992), pp. 331–52

Jeremias, J., *Jerusalem in the Time of Jesus* (SCM, 1969)

Kenyon, K., *Jerusalem: Excavating 3000 years of history* (Thames & Hudson, 1967)
    —*Digging up Jerusalem* (Benn, 1974)

Kochav, S., 'The Search for a Protestant Holy Sepulchre in Nineteenth Century Jerusalem', *Journal of Ecclesiastical History* 46 (1995), pp. 278–301

Ladd, G. E., *I Believe in the Resurrection of Jesus* (Hodder & Stoughton, 1975)

Lee, A. H., *A Good Innings: Private Papers of Viscount Lee of Fareham* (privately published, 1939–40)

Lewis, C. S., *Surprised by Joy* (Geoffrey Bles, 1955)

Mackowski, R. W., *Jerusalem, City of Jesus: An Exploration of the Traditions, Writing and Remains of the Holy City from the Time of Christ,* (Eerdmans, 1980)

Mare, W. H., *The Archaeology of the Jerusalem Area* (Baker, 1987)

Martin, E. L., *Secrets of Golgotha: The Lost History of Jesus' Crucifixion* (Associates for Scriptural Knowledge, revised edn, 1996)

McBirnie, W. S., *The Search for the Authentic Tomb of Jesus* (Acclaimed Books, 1975)

McDowell, J., *The Resurrection Factor* (Scripture Press, 1988)

McRay, J., *Archaeology and the New Testament* (Baker, 1991)

Millard, A., *Discoveries from Bible Times* (Lion, 1997)

Morison, F., *Who Moved the Stone?* (Faber & Faber, 1930)

Murphy O'Connor, J., *The Holy Land: An Oxford Archaeological Guide from Earliest Times to 1700*, (OUP, 4th edn, 1998)

Pearson, L. T., *Where is Calvary?* (privately published, 1946)

Perrot, B. de, *Le Calvaire et la Tombe du Christ* (Editions Spes, 1935)

Pixner, B. 'Church of the Apostles found on Mt. Zion', *Biblical Archaeological Review* 16.3 (May 1990), pp. 16–36

— *With Jesus in Jerusalem: His First and Last Days in Judea* (Corazin, 1996)

Pollock, J., *Gordon: The Man behind the Legend* (Constable, 1993)

Reinhardt, W., 'The Population Size of Jerusalem and the Numerical Growth of the Jerusalem Church', in R. J. Bauckham (ed.), *The Book of Acts in its First Century Setting*, (Eerdmans and Paternoster, 1995), vol. IV, pp. 237–65

Richmond, E. T., *The Sites of the Crucifixion and the Resurrection* (Jerusalem, 1934)

Robinson, E., *Biblical Researches in Palestine* (London, 1841; 2nd edn Crocker & Brewster, 1855)

Sanday, W., *The Sacred Sites of the Gospels* (OUP, 1903)

Spafford Vesper, B., *Our Jerusalem* (The American Colony, Jerusalem, 1950)

Stein, R. H., *Jesus the Messiah* (IVP, 1996)

Stern, E. (ed.), *New Encyclopaedia of Archaeological Excavations in the Holy Land* (4 vols., Israel Exploration Society, 1993)

Strauss, D. F., *New Life of Jesus* (Williams & Norgate, 1865), vol. I

Taylor, J. E., 'Golgotha: A Reconsideration of the Evidence for the Sites of Jesus' Crucifixion and Burial', *New Testament Studies* 44 (1998), pp. 180–233

Vincent, L. H., 'Garden Tomb: Histoire d'un mythe', *Revue Biblique* 32 (1925), pp. 401–31

Vriezen, K. J. H., *Die Ausgrabungen unter der Erlöserkirche im Muristan, Jerusalem, 1970–1974* (Harrassowitz Verlag, 1994)

Walker, P. W. L., *Holy City, Holy Places? Christian Attitudes to Jerusalem and the Holy Land in the Fourth Century* (OUP, 1990),

—*Jesus and the Holy City: New Testament Perpectives on Jerusalem* (Eerdmans, 1996)

Wenham, J., *The Easter Enigma: Are the Resurrection Accounts in Conflict?* (Paternoster, 1984)

White, W. L., *A Special Place* (Stanborough Press, 1989)

Wightman, G. J., *The Walls of Jerusalem: From the Canaanites to the Mamluks* (Mediterranean Archaeology Supplement 4, 1993)

Wilken, R. L., *The Land Called Holy: Palestine in Christian History and Thought* (Yale University Press, 1992)

Wilkinson, J., 'The Tomb of Christ: An Outline of its Structural History', *Levant* 4 (1972), pp. 83–97

—'Ancient Jerusalem, Its Water Supply and Population', *Palestine Exploration Quarterly* 106 (1974), pp. 33–51

— *Jerusalem as Jesus knew it* (Thames & Hudson, 1978)

— *Egeria's Travels to the Holy Land,* revised edn (Aris & Phillips, 1981)

— 'The Inscription on the Jerusalem Ship Drawing', *Palestine Exploration Quarterly* 127 (1995), pp. 159–60

Wilson, C. W., *Golgotha and the Holy Sepulchre* (Palestine Exploration Fund, 1906)

Wilson, E. L., *In Scripture Lands* (London, 1891)

Wright, J. R., *The Holy Sepulchre and the Church of the Resurrection* (Ecumenical Theological Research Fraternity in Israel, 1995)

Wright, N. T. *Jesus and the Victory of God* (SPCK, 1996)

FIGURE AND PLATE CREDITS

Figures

16. Adapted from J. Murphy O'Connor, *The Holy Land: An Oxford Archaeological Guide from Earliest Times to 1700* (OUP, 4th edn. 1998), p. 10, used by permission of the author.

19. Based on Figure 46a in M. Biddle, *The Tomb of Christ* (Sutton Publications, 1999). Used with his permission.

21. Adapted from R. M. Mackowski, *Jerusalem, City of Jesus: An Exploration of the Traditions, Writings and Remains of the Holy City from the Time of Christ,* (Eerdmans, 1980). © 1980 Wm. B. Eerdmans Publishing Company (US). Used by permission of the publisher.

23. Madaba Map. © Ancient Art & Architecture Collection.

24–25, 32. © The Garden Tomb (Jerusalem) Association.

27. From *Palestine Exploration Quarterly* 15 (1885), used with permission of the Palestine Exploration Fund.

30, 33. Reproduced from *Revue Biblique* 34 (1925), pp. 55, 47, courtesy of Ecole Biblique, Jerusalem.

34. Adapted from the drawing by S. Helm in S. Gibson and J. E. Taylor, *Beneath the Church of the Holy Sepulchre: The Archaeology and Early History of the Traditional Golgotha* (Palestine Exploration Fund, 1994), p. 29, used with permission of the Palestine Exploration Fund.

36. Adapted from an original drawing by Bargil Pixner, used with his permission.

Plates

1, 6, 9, 15–16, 18. © Brian C. Bush.

2, 4, 24. © Elia Photo Service, Jerusalem.

3, 13, 53. © Peter Walker.

5, 12, 14, 19. © Michael Cooper.

7–8, 26. © Ecole Biblique et archéologique française de Jérusalem, Couvent Saint-Etienne.

10–11. © Alec Garrard (The Splendour of the Temple), Fressingfield, Suffolk, UK.

17. © Graham Tomlin.

20, 36. © Pantomap Israel Ltd.

21. © Carlos Reyes-Manzo/Andes Press Agency

22. © Ian Scott-Thompson.

23. Reproduced from F. M. Abel and L. H. Vincent, *Jérusalem: recherches de topographie, d'archéologie et d'histoire* (Gabalda, 1912-26), vol. II.ii, p. 121, courtesy of the Ecole Biblique, Jerusalem.

25, 27–30, 32–34, 38, 42–43, 48–51. © Archives of the Garden Tomb (Jerusalem) Association.

31, 35. © Palestine Exploration Fund, London.

Pls. 37, 39–41, 44–47, 52, 54–57: © Garden Tomb (Jerusalem) Association, taken by Brian C. Bush.

For further information about the Garden Tomb and its ministry:

POB 19462, Jerusalem 91193, Israel.